The Great Red Sox
Spring Training Tour of 1911

The Great Red Sox Spring Training Tour of 1911

Sixty-Three Games,
Coast to Coast

BILL NOWLIN

McFarland & Company, Inc., Publishers
Jefferson, North Carolina, and London

LIBRARY OF CONGRESS CATALOGUING-IN-PUBLICATION DATA

Nowlin, Bill, 1945–
    The great Red Sox spring training tour of 1911 : sixty-three
games, coast to coast / Bill Nowlin.
        p.   cm.
    Includes bibliographical references and index.

    ISBN 978-0-7864-6124-0
    softcover : 50# alkaline paper ∞

    1. Boston Red Sox (Baseball team)— History — 20th century.
2. Spring training (Baseball)— United States — History — 20th
century.   I. Title.
    GV875.B62N6934   2010
    796.357'640974461 — dc22   2010039576

British Library cataloguing data are available

On the cover: Red Sox players on an automobile tour of downtown
Los Angeles (Boston Public Library, McGreevey Collection)

Manufactured in the United States of America

McFarland & Company, Inc., Publishers
    Box 611, Jefferson, North Carolina 28640
    www.mcfarlandpub.com

Acknowledgments

One of the wonderful things about the Society for American Baseball Research is that its members enjoy doing baseball research. Most members are willing to take time out of their lives to help out another member with his or her research. In trying to pull together the material for this book, I wanted to try and get local newspaper accounts from the various cities and towns where the two Red Sox teams played in the springtime of 1911. Because others have often been so helpful in the past, I went to the SABR Directory and reached out to members who lived in the communities where the Red Sox played. I wrote individual e-mails, explaining what I was researching and that I was looking for news accounts of the day the Red Sox played in, say, Topeka. Within 24 hours in some cases, I received scans of articles from local newspapers. Within 10 days, I had received either scans or photocopies from most of those to whom I had reached out. I remain impressed with, and grateful for, the dedication of SABR members to help with research.

Thanks to SABR members Bob Burns (El Paso), Robert Elias (San Francisco), Gary Fink (Reno), Craig Fuller (Salt Lake City), Bob Hersom (Oklahoma City), Laura Janssen (Los Angeles), Jan Johnson (Topeka), Brian Kenny (Denver), Walter Leconte (Kansas City), Paul Lovelace (Abilene), Liisa Lyon (Oakland), Bill Lyons (Lincoln), David Martinez (San Jose), Andy McCue (Pomona, Redlands, and Riverside), Bob Millhollen (Hanford), Robert Nash (Omaha), Alan O'Connor (Sacramento), Dwight Oxley (Wichita), Wayne Pedersen (Sioux City), David Raith (Pueblo), Bob Rutishauser (Modesto), Rick Smith (Bakersfield), and Eric White (Dallas and Fort Worth). Each of these members scanned or photocopied nearly 100-year-old game accounts from newspapers in their area and got them to me.

    Other SABR members helped with connections or referrals, or the odd question here and there. They include Dave Baldwin, John Moist, Mark Rappaport, Tom Ruane, Bob Timmermann, and Mike Webber.

    There were, of course, some communities where there was no SABR member. I reached out to public libraries and local newspapers in those communities and also received considerable assistance. Thanks then are also due Barbara Burns, Brian C. Burns, Richard Bussell of the El Paso County Historical Society; Elizabeth Gillis, Sherman Lee of the Kings County Library; Don McCue of Redlands; Paula Murphy, Erika Myszinski, Pauline Nash, Beverly Roy of Hebron Academy; Dr. Arlene Shovald of Salida, Colorado; and Alicia Thomas of the Yuma County Library District.

Table of Contents

Preface

Some years ago, while researching my book *Red Sox Threads: Odds and Ends from Red Sox History*, I decided to try to determine every place the Red Sox had ever played. I found regular-season games in places such as Canton, Ohio, and a meadow known as Jailhouse Flats in Fort Wayne, Indiana — a place once used for public hangings. Let me just emphasize the point — those were regular-season games played there. Needless to say, once one gets into spring training, well, the Red Sox have played all over the place, including Cuba, the Virgin Islands, Mexico, and Japan. And almost every state in the United States.

One of the reasons the Red Sox covered so many states traces back to spring training in 1911, when they made this extravagant exhibition voyage. In early 2010, I focused on the fact that the 100th anniversary of the 1911 odyssey was upon us and so I sat down and pulled this whole book together over the period of just a very few weeks.

Could I have picked a more esoteric subject? Hey, that's part of the fun. When McFarland showed initial interest, I decided to go for it and to see if I could wrap it up in time for publication in early 2011. I started on February 23, 2010, and finished 55 days later on April 19.

Most of this book is based on accounts from contemporary 1911 newspapers. All unattributed quotations are from the *Boston Globe*. It was only after gathering and organizing all that material that I went back and checked to see if there had been any additional details in previously-published books on the Red Sox. There was rather little, but it is always helpful to have a number of perspectives on the season in context.

Introduction

"The greatest joy ride in baseball history."
— *Boston American*, April 9, 1911

Does spring training really matter that much? Clearly, players have to get ready for the championship season to come. In earlier days, players tended not to keep in condition over the winter months. Economics typically forced players to take offseason jobs. The fortunate few whose salaries were large enough that they need not work often let themselves get out of shape, and one of their goals for spring training was to shed 20 pounds and sweat themselves back into form. The climate in California permitted players there to play nearly year-round, and winter leagues were fairly common, but otherwise most players just took time off. There were few places like today's Athletes' Performance Institute catering to year-round training of the professional athlete.

Spring was thus a time to catch up on physical conditioning, as well as to develop teamwork (the double play, getting into position as the cutoff man, and so forth), and imparting skills to prospects (instruction in sliding and the like).

It's possible, though laborious, to look up spring training results in a given season. For most of the 20th century, no one maintained even simple lists of date, opponent, and final score — because most people didn't really care all that much which team won and which team lost. The goal of play was to get your players and your team ready for the regular season. In the first part of the spring exhibition season, starting pitchers might pitch an inning or two, maybe three. It was that way 100 years ago and it is that way today.

On an individual basis, it's almost impossible to find spring training player statistics, because pretty much everyone realizes they are largely irrelevant. Can anyone say how many homers Ted Williams hit in spring training? There have been more than a dozen books about him, but so far as we know, no one has ever tried to compile those stats. We do know how he did on Opening Day (he hit for a .469 average, 23 hits in 49 at-bats, and drove in 15 runs during the 14 season openers he played in). But how did he do in his many years of spring training? We don't know, and it wouldn't be easy to research. Finding the line scores is one thing; finding box scores or detailed game stories is another thing altogether.[1]

Do baseball managers and GMs even care if their team wins or loses a given spring training game? There's something to be said for developing a winning spirit. On balance, it's better to win than to lose, but as Don Zimmer has pointed out, there are lessons to be learned through losing. You wouldn't want to lose in the regular season, but a loss in spring training can be instructive — if nothing else, for teaching younger prospects how to handle a degree of adversity that some of the better ones might not have suffered as much to that point in their careers. Winning one or two games more than you lose can be the ideal scenario, because you get the benefits of both experiences — though, in the end, winning is better.

Has anyone ever done a study comparing a team's spring training success to the ultimate success of that team in the regular season? Is there any point to such a study? No one really expects the spring season to be other than an exercise in training, particularly early on with players wearing uniform numbers ranging into the 90s (when the Red Sox played a couple of spring exhibition games in Tokyo in 2008, there were a few three-digit players among the Hanshin Tigers and Tokyo Giants prospects). In 2010, the Red Sox had 64 position players appear in games and 36 pitchers take part in one or more of their spring training games — an even 100 players. That's not because manager Terry Francona was going all-out to win games. It's because the manager, his coaching staff, and the team's talent evaluators wanted to see these players get even just a taste of playing in a regular game, which is sometimes a side benefit of just getting a warm body in to fill a slot so someone else could come out of a game and not over-extend himself. The Red Sox did not wear uniform numbers until the 1931 season. In 2010, despite having 100 players at one point or another, there were no triple-digit numbers used, since players were coming and going and there was no real problem with occasional doubling-up if it might have occurred.

Mark Rappaport, chair of SABR's Spring Training research committee, has nonetheless done a study relating winning percentage of teams in spring training to their performance in the championship season that followed. "People always point to teams that are hot in spring training but flop in the regular season as evidence that spring training is meaningless," he writes. "But spring training records are not meaningless. There are just as many teams that have a hot April (in the regular season) and then flop as there are teams who have a hot March and then flop."[2]

"The baseball season is very long," Rappaport adds, citing a couple of teams in recent years and how even their early-season records are not predictive of their finish. "Just because a team isn't playing the same way they did in spring training by the time September rolls around doesn't mean that the spring training games were meaningless. Look at the Houston Astros in 2005. They were 9–13 in April, and 10–19 in May, yet they won the NL pennant. You can't predict how a team might change in midseason. In 2007 the Colorado Rockies were floundering along just above .500, then won 21 out of 22 to rampage to the NL pennant. Blaming spring training records for their failure to predict the unpredictable is unfair."

Mark looked at data for the 1955–2000 period, considering teams who were either above .550 or below .450 in spring training, and then tracking whether they were above or below .500 in the regular season. He found that teams who were above .550 in spring training were significantly more likely to have a winning regular season than one would expect by random chance, but that there was no clear pattern for teams who were bad in spring training. This led him to three conclusions, in addition to the points made above. In his words:

> 1. Winning in spring training is an indicator that the probability of the team having a winning regular season is greater than 50 percent. Winning always takes skill, so if a team shows skill in spring training there has to be some real skill on the ballclub.
> 2. Losing in spring training is not much of an indicator either way. This is because it is impossible to tell whether a team is bad, or whether they were just not trying. It is easy to lose on purpose if you don't try.
> 3. The standard deviation of a team's records in spring training (which is about a month worth of games) is approximately equal to the standard deviation of a team's records in any month of the regular season.

On an individual player level, there are plenty of flash-in-the-pan prospects with whom fans fall in love, based on the promise they showed in spring play. Someone can put up great stats, but sometimes the player is never heard from again.

Spring training no longer needs to be a losing proposition economically, a cost to be borne while preparing the team to play ball. The Red Sox have sold out every spring training game at City of Palms Park in Fort Myers since 2003, over 100 consecutive sold-out games to go along with the 550 sold-out home games at Fenway Park through the end of the 2009 regular season. The team has made arrangements to build a larger ballpark in the area, increasing capacity from around 8,000 to 11,000 per game. In 2010, there were 35 scheduled exhibition games. Eleven of the 35 were telecast either by the New England Sports Network (NESN) or by ESPN. There were 15 games broadcast on the club's flagship radio stations.

In the earliest days, attendance at spring training games was light, but the 1911 cross-country trip saw the team come out ahead economically, despite the numerous rainouts and some of the hard-to-fathom choices as to venues and opponents — for instance, the Red Sox had to loan the Yuma, Arizona, team five players when only four Yumans turned up to play before a crowd of 350, some 300 of which were from Troop A of the United States Cavalry encamped in the town. Some of the fields were crude, to say the least. In Yuma, the *Boston Post* said the ball field had "an army encampment for the left-field boundary, a big horse corral in centre field, and an outfield composed mostly of cactus, sage brush, and glittering sand."[3]

Nonetheless, the team came home with a little money in their pockets despite a trip which wound its way through 10 states and the Arizona Territory, and played in some 30 different communities across the country.

Was 1911 spring training a success? All told, they put up a record of 41–21–1 in this marathon springtime. The Regulars posted a 27–3 record. In the regular season, the Red Sox also had a winning record, but just barely. The Sox finished in fifth place in the eight-team league, 78–75, but were a full 24 games out of first place, behind the pennant-winning Philadelphia Athletics.

In 1912, the Red Sox won both the American League pennant and the World Series. By 1912, the team was under different ownership. In the springtime, that year's Red Sox had returned to Hot Springs, Arkansas, for a more conventional spring training. There was a very small number of games scheduled, and a great deal of rain, resulting in more games than usual between the Regulars and Yannigans and in more idle days than usual for games against other teams. This was the first season in which the Red Sox posted a losing record in exhibition play.

The 1912 record was 2–3, two losses to the Phillies, a win and a loss to the Reds in Cincinnati, and a 2–0 win over Harvard College. There were eight intrasquad games, all but two won by the Regulars over the Yans. In the regular season, they cruised to a record of 105–47, winning the pennant by a full 14 games over the second-place Philadelphia Athletics. The World Series was a back-and-forth affair, one of the greatest ones ever played.

1

The Origins
of a Road Trip

Spring training 1911 was quite an adventure for the Boston Red Sox.

The team was nominally based in Redondo Beach, California, which was strange enough, given their habitual home in Arkansas both before and after 1911. But despite being based in their city, the good folks of Redondo Beach may have felt a little shortchanged. The Red Sox only played three intrasquad games, and never took on a competing team there. Then they were off, playing 40 games in 12 other California communities. After splitting into two Red Sox teams, they crossed the country playing an astonishing 62 preseason games in 10 states and another one which was technically outside the country.

The season which followed was nothing special, almost the sole highlight being the work of Smoky Joe Wood who won 23 games, including a no-hitter. The following year, the Red Sox won their third pennant in their first 12 years, and again became World Champions after fighting off the New York Giants in one of the most exciting World Series of all time, which ran to eight games because of a tie in Game Two and only resolved itself in the bottom of the 10th inning of Game Eight, when the Sox came from behind to win it all.

Why Go to California?

The Red Sox held spring training in Arkansas every year from 1907 through 1918, except for one year: 1911. In 1910, they'd played 16 games against the Cincinnati Reds, giving them the opportunity to face big-league competition. Why suddenly veer off to go over 1,600 miles further west, all the way to a small beach town of about 900 people in southern California? The closest major-league city to Los Angeles was St. Louis, over 1,800 miles away. It couldn't have been a strategic move to build up a national radio following for the team; the first commercial radio broadcast was still more than nine years in the future and broadcasting of baseball games as a business proposition was 20 years away.

Several reasons for the Golden State adventure seemed to come into play, including Red Sox owner John I. Taylor's infatuation with the state of California, and the opportunity to make a good amount of money. What made it much easier to conceive of is that the White Sox had taken a similar trip just the year before, the third of three trips to train on the West Coast, and that had proven rewarding. There were two players who played on both tours: Billy Purtell and Frank "Piano Mover" Smith, both of whom were traded to the Red Sox on August 9, 1910. Given the two cities' geographic positions, Chicago in the Midwest and Boston in the East, the Red Sox excursion was of substantially greater mileage, a truly-transcontinental trip.

There was a little competitive rivalry between the two Sox teams, a bit of one-upsmanship. The White Sox had trained in Mexico in 1907, then made three trips to California (1908–1910), and even flirted with trips to Hawaii and Ireland in 1908.

Initial plans for the Boston ballclub's trip were made early in 1910. In February 1910, President Taylor announced that if the White Sox were not going to return to California in 1911, he'd take the Red Sox there. By April, when Comiskey's White Sox took a lease on a training site at Mineral Wells, Texas, Taylor began planning. On May 2, it was announced that former ballplayer Norris "Tip" O'Neill had been retained to organize the trip; O'Neill had arranged the prior trips by the White Sox and, since 1905, was president of the Western League. By the first week in September, most of the contracts were in place for use of the various ballparks.[1]

After the details were in place, John I. Taylor's ambitions were still not realized. He began to envision sending a team to Honolulu right after New Year's Day to take up an invitation he'd received to play there. The *Washington Post* explained:

President Taylor has received a liberal offer from Honolulu for a Boston team to play a series of games. He has it figured out that this can be done. His idea is to take over a team made up mostly of youngsters, and leaving San Francisco about January 1. The veterans would go to California later, as at present arranged, going to one of the California health resorts for a course of baths, while awaiting the return of the Honolulu party. Then the youngsters and veterans would be divided into two squads, and begin practice. Taylor figured that the Honolulu trip would give his manager a good chance to size up his new talent in advance of the regular training season."[2]

The course of baths was one of the reasons Hot Springs was a prime destination. In the early days, it was common for ballplayers to use (and need) spring training to get into good physical shape and also to get into playing shape. One of the reasons the Red Sox and other teams sometimes located themselves in a place like Hot Springs was to take advantage of the thermal waters to "boil out," to take off the extra weight they'd put on over the winter. For instance, a February 20 *Boston Globe* subhead read, "HEINIE MUST WORK OFF FAT TO GET DOWN TO WEIGHT."

Furthermore, the Red Sox were undergoing some roster revision and were quite uncertain who was really going to make the team. Because of the large number of games, no one player would be overworked — and there would be more time for returning manager Patsy Donovan to sort out which players would become regulars and which might need more seasoning, or just weren't going to prove helpful to the team. There was considerable turnover from 1910 to 1911. A full 56 percent of the players on the 1911 team were not on the prior year's team (24 of the 43 who played one or more games in 1911 had not been with the Red Sox in 1910.) Playing a few dozen preseason exhibition games permitted the manager and his coaches more opportunity to evaluate candidates for the big-league team.

Spring Training Headquarters: Redondo Beach

The decision to base Red Sox spring training in Redondo Beach was made only five weeks before the season began. Tip O'Neill was President Taylor's representative in California and he telegrammed the Red Sox owner on January 14, reporting that he had selected Redondo Beach. The small beach town had facilities for baseball and other athletic conditioning.

Redondo Beach, with the Hotel Redondo overlooking the bay (courtesy of the Redondo Beach Historical Society).

They'd even had their own team for one season, the year before, the Redondo Beach Sand Dabs in the short-lived Southern California Trolley League. Other teams in the league were the Long Beach Clothiers, Los Angeles Maiers, Los Angeles McCormicks, Pasadena Silk Sox, and the Santa Ana Walnut Growers. There was, however, suspicion that local businessmen had prevailed upon O'Neill. In early March, after a week or so on site, *Boston American* correspondent Merton Burke wrote, "The team were inveigled into Redondo for advertising and promotional purposes. The coming of the Red Sox to the little shore resort has boosted the place as nothing that has gone before."[3]

All told, Redondo Beach was a relatively new community — other than for the indigenous Chowigna Indians. It had only been "developed" beginning in 1887, when two riverboat captains in effect founded the town. The Redondo Company purchased 1,400 acres of land and brought in William Hammond Hall to design the layout of the streets. Hall had previously designed San Francisco's Golden Gate Park. The city incorporated in 1892, less than 20 years before the Red Sox came calling. It had already become a resort of local renown. "Redondo Beach in the 1910s and 1920s was one of the best-attended weekend getaway spots in America," writes the city's Historical Commission. "The beaches, piers, and downtown were jammed with vacationers and the Hollywood crowd. Water sports mavens drawn to the area included the great surfing pioneer George Freeth, who became a local icon. At one time, Redondo Beach boasted the world's largest indoor plunge along with visionary tycoon Henry Huntington's enormous Hotel Redondo overlooking the Pacific Ocean. The town grew as an import-export point for the City of Los Angeles until political powers decided to put its main port in nearby San Pedro. Since World War II, Redondo Beach has evinced a quaint charm as the jewel city of Santa Monica Bay's southerly shore."[4] Period photographs show wide boardwalks on the pavilion, the Mandarin Ballroom (which seated up to 4,000), and numerous shops and elegant homes.

The Huntington connection was an interesting one. Henry's uncle was Collis P. Huntington who had helped found the Central Pacific Railroad with Leland Stanford, Mark Hopkins, and Charles Crocker. The four men thus provided the western end of the transcontinental railroad. In 1868, the four purchased the Southern Pacific Railroad. Henry took up work for the company, before branching out on his own. He developed the Los Angeles street railway system into a system that had 20 streetcar lines and a reported 1,250 trolley cars. The city of Huntington Beach, California, was built on land he owned and is named after Henry Huntington.

While the Red Sox were in Southern California, they were staying at the Redondo Beach hotel he had built and took streetcars around Los Angeles on Huntington's Pacific Electric Railway. They had arrived from El Paso on his Southern Pacific Railroad, and when they traveled back east in two groups, both started off on the South Pacific, one contingent heading back via El Paso and another leaving San Francisco to Reno and on to Ogden, Utah. And when they arrived back in Boston for the regular season, they played at their home park, the Huntington Avenue Grounds, named after Ralph Huntington, another family member, who'd built his fortune running rum back and forth from the West Indies, where he lived for 10 years. It was Ralph's inspiration to build roads, such as Western Avenue (later renamed Huntington Avenue in his honor), and to fill in the area of Boston known since as the Back Bay.

Ralph's base of operations in the West Indies rum trade was in Santo Domingo, which currently specializes in exporting major-league baseball players to the United States. Chuck Huntington, the secretary-treasurer of the Huntington Family Association, responded to an inquiry: "Henry Edwards Huntington and Ralph Huntington are third cousins one time removed. Their common ancestors are Samuel Huntington and Mary Clark." In his spare time, Collis Huntington also founded the city of Newport News, Virginia.[5]

The Red Sox planned was to divide the larger-than-usual contingent of contenders into two groups, with the regular players working with the younger pitchers and the veteran pitchers paired with the younger position player recruits. There was the initial possibility that one of the groups would train for a while in Paso Robles, after the two were separated. The division into two teams, each of which would play opponents on the road, was not unheard of. The Red Sox themselves had done it for four games in 1909, and other teams such as the White Sox had divided into a younger "Colts" team and a "Regulars" team each of which played opponents in the springtime.

The *Boston Globe*'s Tim Murnane wrote on January 22 that the trip was "likely to be a real money-maker" and asked, "How much better condition will the boys be after this long trip, and how much better to stand the strain of a six months' playing season, than if they started a month later, and trained in some smug little corner of old Virginia?" He predicted that if the trip was a success, the team would probably begin to train on the Pacific Coast each year.

The team was to be housed at the well-appointed Hotel Redondo, built for an estimated $500,000. The hotel was on a slight elevation overlooking the Pacific, built as a sister property to San Diego's luxurious Hotel del Coronado. It was set among giant palm trees and at the foot of extensive gardens of carnations. On the hotel grounds were scores of orange trees, fairly laden with fruit. The entire third floor of the hotel, and some of the second, was reserved for the Red Sox. Players were able to avail themselves of hot salt-water baths. The "plunge" was said to be the largest saltwater heated pool in the world, big enough to accommodate between 1,000 and 2,000 swimmers at a time — though they would have had to stand rather close to each other since the pool measurements were 200 feet by 70 feet. It contained a water slide, a diving pool, and a wading pool, heated through an underground system of pipes from the nearby Pacific Light and Power steam plant. That facility was, boosters at the time of its 1906 opening crowed, "the greatest steam plant west of New York." The Bath House opened in July 1909 and featured 1,330 dressing rooms.

The hotel itself was of wooden construction, "an imposing structure of turrets, gables and chimneys," the gabled rooms being on the fourth floor. It was on a grand scale, a 225-room establishment which opened in

May 1890, with festivities and area-wide acclaim. The city's website adds, "The elegant grounds offered tennis courts as well as landscaped gardens. With the beach only a few steps from the lobby, the view was sweeping and unobstructed. Each room was individually decorated.... Not only did Hotel Redondo have everything a guest could desire, it was the cultural hub of the city with its reading rooms, a billiard room, a ballroom, and steam heat." Furthermore, the hotel boasted a bathroom on every floor. One amenity the hotel lacked was alcohol, due to deed restrictions. The Stag Bar on Pacific Avenue and other drinking establishments, however, weren't far away—"within staggering distance." The hotel had a British look to it, as there were hunting scenes painted on the walls of the hallways. It was ultimately demolished in 1926. Right behind the hotel was the Redondo Beach railway station with car barns that served as terminus for the Red Cars that carried patrons by rail to and from Los Angeles for a fare of 25 cents.

The stay in Redondo Beach wasn't expected to last all that long, from February 23 to March 1, at which point the Red Sox would break into two groups, each on their own schedule and only to meet again in Boston.

2

1911:
The Season Ahead

An accident at the very beginning of February could well have turned the season upside down. Both AL president Ban Johnson and Chicago White Sox owner Charles Comiskey were involved in a train crash near Fulton, Kentucky. Johnson suffered only a "few bruises" and everyone else was unscathed.

For the Red Sox, getting all the players signed in January, and even into February, was no simple task. It was only in early February that it became clear that eight-year veteran first baseman Jake Stahl would not be returning to the Red Sox in 1911. He chose to pursue a career in banking in Chicago; he was part-owner with his father-in-law of the Washington Park National Bank on Chicago's South Side. Stahl not only returned in 1912, but did so as player/manager and led Boston to a world championship. Catcher Bill Carrigan might have been another who elected not to play; he had a thriving tobacco business in Lewiston, Maine. On February 10, however, Carrigan came around and signed his contract, but only after he and Patsy Donovan had taken in a vaudeville matinee did he sit down with Taylor to work things out. He had a good year, but when the month had begun, this was by no means certain.

Looking ahead to the season to come, John I. Taylor wrote a column in his family's *Boston Globe* shortly before the traveling party left Boston to wend its way across the country to Southern California. The column was headed "RED SOX NEED FEAR ONLY THE ATHLETICS." "It is certainly a long way to go for a training trip," he began, "but the delightful climate of California more than makes up for the long ride, trouble and expense. California baseball fans are always glad to extend a hearty welcome to a good major league ball club. This takes care of most of the expense, particularly as there is Sunday baseball in most of the Pacific coast cities." His expectation of the Golden State's "delightful climate" may have been dashed a few weeks later. Taylor continued:

> The Red Sox' outfield is certainly the best in the country, as formed at present. Two new men, Riggert and Perry, will strengthen it still more. The infield, in spite of the absence of Jake Stahl, looks good to me. Of course, I would like to have Stahl with the club, but I consider Bradley a fine first baseman, and, played regularly, he will undoubtedly bat for .275 or better. He is not a clean-up hitter like Stahl, but a less erratic batter.
>
> At second, Gardner ought to have a better year than last, with one season's steady experience in the same position.
>
> At shortstop it is needless to say much about Wagner, except that

John I. Taylor, son of *Boston Globe* publisher Charles Taylor, owned the Boston American League team from 1904 to 1911. While the team did not win the World Series under his direction, he renamed the team the Boston Red Sox in 1907 and started construction of Fenway Park in 1911 (Bain Collection at the Library of Congress).

> he is one of the gamest men that ever took part in any sport. He will play at times when he should be on the bench owing to injuries that would keep many another ball player in bed.
>
> At third either Purtell or Engle can fill the bill. Engle is a much harder hitter, but Purtell is much better in the field. Which one gets the position will be decided by manager Donovan on the spring trip.
>
> The Red Sox may be weak in the box, but we have a lot of new men with fine minor league records, and are doing the best we can to dig up some consistent pitchers.
>
> Certain members of the present staff may do better work next year. If they do not, they will be traded or sold and new men given a chance.
>
> Behind the bat Boston looks bad, but Carrigan may have a year like 1909, in which case it will help a lot; and he will not be over-worked. He is one of the hardest workers that ever played ball, and is fighting every minute of the game. I hope he comes back, and certainly think that he will.

Kleinow caught good ball, but did not hit. He will have to hustle a little bit this year and make good or go. This is no secret, as he has been told so.

Madden weighs less this spring than he did after the training trip a year ago. He is lazy, and has been told to get down to weight, and stay there. He is the proud possessor of a $15 rubber shirt, which may help some!

I have four new young catchers, and expect to get at least two good men out of the four. The new catchers will be a chance this year as they never have been before.

As to manager Donovan, I have every confidence in the world in him. He is liked by everyone who knows him, and he ought to do even better work next year than in the past.

Discipline will be more rigidly enforced than in former years, and no man, no matter how good, will stay with the club unless he takes care of himself and is working every minute for the club's best interests.

It looks to me like Philadelphia for the one club in the league to beat for the pennant. New York and Detroit may be dangerous, but I should place the same four clubs in the first division, as last year, with Cleveland and Chicago stronger than then in spots, and with a much better chance to fight their way into the first division.

Before Heading West

When the year opened, President Taylor needed to get his players on board and get fully staffed for the season to come. This was something more easily said than done.

January 1—Strange as it may seem to anyone familiar with the Red Sox of the late 20th century, there was a time when they were known as the "Speed Boys" for their fleetness on the basepaths. When readers of the *Boston Post* opened their newspapers on Sunday, January 1, they read, "DONOVAN TO INSIST ON SPEED." The team had slowed down near the end of 1910, and manager Patsy Donovan pointed to Duffy Lewis in particular as someone who, though only 22, could have boosted his .283 average by 30 points had he been a step faster running out batted balls. "He realized how many safe hits he lost by his unnecessary slowness last season, and he is now in the hands of a competent speed trainer."

January 2—The *Boston Herald* reported that it didn't look like the Boston Nationals were going to be able to sign Hal Janvrin for at least a year, because of the objections of his parents to him playing professionally.

Pitcher Ray Collins wrote a letter to the *Post* from his home in Burlington, Vermont, to say how much he was looking forward to the coming season. He'd been doing offseason work as a yardman for a coal company and then moved to writing insurance.

January 3 — Hugh Bradley stopped by the Red Sox offices on Washington Street for a talk with Taylor and came out pleased. The Red Sox had signed "the Caruso of the league," guaranteeing that Bradley would be able to entertain with his singing (and maybe also play some first base, too). Of his flourishing vaudeville career, he told the press, "I'm singing nine songs a day. Keeping them satisfied." Pitcher Marty McHale, another singer in the Red Sox Quartette and a graduate student in Maine, came to Stoneham to visit his mother and signed his contract the same day as Bradley.[1] Taylor already had the whole outfield signed — Lewis, Speaker, and Hooper. And he had three other pitchers — Hunt, Hall, and Piano Mover Smith. Heinie Wagner and Billy Purtell were under contract, too, as was Tommy Madden.

January 4 — In the day's *Boston Journal*, Herman Nickerson wrote, "If President John I. Taylor was in a football league, he would have just enough men to start a game with, eleven having signed up for 1911." During the day, President Taylor went over to pay a social visit to his National League counterparts, most frequently known as the Boston Braves but going as the Rustlers in 1911. Red Sox pitcher Frank Arellanes, "the Mexican," had pitched for parts of the three prior seasons and was a 16-game winner in 1909. In 1910, he'd not gotten into shape, declining to take the hot baths at Hot Springs, and was finally suspended, then sent to Sacramento in mid–August 1910. He did well there and was going to be given another chance to make the team. Taylor also let it be known that a group in Santa Barbara, California, was angling to have the Red Sox base themselves there when they came to Southern California for spring training. Taylor talked of two key prospects, saying that Hank Perry was Patsy Donovan's man and Joe Riggert was his. Competition would see who came out on top.

Taylor said he tended to favor Fresno, largely on the recommendation of Hugh Duffy, who had been there with the Chicago White Sox the previous spring. One thing that Taylor was clear about, though: Red Sox players were to be discouraged from taking hot baths, "since there is no question but that the too liberal use of hot water has weakened the arms and general condition of many ball players." There may have been other aspects of Hot Springs taking a toll on the men, too; in his work on spring training 1912, Mike Foster has written about the temptations and corruption which plagued Hot Springs at the time.[2]

January 5 — Infielder Billy Purtell wrote the *Post* from his home in Columbus, Ohio, that he was doing a lot of walking in the winter and keeping in shape.

January 7 — By coincidence, the signed contracts of Frank "Piano Mover" Smith and Billy Purtell turned up on the same day in the Red Sox mail. The two had both been obtained in the trade Taylor engineered to get Harry Lord off the team in the summer of 1910. Smith agreed to a bonus arrangement based on the number of wins he achieved in 1911. Club Secretary Eddie Riley was busy making arrangements for the transcontinental trip.[3]

January 8 — By the time the season is over, including the cross-country jaunt, the Red Sox will have traveled an estimated 25,500 miles — just enough to circumnavigate the planet. The transcontinental tour was to cover 8,500 of those miles. Fresno, Santa Barbara, and Long Beach were the three leading contenders for the California base of operations, with Tip O'Neill out west scouting operations. O'Neill had lived in Oakland for the previous 10 years and knew the West Coast fairly well. The total cost of the trip was expected to run about $16,000, something over $430 per prospective team member. Already in December, the Red Sox had ordered up special stationery with a rendition of a train across the top and the legend "Red Sox Special, Coast to Coast" appearing underneath.[4] It seemed that few expenses would be spared.

Boston English High School track star Hal Janvrin was signed, the youngest of the recruits hoping to make the team. He had just turned 18 in August. Boston's NL team had first claim on his services, but had recently changed owners and the new group felt the cost to sign him was too great. Janvrin's family opposed his signing, wanting him to continue his studies but Taylor was able to talk them into seeing what use he could make of his athletic abilities. Janvrin had captained both the baseball (third base) and football (halfback) teams at English High. He was a track star, holding a record in hurdles with an athlete from Yale, and active as a forward on the hockey team, too. He was working at a leather concern in the winter.

January 9 — A letter from Joe Wood arrived in Boston, occasioning a headline in the *Herald*, which commented, "Wood has contended that he deserved a raise in salary. President Taylor could not bring himself to take the same view of the matter." It appeared that Wood blinked first. Wood was farming in Pennsylvania. Both in 1909 and 1910, Wood had hurt himself while practicing his talents at other positions. In 1911, manager Donovan was determined to confine him to pitching. "I know that I will virtually have to put him in a straightjacket ... but I shall put my foot down from now on and refuse to allow him to mix it. He has a $20,000 arm and a great head, but when he sees the hide being batted and thrown around, he wants to get right into the fray." Donovan saw in him the potential to be another Walter Johnson, but only if curbed and cured of the desire to play other positions, too.[5]

January 13 — The Red Sox Quartette added another member when two more players signed Red Sox contracts — Chris Mahoney, a former pitcher for Fordham who'd appeared in two games for the 1910 Sox, and Buck O'Brien from Brockton, the "Zenetello of the Operatic Duo" (a reference to a singer of the day) and a 20-game winner for Hartford in 1910. O'Brien apparently had a firm handshake. Nickerson wrote, "Along toward dusk, John I. had just got his fingers so they worked naturally." Nickerson also recounted Taylor picking up a letter from Eddie Cicotte and reading it out loud, as "Knuckles" told how he was rounding into shape. "The man who said I was hog fat was not telling you the truth," wrote Cicotte. "I am tipping the scales at 171, and working hard to keep in condition." Taylor wanted him at 165 and wrote him back to "get wise and hustle" if he wanted to join the Red Sox train heading west. Otherwise, it was a long and rocky walk.[6] A special wire to the *Journal* reported that the Redondo Beach Hotel had been selected as the site for the spring camp.

Why a beach location had been chosen is not known. *Sporting Life* had reported in May 1910 that the White Sox had had a bad experience with ocean winds, and that consequently inland locations such as Redlands and Fresno were likely to be chosen.[7] This decision to locate on the coast may even have had fatal consequences for one of the Red Sox infielders. Pitcher Charlie Smith was in Hot Springs on his own, "boiling out" to help him get into shape.

January 14 — Only those who had signed contracts would be permitted to board the Red Sox Special as it traveled to the West Coast. Taylor had reportedly offered a number of returning men substantial increases over their 1910 salaries, but those who returned the contract unsigned asking for more were instead sent a revised contract at a lower amount. Anyone who wasn't on board contractually would not be provided transport and would need to find his own way to the coast. Joe Wood's contract arrived in the mail on the 13th, though it was already pegged at a lower amount than in 1910. Taylor "figured he did not work as hard as he was capable of working, and the cut down came merely as an object lesson to him — a gentle hint that ball players must work for what they earn, and that magnates in these days do not intend to pay a man for his reputation alone." The break came when Taylor offered to restore his old salary if he showed that he was giving his best.[8] Wood went on to win 23 games in 1911.

The main hole was second base, where Vermont's Larry Gardner had still not signed on. Gardner had played well in 1910, so well that his salary had been "boosted several times owing to the appreciation of his work by Owner Taylor." But he was still seeking more, in straight salary without bonus clauses allowing him to earn more than his base salary. Nickerson noted that Gardner had missed over 40 games in 1910, and that his .283 average was hardly Eddie Collins territory. Catcher Carrigan was still holed up in Maine and still holding out. He'd suffered the same sort of cut in his base contract as had Wood. It was part of what Taylor called a "bonus plan," to have a base contract and the rest of the money earned by attaining certain performance-based thresholds.

January 15 — "Bullet Jack" Thoney claimed he was ready to return. The "fastest man in baseball" was a hard-luck case who had broken his leg early in his baseball career, then his arm, and had thrown his arm out so badly in spring 1910 that he missed the whole season. Taylor said he would invest a railroad ticket on the man who had once cost him $10,000 to acquire from Toronto.

January 17 — "The Mexican promised to turn over a new leaf and do his utmost for the club's success," said the *Herald*, as Taylor had agreed to give pitcher Frank Arellanes another chance in 1911.

January 19 — Unlike Duffy Lewis, Frank Arellanes, and some of the other Californians on the team, Harry Hooper was not taking advantage of the climate to play winter baseball. He wrote Paul Shannon of the *Boston Post* that he was taking it easy, hunting and fishing around his town of Capitola on Monterey Bay. He was prone to seasickness so didn't venture out for deep sea fishing but had already caught close to the limit of 50 for trout, fishing within 200 yards of his house. He'd received a letter from trainer Doc Green, giving him some pointers on staying in shape, but said he'd been doing so much walking he was maybe even a bit under weight at the time.

January 28 — A sensational headline in the *Boston American,* "BILL CAR-RIGAN QUITS RED SOX," was not exactly accurate. Taylor had sent an ulti-matum to the star catcher of the Red Sox and Carrigan declined to sign the proffered contract with the paycut and bonus clause. Shannon of the *Post* called it "open war" between Carrigan and Taylor. Without Jake Stahl for 1911, and with it now looking that Carrigan would be gone, too, the year ahead was looking bleak. Within a week, the *American* was saying it wouldn't be surprised were Carrigan to stop by Taylor's office and sign on.

January 29 — Taylor said that because Carrigan would not agree to a large portion of his contract being based on achievable incentives — the "bonus" plan — he would be sending a contract to Jack Kleinow to serve as catcher for the Red Sox. Tommy Madden, a catcher from Roxbury, Massachusetts, might find this the opening he needed to break in as backstop for Boston. He'd appeared in 10 games in 1909 and 14 games in 1910, and was number one on the depth chart after Carrigan.

January 30 — "HOLDOUTS GET OUT OF WET," read the *Boston Post* head-line the next morning. The two Vermonters on the team, Ray Collins and Larry Gardner, both met with Taylor and both came out with "beaming faces" and new contracts. "I don't know why it is," Taylor said, "but every time I sign up a player, I am the sucker. I was an awful sucker in this case. They got what they wanted, and that was the way we compromised."[9]

They hadn't gotten a salary increase; they had just declined to sign on to his bonus scheme, but Taylor gave way. Noted sports columnist Hugh S. Fullerton observed generally, "Taylor treats his players better and more liberally than any man in either major league, does more favors for them makes their lot as pleasant as that of any crowd of athletes in the country."[10]

February 1—It would mean breaking up the best outfield in baseball, but there was thought being given to having Tris Speaker play first base in the absence of Jake Stahl, should the Chicago man stick to his planned retirement. Paul Shannon of the *Post* was more or less appalled: "It would be the height of foolishness to try and develop one of the greatest outfielders the game has ever known into an indifferent infielder."[11] News was that infielder Steve Yerkes had been signed.

February 4—The Red Sox uniforms for 1911 would be the same as for 1910, except that buttons would be used on the jerseys instead of lacings.

Earlier days at Hot Springs. Tommy Madden dressed as an American Indian and Bill Carrigan (center) and an unidentified player dressed as cowboys pose on burros during a rabbit hunt at Hot Springs, Arkansas, 1907 (courtesy Boston Public Library, Print Department, McGreevey Collection).

The sweaters would be red with a white Old English B. They were to be ready in time for the March 2 opening of the new ballpark in Los Angeles.

February 6—Jack Thoney said he could play first base. He said he'd been working out all winter and walking eight to ten miles a day. He and Doc Green had both gone to college together.

February 9—Bill Carrigan said he could play first base: "I'd just as soon play first base as catch ... and I have a hunch I could do even better work there than behind the bat."[12] He'd come to Boston to buy a fresh load of tobacco for his cigar-making plant in Lewiston and was asked by reporters about his plans. Nonetheless, he was adamant about signing for a cut in pay, even with a compensating bonus arrangement.

February 10—Bill Carrigan signed, a week to the day before the team's scheduled departure for the West Coast. He had dropped by Red Sox headquarters, but firmly refused to meet Taylor's terms. After Patsy Donovan invited him out to lunch, they took in a matinee show, talking much of the time to somehow pave the way to bridge the gap between Carrigan and President Taylor. A sports page cartoon in the February 16 *Boston Post* depicted the drama.

Destination: Redondo Beach

In the earliest days of the franchise, it wasn't always the case that newspaper sportswriters attended road games. Boston newspapers were more active in covering away games than the papers of many cities, but game accounts were frequently provided by the Associated Press. For the 1911 cross-country road trip, however, there were reporters from four Boston newspapers who accompanied the team: Tim Murnane of the *Boston Globe*, Paul Shannon of the *Boston Post*, sporting editor Herman Nickerson of the *Boston Journal*, and Merton E. Burke of the *Boston American*. *Globe* sports cartoonist Wallace Goldsmith, whose images provide some sense of the atmosphere, linked up in Los Angeles later on. The *Post* either sent cartoonist Scott on the trip, or he conjured up his cartoons from the stories Shannon filed (which we suspect was the case). The *Boston*

Herald provided no bylined coverage but relied on special reports. Gold-smith's 82-year-old father lived in Oakland and the two had a chance to spend time together in early March.

The *Globe* printed details of the trip on February 9. A party from Boston would make its way to Chicago, meeting up with others there, before a special "train de luxe" would head west. There were six rail cars devoted to the Red Sox party, expected to number 75 including the news-men. Three of the cars would be sleeping cars. There would be a dining car, an observation car, and a buffet/baggage/library car which would con-tain a barber shop and baths as well as "all of the latest authors and some of the old ones." The train would have completely furnished state rooms

On August 12, 1908, John Irwin, owner of the Sweet Summer Dream Hotel on Peddock's Island, invited Boston baseball men, including the Rooters, former players and members of the sporting press, to a day of baseball-related events. Pictured here, in front of the hotel, are Boston's most prominent sportswriters. Top, left to right: O. W. Brown, *Boston Traveler*; Mose Chandler and S. P. Car-rick, *Boston Journal*; Charles Leary, Fall River [newspaper unidentified]; Timothy Murnane, *Boston Globe*; Sam Crane, *New York Journal*; and O. J. Burke, *Boston Journal*. Bottom, left to right: Wallace Goldsmith, *Boston Globe* sports cartoon-ist; Arthur Cooper, *Boston Post*; Herman Nickerson, *Boston Journal*; Ralph McKenna, *Boston Herald*; J. C. Morse, *Baseball Magazine*; and Paul Shannon, *Boston Post* (courtesy Boston Public Library, Print Department, McGreevey Col-lection).

and would "seem more like a home than a few coaches on rails."[13] The trip from Chicago to Los Angeles was expected to take almost three days.

There was plenty planned for them once they reached Southern California. The *Los Angeles Times* described a "programme of courtesies" arranged by the Chamber of Commerce which would include "dances, special launch trips for deep-sea fishing, ocean trips and a three-day carnival of athletic sports." They would be free to avail themselves of the billiards room, play cards, or simply "lounge around at will"; indeed, all of the exclusive club rooms of the hotel were to be made available, along with "all the privileges of the bath house and plunge." Free transportation would be provided for those who wanted to take the 50-minute trip to Los Angeles. Even those who whiled away the hours by sitting and fishing on the wharves had agreed to offer up "the choice seats to be had along the pier."[14]

Redondo Beach was, according to a story in the February 20 *Globe*, "a nice, bustling little sea-side village waiting for them with open arms. The place is far enough from a big city to be safe from its nightly allurements, yet near enough to permit daily trips with no inconvenience." Los Angeles was about a 50-minute trolley ride away. The residents were, readers were assured, "awaiting the coming of the Red Sox with bated breath." Never had they "entertained athletes of such distinction. In its time it has developed championship water polo teams, champion swimmers, and other aquatic wonders, and has entertained presidents and admirals, but never has [the community] had the opportunity to prepare a big league baseball team for its championship season." The story listed in some detail some 12 species of fish that the men could seek and the kind of line and tackle they could use, all the diving stunts they could enjoy, the exhilarating pleasures of surf bathing, and the chance to do some "gunning" for cottontails and jackrabbits as long as the non–Californians among them purchase a game license.

Judge L. F. Wells was a busy man. He chaired the committee planning a welcome banquet and reception on behalf of the Chamber of Commerce, oversaw the crew of men working on the ball field, and was also the manager of the Hotel Redondo which opened for the season specially for the arrival of the Red Sox.

The *Boston Journal* was a little less romantic about Redondo Beach than the *Globe*. It was actually a city, not a quaint seaside village, incor-

The Sox set off for California. Sports page cartoon in the February 18, 1911, *Boston Post*.

porated in 1892. Four years earlier, the first Santa Fe excursion train visited the area and a pier constructed of iron reached into the Pacific. The city had two sides. It was "really the shipping port of Los Angeles, where the coastwise steamers to San Diego, San Francisco, and Seattle touch as well as the boats for Hawaii and Japan. With this there is the recreation side of a fashionable resort, with its dancing pavilion and band. At the beach there is the largest hot salt water plunge in the country, with a fine pool and a good stretch of sandy beach." President Taylor had particular ideas about water temperature and his player. Though he said that hot water "boils all the baseball out of them" he somehow felt that "hot salt water is fine for ball players."[15] At Moonstone Beach, it was said that semi-precious stones washed up on shore: onyx, jasper, and moonstone among them.

3

A Grand Send-Off
from Boston

There was a surprisingly large crowd of some 2,000 people who gathered at Boston's South Station to see the team off on the first leg of its journey. It wasn't the whole team by any means, as there were only a half-dozen players in the advance party. They would pick up other players at convenient hopping-on stops along the way west, with the California players joining in on arrival. Although Boston had won the pennant in 1903 and 1904, this was a team which in the prior six years had only once finished as high as third place and had a cumulative record of 430–483.

This year, the idea of a cross-country trip gripped the public imagination in the Hub. That so many crammed into the station to see a few out-of-uniform ballplayers get onto a train was a testament both to the thirst for baseball in what has always been one of its best cities but also the publicity accorded this adventure. That four of the major newspapers of the city assigned full-time sportswriters to go on the entire trip testified to that as well. Several of the New England–based players assembled at the downtown Boston offices of the Red Sox and posed for a photograph with one of John I. Taylor's Decatur trucks (Taylor had an automobile business); Taylor then drove them to the train station.[1]

Departure was at 1 P.M. on February 18 on Track 16. President Taylor and treasurer Hugh McBreen were there to see them off for the first stop, New York City, under the leadership of secretary Edwin Riley. Other luminaries in the crowd of well-wishers included Hugh Duffy, Fred Lake, Tommy Connolly, A. H. C. Mitchell, and Dan Howley. "The crowd was so massed on the long platforms and about the gates that late departing passengers had to execute mass plays behind the broad backs of patrolmen in order not to miss the train."[2]

In the advance group were Bill Carrigan, Hugh Bradley, Larry Gardner, Hal Janvrin, Tommy Madden, Marty McHale, Buck O'Brien, Chet Nourse, and Chris Mahoney. Trainer Charles Green traveled with them, as did three of the newspapermen and three fans, one of whom was legendary Red Sox Royal Rooter "Nuf Ced" McGreevey. There was also "Uncle Bill" Cahill of East Boston and Joe Burns from Taunton, who wound up umpiring some of the games. He was a former ball player who served as a "warmup umpire" often in the past. The three "regulars" typically made every spring training trip and weren't about to pass on the biggest one of them all. Assistant business manager Arthur D. Cooper was on board as well, though he somehow managed to forget his trunk (not that reassuring in a business manager) and looked to have it join him in Chicago.

The talk on the train was of their winters, and of baseball. Neither Bradley nor O'Brien started in singing as yet. Janvrin had his nose buried in a book. Nourse's major-league career consisted of five innings for the Red Sox in 1909 (in which he gave out five walks and gave up five hits); he was only along for the company, heading out west for his second season pitching for Sacramento. The team stayed overnight at the New Marlborough Hotel, its habitual team hotel of the period, where they were greeted by a good crowd including Joe Wood smoking a long black cigar (he'd given up the cigarette habit). Dinner consisted of "blue points, olives, radishes, consommé, guinea chicken, spaghetti, asparagus tips, sugar-cured ham and all the rest that goes to make life worth living."[3] Some took in a theater show in the city and other just strolled about. Tongue in cheek, McHale said the city was so different it reminded him of Orono, Maine.

There was great optimism regarding the trip. Taylor told the press before the party set off, "If this trip doesn't shake together the finest team on earth, it won't be for lack of inspiration. After this our boys ought to be all of one mind and in the finest fettle."[4] The emphasis on being "all of one mind" after a trip that forged stronger bonds of teamship was an important one after the 1910 imbroglio; Hugh Fullerton claimed the "disruptions and quarrels within the club, centering around Taylor, Lord, and Engle, and involving half the players, wrecked the team.... The team went all to pieces and finished floundering."[5] Though his family owned the *Boston Globe*, it was for the *Sunday American* that Taylor wrote a bylined story predicting a successful trip and providing his assessment of their strengths and weaknesses at each position.

"A trip across the continent is certainly a long way to go for a training trip," Taylor acknowledged. "But the delightful climate, the beautiful scenery and natural wonders of California will more than repay us for the long ride, the trouble, and the expense." He expected good crowds in California, in part thanks to Sunday baseball. He expected a "handsome return for the money we expend." Taylor felt that no team in baseball had a better outfield. He said that the infield looked good to him. The pitching had some question marks, but they had a lot of men with strong minor-league records ready to work. He was candid about what he saw as their primary weakness: "Behind the bat, Boston looks bad." He was counting on Carrigan to come back a bit to the form he'd shown in 1909. With Kleinow and Madden ready and waiting to back him up as catcher, Taylor thought they'd be fine.

A special guidebook which the Red Sox had printed for the trip — it sounds like an early edition of today's media guide — described the setting of the team's spring training site as "where the fragrance of the orange blossoms mingles with the cooling breezes from the snow-capped peaks and the warm tingling salt-laden zephyrs of the Pacific.... In the shadows of the romantic missions, practice will be carried on and in California's energizing air, the players composing the Boston Red Sox will receive the impetus that will carry the team through the season's nerve-trying battles for the American League pennant during 1911."[6]

There may have been other reasons for the trip, too, more personal ones for John I. Taylor, who had married a woman from the West Coast, San Francisco's Cornelia Van Ness. He enjoyed scouting for baseball talent on trips to California. He signed both Harry Hooper and Duffy Lewis, though they were brought to his attention by baseball men on the coast. The *Boston Post* commented on the trip, noting, "Taylor has been giving the folks out in that California more than a large earful about his outfit's prowess. It has been on the schedule for some moons that said outfit was to be shipped out for the benefit of said folks, the crop of ensuing admiration being slated to break all records, both for quality and proportion." In other words, he wanted to show off his baseball team.[7]

A Taste of Early Rising

The early-morning call at the New Marlborough Hotel was 5:45 A.M. for a 7:50 A.M. departure, and the players breakfasted in a room decked out in American flags. Those boarding the Red Sox Special got to see sunrise in Manhattan, as did fresh crowds on hand despite the early hour, one at the hotel and another at the West 23rd Street ferry terminus. There being neither a George Washington Bridge (1931) nor tunnels under the Hudson River, railcars were transported to the New Jersey side by ferryboat. Taxis sped everyone to the terminus, traveling so fast on the empty early-morning streets that Nuf Ced McGreevey cried out for them to slow down. Jack Kleinow lived in the city. Team captain Heinie Wagner lived "45 minutes from Broadway," albeit on a chicken farm. Both were waiting at 23rd Street. Trainer Doc Green had already lost one of his bags, but was relieved to learn it had been recovered.

Others joining the team in New York were Steve Yerkes, Walter Moser, and Cecil Thompson and Mrs. Thompson, on their way to Sacramento. Right-handed pitching prospect from Wilton, Maine, Willard Sawyer, late of Hebron Academy, was on board, a Bill Carrigan find.

It was first-rate travel, each player assigned a lower berth by passenger agent E. E. Baekey of the Baltimore and Ohio along with S. L. Parrot of the Rock Island Line. The makeup of the train, exclusively devoted to the Red Sox party was one 16-section car, two 12-section drawing room cars, and one 10-section observation car, along with the combination baggage and buffet car and the dining car, which would remain the same diner all the way to El Paso. It was, as the *Journal's* Nickerson wrote, "about as complete in every particular as is possible in this enlightened railway age and the boys will have every possible comfort on their long journey."[8] Eddie Riley saw them off, then headed back to Boston.

Joe "Patsy" O'Rourke (bound for Sacramento) and Izzy Hoffman (bound for Oakland) joined the Red Sox train in Philadelphia, as three others hopped on board at 9:00 in the evening in Pittsburgh: Frank "Piano Mover" Smith, Hugh Bedient, and Richard Nebinger. The train passed through a blizzard in the mountains without incident.

Treasurer Hugh McBreen left Boston the following day, directly to Chicago, traveling with his wife and young daughter. There were fully 20 players scheduled to join the party in Chicago: Eddie Cicotte, Hack Engle,

At Last Come Signs of Spring, the Red Sox Are on Their Way

Detail from **Boston Post** sports page cartoon, February 20, 1911.

Billy Purtell, Jack Buzick, Hank Perry, Curt Elston, George Pierce, Jack Thoney, Blaine Thomas, Larry Pape, Jerry Sheehan, Dutch Lerchen, Rex DeVogt, Herman Priepke, George Hollis, Chick Farrell, Ralph Pond, and manager Patsy Donovan. Ray Collins arrived from his home in Vermont by way of Montreal. It surprised some of the newsmen that pitcher Charlie Smith joined the group, but he was being offered a chance to make the team. Purtell was one of the last to arrive, his train coming in five hours late from Indianapolis. An outfielder named Anderson was due to join the party in Chicago, but he never turned up.

President Taylor had come separately from the east to see Donovan take charge of the party in Chicago at the Great Northern Hotel. One would have thought Taylor was bound to join the team at some point, but it was not to be. As the Special headed west, Taylor would travel back to Boston. His wife was ill, and he also wanted to stop into Detroit in conjunction with his new Taylor Motor Sales Company in Boston. There was hope that Jake Stahl could be induced to join the party once it assembled in Chicago, but it was not to be. He remained deaf to Donovan's offers, preferring to stick to "real business" as the vice-president of his bank. The two talked for two hours, but Stahl was unshakeable.

During the day in Chicago, there was sightseeing and many availed themselves of the hotel barber shop to get themselves a shave and "the last chance for a civilized hair cut." Asking about the sudden influx of patrons, one of the barbers asked if they were in town for the cement and concrete convention. He wasn't enough of a baseball fan to get the riposte that some of them were probably entitled to join a convention of cement workers but they were Red Sox.[9]

Though he'd told McBreen he would forego coming by, at the very last moment, Jake Stahl turned up at the hotel to greet the players and saw them off at the train station along with a "good-sized crowd." Taylor was there to see them off, too, when they pulled out of the station at 9:00 P.M. In Stahl's case, Paul Shannon said he was "a rather forlorn figure, the only down-hearted personage among the vast crowd ... [he] must have figured that baseball had gone out of his life forever. It was a very sad parting and all parties concerned felt it. The Red Sox saw their mainstay left behind, and Jake must have experienced many a pang as he saw his old brothers in arms steam slowly out of sight in the distance."[10]

The most colorful accounts of the trip were provided by one of the least-known Boston sportswriters, Merton E. Burke of the *Boston American*. He let readers know that Carrigan's man from Maine, Sawyer, had "got lost in New York and rode round and round in the subway till 1:30 A.M." He summarized the sentiment about the trip in his last transmission before they left the Windy City:

> A Broadway hotel and a hard night on the rail are not conducive to rest. However, we board the Golden State special to-night, and when we wake up tomorrow morning will be speeding through next Spring. Everyone seems content to forego a little hardship for the sake of gay times to come. The old timers have begun to get together and swap yarns of their many adventures and wonderful deeds.
>
> Up to date Captain Wagner seems to be a few points in the lead. He allows his eyes are so keen he can see a fly wink a thousand feet in the air. He hasn't much on Tom Madden, however, for he swears that while duck hunting last fall he shot a thousand birds with a rifle loaded with a foul ball.
>
> Bill Carrigan went to sleep on landing in New York and hasn't woke up yet. Doctor Green thinks he smoked one of this own make of cigars.[11]

The *American* ran Burke's column on the front page of the newspaper all the way up through the March 11 issue.

Hugh Fullerton's predictions for the season picked up on the discord from the 1910 team. "Here is rich material for a winning ball club, in my estimation," he wrote. "Patsy Donovan is not a strong manager, although a clever baseball man and a gentleman. The feeling among the old players still is uncertain, and although Carrigan has come into the fold, Stahl quit the team and there are others still affected by the disturbance that cost the club the services of Harry Lord and McConnell." He saw deep wealth in the number of recruits, but frowned on the excursion. "The team is opening under an immense handicap. It is to train in California, making a spectacular special train tour from Cape Cod to the Golden Gate — six days' ride — and it is routed all over the West and Southwest on the homeward march. The training plan, abandoned by Comiskey after three ruinous years, will rob Donovan of a chance to see many of his young players and will bring them East in bad condition from hard traveling."[12] He suggested that on paper, the Sox ought to finish in the top three, but, presciently, picked them for fifth place.

Passing Through Kansas

They weren't done yet picking up players. By the time Nickerson filed his dispatch from Topeka, there were 73 people in the traveling party. When the train reached Kansas City, Alva "Rip" Williams, Joe Riggert, and Les Nunamaker swung on board, and Gene Dale and Chet Thomas hopped on at Hutchinson. Nickerson was no longer impressed with the rail accommodations: "Believe me, there is no Pompeiian bath on this train. In general character of rolling stock and speed, it resembles a B. and A. [Boston and Albany] local. In other words, the brilliant picture of the palatial train painted by the railroad officials of the past month led everyone to expect something. In reality, it is no different than a tourist train. The goods are not up to prospectus." The train left Chicago 15 minutes early, but no one was left behind. The first part of the trip passed through a cold and snowy landscape, and the sleeping cars were cold, too, "all the steam being used for the engine."[13] Worse, there weren't enough blankets to go around; most of the men complained of cold feet during the night.

Nuf Ced McGreevey hopped off at every stop and took photographs with his camera. Others scribbled quick postal cards from the various stops along the way. Bill Carrigan set up shop with a deck of cards. Treasurer McBreen was already "hustling from one car to another to dodge the calls for help and advance money."[14]

Some of the food became a little monotonous at times. "Oh, quite a variety of meats offered to-day," said first baseman Bradley. "Come off; there's only steak," remarked the practical Carrigan. "Begging your distinguished pardon," replied the observing first baseman, "but I see three kinds, rare steak, medium steak, and well-done steak." Jack Kleinow piped in: "Fellow wanted to commit suicide, so he went out and laid down on the Rock Island tracks. He starved to death." Sawyer had come prepared. He'd been seen aboard the train with a "mysterious round bundle under his arm." It turned out to be a can of corn from Maine, which he had the chef warm up for him."[15]

When the train stopped to take on water, Joe Wood said, "I knew a man once who didn't know what water was. I was trying to tell him when he surprised me by exclaiming, 'Oh, that's the stuff they have to put under bridges.'" Such were some of the ways that the party tried to entertain themselves.[16]

High drifts of snow had to be cleared from the track outside of Liberal, Kansas. As the train traveled even further south, to Tucumcari, New Mexico, the temperature dropped to 10 degrees and snow-banked cactus caught the eye. The trainmen said this was most unusual weather. There were even reports of earlier trains being stuck in the snow for as much as 24 hours, with temperatures as low as 25 degrees below zero.[17]

A train of Mexican workers headed north from El Paso provided some color, but for the most part it was the land of the prairie dog and the jack-rabbit and cotton-tails, with pathetic-sounding little homestead claims where hopeful yet desolate people had erected little huts to stake their claim. They even saw a cowboy and cowgirl ride alongside at one point, eliciting cheers.

The train got to El Paso four hours late, squelching a scheme to take the whole group across the border for a team photograph by Tresillian, a photographer from Boston who had gone on the trip. Ed Karger, Tris Speaker, McLeod, and Scott Stanfield boarded in El Paso. Only briefly in the border city, Ray Collins, Larry Gardner, and Ralph Pond joined Nuf

International Bridge from Juarez to El Paso (Bain Collection at the Library of Congress).

Ced McGreevey and some of the others and took automobiles to cross the border (the bridge across the Rio Grande) into Mexico where they saw some soldiers, some gambling, and bought some trinkets.

Some of the players were more concerned than adventurous. Jack Thoney and Charlie Smith were among those fearful that the Mexican insurgents might hold up the train; they both decided to hide their "rolls." Paul Shannon admitted that he and the other journalists on the train might not be averse to a holdup: "There is an awful dearth of live news as the players seem to be pretty well fagged out already by their long confinement in the train. Then, too, there are a large number of strangers on board, and the big leaguers and 'bushers' do not seem to mix very well. The Red Sox players keep pretty much to themselves, while the California leaguers hold nightly sessions and some of them are bound to be pretty well cleaned out by the time they reach Sacramento."[18]

Nickerson shared observations on the brief foray into what he called the seat of the Mexican Revolution:

> The old Spanish town is a picture, with the added interest of martial law, Mexican cavalry patrol, the quiet streets, while at the corners sentinels are posted.

The plaza in front of the curious Guadeloupe, Juarez, is a blaze of light, that the troops stationed on the roof of the church may see what is going on around them. Over 150 men were on the roof of the structure last night, while groups of soldiers kept warm beside fires on the sidewalks. Buildings have sandbags along the edges, from behind which the glistening muskets can be seen.

Our auto was held at the bridge and a close inspection made of the contents. The Mexicans evidently are not taking anyone's word for it, and the Red Sox had to pass muster. It was just a flash of warfare, and yet it looked like the real thing. The natives of El Paso do not regard it as comic opera, pointing to the number of killed and wounded. Our driver told us of taking an American visitor out to the firing line, for which he was paid $50. This man had been a sharpshooter in the Spanish War and gave evidence of his marksmanship by borrowing a gun, with which he picked off a few insurrectos.

Keno games, operated by electricity, are in full blast and were patronized by Texans and Mexicans alike in the old town.[19]

Some of the drama was of a little more innocent nature. Mrs. Patsy Donovan nearly got left behind in Santa Rosa. She'd climbed down from the train to look over the town from the platform when the train started to pull out without warning and she had to run to get back on board. Nickerson said she seemed to enjoy the thrill of the moment. Thoney had a bit of a scare when he decided to chase a jack-rabbit (he wasn't really *that* fast), but when it scurried into a hole, he unwisely reached in after it and suffered the only reported rabbit bite of the trip. The weather remained very cold, down into single digits in El Paso and even into Arizona and Burke wrote that the outfit slept in raincoats, bathrobes, and sweaters.[20]

The special train of the Red Sox had apparently been following the Golden State Limited all the way from Chicago, but when the two trains reached Bowie, Arizona, Tip O'Neill somehow prevailed on the local agent to shift the other train onto a sidetrack. The Red Sox train rumbled ahead of it, sending up cheers from the men at the notion of having captured first place.

From endless fields covered with snow, the train sped into Yuma, Arizona, one of the hottest places in the country. The heat became so intense that many crowded out of the stuffy cars onto the observation platforms for a little fresh air, though it was so dusty with alkali that breathing was difficult. The team passed through an Indian reservation just after crossing the Colorado River from Arizona into California "and escaped without scalping" since "the aborigines were safely corralled." Paul Shannon's politically incorrect prose was more common for the day. Shannon might have known better; the first Native American to play for the Red Sox occurred just the prior year, Louis Leroy, appearing in his third year of major-league baseball.[21]

When the train reached Redlands Junction, some of the men hopped a fence and purloined oranges from the groves. Some players in the party, the bushers, broke off to go to Portland, Oakland, and eight of them for Sacramento.

At Colton, just south of San Bernardino, a party of Los Angeles newsmen clambered on board and rode into L. A., dining with the Red Sox party and gathering news of the trip for their papers. It was actually quite warm on the desolate and recently created Salton Sea in the California desert.

The train arrived in Los Angeles at 7:45 P.M. on the evening of February 23, about four hours late. There they enjoyed a "rousing welcome from the Angelenos, several hundred of whom lined the station platforms each wearing on his coat a pair of bright red sox." They were too late for the planned welcome banquet, and continued on to Redondo Beach by electric train ("appropriately decorated" trolleys), arriving between 9:00 and 9:30. Other trolleys had been sidetracked so they could get to Redondo Beach more quickly; the ride seemed so perilously fast that Doc Green was delegated "to go forward to determine if the motorman was an escaped lunatic."[22]

There were hardly any other guests, since the hotel had been opened early in the season especially for the Red Sox, so it gave off a deserted air but check-in was quick. It was the first time since the 18th that most in the party had enjoyed real hotel rooms. Despite the rapid drop in temperature on the coastline that brought out the sweaters once more, many of the players walked down to the beach to see the surf of the Pacific.

Those meant to join the team in California were Charley Hall, Ben Hunt, Doc Moskiman, Duffy Lewis, Harry Hooper, Jack Killilay, Frank Arellanes, and Hap Myers.

Taylor let the men know that he wasn't prepared to countenance any carousing. "There will be a great list of fines," he declared. "Automobile riding is barred this season. It has done more harm to ball players than rum. Cigarettes are next, and so on down the line. Eleven-thirty will be the latest hour for retiring and, believe me, it goes. I have to get even some way for these advances in salary."[23]

8000 MILES—COAST TO COAST

Red Sox Off for California Training Ground, Where Patsy Donovan Will Have 40 Players From Whom to Develop a Winning Team

The original itinerary for the 1911 trip is depicted on this map from the February 11, 1911, *Boston Globe.*

By the time it was all over, this was to be an 8,000-mile journey, coast to coast, with plenty of traveling up and down the West Coast and then, as originally planned, each one of the two traveling teams taking seven or eight stops as they each made their way from California to Chicago.

There were some cities on one of the two original itineraries that never saw the Red Sox play: Whittier, Ventura, Ogden (Utah), Amarillo, and Sioux City (Iowa). They did play in some communities not on the original schedule: Vernon, Pomona, Riverside, Salt Lake City, and El Paso. Precise train schedule times throughout the trip were planned out and printed in the newspaper. Both Tucson, Arizona, and Grand Junction, Colorado, were added before the men had arrived, but neither place saw a game, as things transpired.

Working Out at Redondo Beach

Manager Donovan had already broken the group into two squads and posted the lists beside the front desk the evening the men arrived, letting them know what time to report for work.

Practice started for the first squad at 9:30 in the morning of the 24th, with the Yannigans under Madden's leadership. The second squad — the Regulars — started at 10:30, overseen by Wagner. There was a 2:00 afternoon workout, too. The ballpark was a short walk from the hotel, and it was a better ballpark than Whittington Park in Hot Springs, even with that park's 1910 upgrade. Many of the recruits had not yet been issued Boston uniforms and so wore jerseys representing an array of different teams from their recent and respective pasts.

The setting seemed idyllic. Waking up from their beds without the rattle of the rails, they were refreshed "to see the sky a brilliant blue, to hear the birds in the gardens about the hotel singing merrily, and below the breakers of the Pacific, washing the white sands of the beach. Nothing could have been more ideal than this day for the workout."[24] Most of them could hardly wait to start playing baseball after the long stretch on the nation's railroads.

The team used the warm salt-water bathhouse, the plunge, as their dressing facility and some of them became a little too exuberant trying out the pool. Gardner got a small bump on his head when diving, and Engle's head hit the bottom of the pool too hard, too. Smoky Joe received "a bad jar" while going down the chute, but trainer Green got him feeling better.

Wood had tried to come down the chute standing up and almost made it before his "feet did a Highland fling, and he sat down between the right ankle and his slab arm, making a noise like a Mexican insurrection."[25] Donovan told the men to "cutout the comedy after this." Word reached John I. Taylor back in Boston, and a disapproving telegram from him arrived the very next day.

Speaker cut the morning practice, but turned up in uniform in the afternoon to the delight of some of the local fans who came out to see the practice. Hall lived the closest to Redondo Beach, in Ventura, yet was the only one who hadn't turned up yet. The weather was perfect and some of the men worked out too hard. Hal Janvrin, just out of Boston English

Players at the plunge at Redondo Beach during spring training: Harry Hooper (second from left), Les Nunamaker (second from right) and three unidentified individuals (courtesy Boston Public Library, Print Department, McGreevey Collection).

High School and the youngest player present at age 19, raised eyebrows even during the first loosening up. Hooper's luggage hadn't arrived so he was unable to suit up the first day.

All in all, it was good to hear the crack of the bats hitting baseballs around the field. It was about the best day they saw on the whole trip.

It was about a 10-minute walk between the hotel and the park. The field was a "skin diamond" (very little grass and in this case mostly sand, occasioning some unpredictable infield bounces). Nonetheless, Tim Murnane, himself a former ballplayer and umpire turned sportswriter, conveyed an enthusiastic initial impression of the setting: "From what I have seen I believe it is a better place to train than even Hot Springs. One important advantage is the splendid facilities for warm bathing after the practice work each day, and another is that the bright lights of Hot Springs are not duplicated, for here it is like the simple life, with fishing on the wharf the most exciting pastime known to the natives." The bathhouse had the "largest plunge in the world."[26]

The climate, wrote team captain Charles "Heinie" Wagner in a bylined column for the *Los Angeles Times*, was "decidedly more bracing and invigorating" than Hot Springs. He was optimistic after the first four hours of workouts, concluding his column, "From all appearances, this year's team will be 25 per cent farther than last year's team, and that's goin' some."[27]

Donovan warned the men against trying to do too much the first day, but "the men were unable to hold themselves in check." Several of the men showed off quite well, with Speaker hitting three balls over the right-field fence. After two "red hot practices" and the cavorting in the salt-water plunge (located a few hundred yards from the hotel via a path through a "semi-tropical grove"), two-thirds of the men were ready for bed within an hour after dinner, soothed to sleep by the sound of the rolling surf.[28] They played their first game the very next day, the 25th.

The other major-league teams trained much further east, the westernmost among them being the Chicago White Sox who were based in Mineral Wells, Texas, and the New York Giants, in Marlin, Texas. Hot Springs, Arkansas, hosted four teams: Brooklyn, Pittsburg, and Cincinnati of the National League and the St. Louis Browns of the American League. Cleveland trained in Alexandria, Louisiana, the Chicago Cubs in New

Orleans, and the Detroit Tigers in Monroe. Jackson, Tennessee, was the spring home of the St. Louis Cardinals. The Philadelphia Phillies trained in Birmingham and the Athletics in Savannah. Georgia hosted the remaining three teams: the New York Highlanders in Athens, the Washington Senators in Atlanta, and the Boston Rustlers in Augusta.

4

Chronology
of the Games

February 25

at Redondo Beach, CA: Regulars 7, Yannigans 3 (5 innings)

The first competition was held at Redondo Beach, a five-inning game free to the public in front of about 250 people, some of whom had come from Los Angeles to take in the practice. There had been no game planned, but Captain Wagner's men were itching to get in something akin to game action and Donovan yielded to their pleas. The weather was perfect. Donovan had two batteries work for each team, but it was a spirited contest in nice warm weather, Carrigan twice having to block the plate in one inning to prevent a pair of runners from the Yannigans from scoring. Both Yerkes and Janvrin were thrown out at home plate, Lewis to Carrigan and Wagner to Carrigan, due to "reckless base running."[1] Pierce and Hollis held the Yans to four hits (though Hollis walked four), while the Regs rang up a dozen. Janvrin had half the Yannigans' hits, one of them over the right-field fence (which was counted as a double, due to the very short fence) and then drove in two runs with a sharply hit single to left field in the fourth. Purtell, Speaker, Wagner, and Hooper each had a brace of hits for the Regulars. Yerkes tripled twice.

The first injury was to Hap Myers; Doc Green treated a split finger when he had his nail torn off by a Duffy Lewis grounder.

Carrigan's blocking of the plate may have presaged his earning the nickname "Rough" but it was perhaps some time in coming. None of the five Boston newspapers used the nickname in their accounts of this year's spring training. The first mention of his nickname found in the *Boston Globe* doesn't come until September 1912.

Second baseman Priepke never made it to the big leagues, but the native of Germany was deemed "the most conspicuous worker" on the field with his bushy red hair (which won him the nickname "Pepper"). He'd played for first-place Huntington, West Virginia, in the Class D Virginia League in 1910 under manager Cy Young, who likely recommended him to the Red Sox.

After the game, the Regulars worked out for another half-hour and then the field was cleared for some rifle practice with old baseballs thrown in the air by a local boy. Ed Karger won first place with three hits, Speaker second with two hits and a miss (but brought down a bird with another shot). Wood and Moser each hit one ball. *Globe* cartoonist Wallace Goldsmith captured the image in a March 3 sports page cartoon.

Tip O'Neill's original recommendation had been that the Regulars stay in Southern California where the weather was warmer, but then travel back across the country on the northern route, where they would be playing in larger cities and could thus attract larger crowds and more lucrative gates. McBreen had only reserved 17 tickets for the southern route back east. After talking with Purtell and Frank Smith about how cold the northern route had been for the White Sox in 1910, Donovan began to think about reversing the original plan and have the Regulars be the team that traveled the southern route while returning east. There was the interest expressed by a number of Texans wanting to see native sons Tris Speaker (from Hubbard City) and Ed Karger (from San Angelo). And perhaps the weather would be better and the first-stringers kept in better shape. This was the plan ultimately adopted. There were so many players in camp that Donovan hadn't actually met them all yet.

This was a problem throughout, and one foreseen by Hugh Fullerton even before the trip had gotten underway. With the division of the team into two groups, inevitably Donovan could only watch over half the men. Since he planned to travel with the first-string players, the ones Donovan would not see were the ones regarding whom decisions had to be made, not the ones who were pretty well fixed. Fullerton added, "Donovan is not a strong manager, although a clever baseball man and a gentleman.... The training plan, abandoned by Comiskey after three ruinous years, will rob Donovan of a chance to see many of his young players and will bring them East in bad condition from hard traveling."[2]

While the White Sox had enjoyed perfect weather on their 1909 visit, and the 1910 trip had some problems with rain, there was no intimation that inclement weather might put a serious damper on 1911 spring training for the Red Sox.

Speaker caught several fish with a hook and line dangled in the water off Redondo pier and Judge Wells had them served up for dinner in the Rotunda dining room of the hotel, where a banquet, reception, and dance had been organized by local businessmen. The hotel also served up banana fritters, and Bill Carrigan became the butt of a few jokes when he turned to Ray Collins and said, "These are the funniest tasting sweet potatoes I ever ate." After he was told what they were, he said, "Well, I guess I'll try some more."[3]

There was a little socializing, and the young blade of the group seemed to be Hal Janvrin. He was, observed the *Los Angeles Examiner*, "the leading social light at Redondo. He has danced with more petite Angeleno maids than anyone else at the shore. 'I've been to dances before,' he confides."[4]

February 26

"REGULARS WIN BY ONE-RUN MARGIN"—*Boston Post*
at Redondo Beach, CA: Regulars 3, Yannigans 2

The Sunday *Los Angeles Times* carried a number of features on the Red Sox, including a lengthy interview with pitcher Ben Hunt, a profile of Donovan, and a column by trainer Green in which he wrote, "It isn't a cinch looking after forty or fifty baseball players in spring training and during the season." He liked the climate and the salt baths, but worried that the ocean breeze was likely to give a couple of the boys a cold. He complimented the hotel: "The meals are wholesome and palatable and everything is fine and dandy for a mighty successful training season here in Southern California."

The *Times* also let its readers know that Red Sox President John I. Taylor's father, General Charles H. Taylor, had purchased some real estate in Boston known as the Dana lands, on Ipswich and Lansdowne Streets, a couple of months earlier. It was sold at public auction for $120,000. The Red Sox were facing their last season at their original ballpark, the Huntington Avenue Grounds, because the Boston Elevated Railway Company, which had leased them the property prior to the 1901 season when the franchise was first established, planned to cut two streets through the property. The permits were granted on the proviso that the 1911 season could be played in full before the roadwork began. The Taylors planned to build "new grounds in the exclusive Back Bay section of Fenway."[5]

There was no morning practice, so the players could attend church if they wished. Father Fitzgerald greeted 20 at Catholic mass and bade welcome to the Red Sox before beginning his sermon.

Admission to the ball game was charged, but neither that nor a cold breeze off the Pacific deterred 1,500 fans (some who'd come on special trains from Los Angeles) from crowding in to watch the game, filling all available seating and also crowding onto the field. After the brass band concert, they saw a good full nine-inning one-run game, a 3–2 win for the Regulars, who pitched Arellanes for four innings, and then Wood, Moser, and Killilay (who hoped to make the big leagues after going 24–10 for Spokane in 1910). Engle, nicknamed Hackenschmidt by Shannon of the *Post*, managed the Yannigans, who took a 1–0 lead in the top of the first when Perry lined one past third, moved to second base on an out, and scored on Yerkes' single. Murnane noted that Perry "cracked two fine singles" but also observed that he "hit in a wild sort of manner." He may have meant Riggert, who had indeed singled twice. The box score only credited him with one hit, however. O'Brien gave up three runs in the bottom of the third on Gardner's double, a single by Purtell, a Speaker double, and singles from Lewis and Bradley. Hunt and Sawyer, the Carrigan protege from Maine, pitched five innings of scoreless ball. Donovan saw to it that anyone who looked like they might be trying too much too hard was replaced. To please the crowd, he also made sure that the Californians in the crew each made an appearance; some 27 players in all took part in the game. The fans were just glad to see some baseball played by some of the stars from back east. "Everyone wanted to see Speaker, Carrigan, Wood, and the other players that they had heard so much about, and no one cared very much which side won as long as the celebrities took part."[6]

The chilly winds were dismaying, and rain was predicted for Monday. There was already a bit of grumbling about the "rather poor hotel accommodations" but they were willing to endure those. The cold winds off the ocean forced the players to depart the field quickly: "The moment a player finishes the workout on the field he is compelled to run hard all the way to the hotel in order to avoid taking cold."[7]

After the game, Tip O'Neill left for San Francisco to oversee preparations for the team to stay there. Hugh McBreen was to go, too, but deferred his plans at the last minute. "Mac" was considered to be quite sharp with figures, not only able to recall the exact number of minutes it took the train to travel from Chicago to Los Angeles and the precise number of pennies each Red Sox player was paid, but he was also able to unerringly state the age of any person who told him the day, month, and year they were born. "A wizard all the way," marveled the day's *Times*.

It seemed to be a sober crew. "Half of the boys don't indulge in joy water of any kind," wrote Lou Guernsey in the *Times*. "The boys that do, drink nothing but beer. Donovan doesn't object if the boys knock over a glass of beer or ale now and then, but he won't stand for any lushing. He is very temperate in his habits, and wants the boys to be the same."[8] All players were expected to be in their beds by 11:00 P.M. and up by 7:30 A.M., but Donovan tended to trust his players rather than tightly regulate them.

There was a lot of card playing (bridge), and the Red Sox Quartette practiced their barbershop harmonies at least once a day under bass singer Hugh Bradley. Marty McHale sang tenor, Larry Gardner baritone, and Buck O'Brien, second tenor. Guernsey reported, "All of the boys have a good word to say for Judge Wells, the fat and jolly innkeeper. He is doing all he can to make it homelike and pleasant for the boys and they surely appreciate it."

The weather was nice enough back in Boston that the next morning's *Globe* noted, "If the Red Sox had been at home yesterday, and if it hadn't been Sunday, they could have played." Under the laws of the day, however, they would have been arrested had they attempted to play ball on the Lord's Day in Boston. It wasn't until 1929, after a state referendum in 1928, that Sunday baseball could be played in Boston,[9]

February 27

A cold rainstorm rolled in on Sunday night. When Donovan saw what it was like in the morning he called off the day's game. Most of the players put on heavy sweaters and went for a long walk of several miles along the beach. Arellanes was excused to play in a handball game, a sport in which he excelled and which helped keep him in shape. The sun only came out for a few minutes, but the weather cleared enough by mid-day to get in some light work on the damp field in the afternoon. The temperature had dropped to 45 degrees and the hotel, too, was "cold and cheerless, save in front of the open fire where there was standing room only."[10]

Two days earlier, Burke had written that Jack Thoney "certainly has gotten back his throwing arm" but now many of the men had sore muscles. Thoney's case was one of the worst, occasioning a front-page headline: "THONEY CAN'T PLAY BASEBALL." He explained part of the reason. The

Third baseman Larry Gardner, first baseman Hugh Bradley, pitcher Marty McHale and pitcher Buck O'Brien in Redondo Beach, California, in March of 1911. The four sang together as the Red Sox Quartette (courtesy Boston Public Library, Print Department, McGreevey Collection).

ocean breezes, previously deemed "refreshing" now were said to "cool off the players a little too quickly and gives them a chill which stiffens up arms and legs more than usual." He now doubted Thoney would make the big leagues again this year. Many of the men were now displeased with the "cold winds of the unfeeling Pacific and withal the squad will be glad to move on to inland towns."[11]

Charley Hall turned up in camp, in time for more songs by the Red Sox Quartette and a lot of card games. Kleinow was the king of the billiards table, with Wood second-best. Donovan thought pool and billiards were good for the eyes and encouraged the sport. There was a fire scare at the hotel when smoke billowed through some of the corridors, but where there was smoke, there was no fire — or at least none which did any damage. During the day, Donovan re-divided the two squads into the northern one (primarily the second-string Yannigans) and the southern one, the Regulars.

The southern team: pitchers Arellanes, Bedient, Cicotte, Hunt, Killilay, Mahoney, Pape, Pierce, and Wood; catchers Kleinow, Madden, Thomas, and Williams; infielders Bradley, Gardner, Nebinger, Purtell, and Wagner; and outfielders Hooper, Lewis, and Speaker. Mahoney could serve as the reserve outfielder. Donovan would travel with the southern team, which would first break off and head for the San Francisco/Oakland Bay area before returning to Los Angeles and traveling east.

The northern team: pitchers Collins, Dale, Hall, Hollis, Karger, Moser, O'Brien, Sawyer, C. Smith, and F. Smith; catchers Carrigan, Nunamaker, and Sheehan; infielders Buzick, Engle, Janvrin, Priepke, and Yerkes; and outfielders Myers, Perry, Riggert, and Thoney. Carrigan was placed in charge of the northern team which, despite its ultimate route, would at first remain in Southern California. For some reason, Hall was to play with the northern team in the south, but then join the southern team at Modesto and come back south. On Carrigan's shoulders, of course, would rest most of the responsibility for the selection process Donovan must eventually undertake. Carrigan was clearly already valued for his baseball insight, reflecting to a degree the successful manager he would quite soon become. Carrigan managed the Red Sox from 1913 to 1916, winning back-to-back world championships in 1915 and 1916.

The highlight of the day was when Tris Speaker hooked a pelican in the wing while trying to fish off the pier. The newspapermen were feted with a banquet at The Alexandria in Los Angeles.

There was already a sense of some dissatisfaction or skepticism in the minds of some. Herman Nickerson of the *Journal* confided to his readers, "The day has been as dead as Chelsea," adding, "As near as I can figure this trip out it is largely in the nature of an advertising scheme. Surely this beach is no place to train a ball club.... The training trip of 1911, aside from furnishing the ball players with a fine view of the United States, is likely to be a fizzle in its effects."

The weather had become worse than disappointing. Writing of the Regulars, who were due to leave for Northern California, Paul Shannon confided, "Most of the party are glad to get away from here, for the cold winds have chilled everybody, and the pitchers do not expect to improve their condition much at this beach resort, but those who leave on Wednesday will have to come back, while the ones scheduled to stay have the consolation of knowing that once they leave they will not have to return."[12] The initial warmth and welcome after the long train ride matched the buildup the party had been given regarding the California climate. The giant palm tree, the gardens of carnations, and the citrus groves on the hotel grounds were all as advertised, but the weather had turned. The bloom was off the rose.

February 28

"YANNIGANS GET BIG END OF GAME" — *Boston Post*
at Redondo Beach, CA: Yannigans 5, Regulars 1 (7 innings)

The men worked at bunting in the chilly morning, and the pitchers worked at covering first base, a weakness the team had shown in 1910. The "heavyweights" (the players who hadn't shed enough weight yet) were sent around the park doing some extra running. Burke noted that even native Californians didn't tend to live on the coast in the wintertime and that, while the area was "sun-kissed," the sun itself was "very fickle and the kisses are a passing fancy that is chilled immediately after the smack."[13]

The Yannigans finally had their day, behind the seven-hitter thrown by Bedient (three innings of one-run ball, pitching to Carrigan) and Buzick (the final four of a seven-inning game, throwing to Madden). Sawyer pitched the first three frames for the Regulars, without giving up a run. O'Brien was victimized with one run in the fifth and four more in the sixth. The Regulars' run came in the second inning when Duffy Lewis singled, moved up on Wagner's out, then scored on Bradley's hit that bumped up against the left-field fence. The game was tied when Riggert doubled over Hooper's head in right, then was sacrificed to third by Janvrin and sacrificed home thanks to Priepke's fly ball.

The game had broken open in the top of the sixth, though, after a single, a walk, and a safe bunt loaded the bases. Hollis's double over that short right-field fence scored both. Yerkes singled in another, and Riggert's sacrifice fly brought in another. Though Speaker didn't play, being a bit lame, he worked out on the bunting but left the center-field work to Mahoney, who covered some ground and made four nice catches. Riggert was a real prospect; he had hit .350 and shown extra-base power in the Kansas State League and with Omaha in the Western League in 1910, with 31 doubles, 27 triples, and 17 homers, and some speed with 36 stolen bases.

The field wasn't the best; it was smallish and left field was kind of "hilly" while the infield was a little too rough for sliding. The regulars were smart enough to be cautious in their play, but Murnane said Donovan was very worried by the "insane desire of young players to make a good showing" regardless of the conditions. Fortunately, no one was hurt save for Myers.[14] There were some truly exceptional fielding plays in the game reflected in newspaper game accounts, remarkable for an early spring intrasquad ballgame. The left-fielder Riggert "was some pumpkins" going back to catch Mahoney's long drive in the bottom of the sixth, and throwing a strike to home plate, getting the runner out by two strides.[15] Lewis made a full-speed running catch over his head with his back to home plate, then whirled and earned an assist on a strike to Wagner.

Donovan proclaimed to the press what wonderful shape everyone was in, better than had they been at Hot Springs. The pitching corps wasn't buying the company line. None had been able to throw anything but straight fastballs yet and the chilly breezes had stiffened their arms.[16]

The win for the recruits, the "second team," most likely pleased Donovan. Winning a game had to encourage the recruits and give them some sense of self-confidence. Losing reminded the first-stringers that they were not invincible. Losing games in spring training can have a salutary effect.

The games at Redondo Beach were over, with all of 21 innings being played and all of them intrasquad games. It was an underwhelming record for a community that was considered the spring training home of the 1911 Red Sox.

The evening's entertainment was courtesy of the St. James Catholic Church at the Auditorium, and Hugh Bradley, Marty McHale, and Buck O'Brien joined in the vocalizing, as did Patsy Donovan's wife. Some of the players bribed one of the waiters to present Bradley with a "huge bunch of wild flowers," which seems to have been a joke of some sort.

March 1

P.J., as some of the more familiar columnists called Patsy Donovan, hadn't really had a chance to assess the men before it was time to separate. He would be traveling with the first-stringers, the Regulars, who were due to take the Owl (the overnight train) to Oakland, departing at 6:00 P.M. and arriving at 9:00 A.M. the following morning, where they would stay at the Hotel St. Mark and be ready for their first game on March 2. As it happens, the train arrived early, at 7:37 A.M. at Oakland's 16th Street Station but was still greeted by around 100 well-wishers and the Prosperity Committee of the Oakland Chamber of Commerce. A dozen automobiles carried them to the hotel for an "elaborate breakfast." They were then driven around the city and shown points of interest.[17]

It was the first warm day since arriving in California and both squads worked out in the morning, but the Regulars (confusingly called the "southern division") had to get ready to head north so they curtailed their own afternoon activities. The squad which was to remain in Redondo Beach worked out for a couple of hours in the afternoon, mostly batting and infield practice.

There was a surprising amount of transcontinental travel so many years ago. Ray Collins and Larry Gardner were invited to lunch at a local restaurant and feted by a group of 25 folks from Burlington, Vermont.

Tris Speaker was due to stay in Southern California so he could play in the inaugural game at Washington Park, Los Angeles. Nuf Ced McGreevey traveled north with the "southern team," the Regulars who would be taking the southerly route back east. At the last minute, Speaker headed north to Oakland, too. Despite both teams playing in California, they weren't due to meet again until April 10 in Chicago.

As noted, the second team (the northern team) was placed under the command of Bill Carrigan and dubbed the Carrigan Colts. The selection of Carrigan clearly acknowledged him as a leader among the men, and foreshadowed his selection to manage the Red Sox in mid–1913.

Hosting the Red Sox on the second of March were the Los Angeles Angels of the Pacific Coast League, under manager Frank "Pop" Dillon. Coast League teams typically played long schedules since the climate permitted extended seasons; after the 1911 season played out, the Angels were dead last with a record of 82–127, 39½ games behind the first-place Portland Beavers. The Angels had played at Chutes Park, Los Angeles, beginning in 1901. It was situated on Washington Boulevard between Grand and Main; an amusement park was located beyond center field. It seated 6,000. They had a brand-new ballpark, Washington Park, built and ready for the 1911 season just 300 yards away from Chutes Park; the new facility seated 12,200. And the Boston Red Sox were the first team to take on the Angels in the new park.

A 1:00 P.M. parade was planned from City Hall to Washington Park, with the players proceeding in automobiles that followed a brass band. The Red Sox had had less than a week to practice, but that was more than the Angels had allowed themselves. However, many of the Angels had played winter ball in California and were generally in good shape. Ed Karger was named to start for the Red Sox and Bill Tozer for the Angels.

The *Los Angeles Times* had a nice feature on Elinor McBreen, the four-year-old daughter of the Red Sox treasurer. She'd made the whole cross-country trip from Boston and was the "official" mascot of the team. She was most impressed with speed. She declared that the reason she liked to see Tris Speaker was that "he runs so fast." And as for Smoky Joe: "I like to see Joe Wood pitch for he pitches so fast that sometimes I can't hardly see the ball." These were the "Speed Boys" after all. "My daddy says the Red Sox is going to win this year, and I think so, too." She had been interviewed on March 1, and the story ran in the next day's paper. Hugh McBreen himself contributed a bylined column in the same edition, running through the team's strengths. He admitted that the team "may be a little weak in the box, but we have a lot of new men with fine minor league records, and sincerely hope that one or two of them will turn out good heavers." Ominous or just a statement of fact, he warned, "Certain members of the present staff may do better work this season. If they do not, they will be traded or sold and new men given a chance."

March 2

"Janvrin's Hit In Tenth Won Game"—*Boston Post*
at Los Angeles, CA: Boston 6, Los Angeles 5 (10 innings)

Facing outside competition for the first time, and playing in front of 4,000 to 5,000 fans, including a large number of Boston fans, both the Angels and the Red Sox acquitted themselves well with an exciting game that even stretched into extra innings. This being the grand opening of brand-new Washington Park, tickets were sold at half-price (25 cents instead of the 50 cents charged during the White Sox visit in 1910) and Los Angeles Mayor George Alexander, 71, kicked off the 3:00 P.M. game by throwing the first pitch — against a live batter. "You might get a little more steam into that pitch than you did last year," taunted Angels owner Henry Berry. "Last season you were a little weak." The batter was Angels leadoff hitter Thomas "Pete" Daley, who went on to hit .302 in 1911. The mayor went into something resembling a windup "and a frightened cheer broke from the grand stand." Alexander was wearing a buttoned-up double-breasted suit and a fedora, and didn't even have a glove for self-protection. The ball actually went over home plate. Daley swung and somehow missed the mayor's pitch by a foot. The band then tore into an "up-to-date" tune. The *Los Angeles Examiner* differed with the *Globe*'s account of the first pitch, claiming he "heaved the nice white ball twenty feet to the fork side of the batsman." Perhaps the *Examiner* was in the pocket of political opponents.[18]

Unlike Chutes Park, the Washington Park grounds boasted a grass infield. Despite heavy dark clouds earlier in the day, and slightly soggy grounds from the day before, the parade had proceeded as scheduled and the game suffered neither rain nor delay. The game was well-played, with only two errors, both by Angels players slipping on the surface, both attributable to the soft field conditions and both deemed excusable. The park itself was as new as could be, as H. M. Walker of the *Examiner* wrote, "It is all that has been said for it, and then some. Outside of the fact that some of us rubbed our elbows against the fresh paint and carried away a few splinters in our shins as souvenirs everything was perfectly lovely."[19]

The fences were deep and on another day with a firmer surface to run on, one or two of the four triples might have gone for inside-the-park

Red Sox players in uniform during an automobile tour of downtown Los Angeles (courtesy Boston Public Library, Print Department, McGreevey Collection).

home runs. Engle batted second for Boston and cracked a triple to deep right field in the top of the first; he scored on a wild pitch from right-hander Bill Tozer (the *Los Angeles Herald* said he "mistook the press stand for the catcher").[20] It was the only run either team scored in the first two frames, though Tozer took a while to gather himself, throwing two wild pitches and seeing a passed ball.

Ed Karger started for the Red Sox and ran into trouble in the bottom of the third when Tozer singled and Daley tripled down the first-base line. A double to the fence in left field off the bat of Ivan Howard gave the Angels the lead.

Pitcher Crips took over for the Angels in the fourth inning. He struck out the first man he faced, but walked Steve Yerkes, who took second on a wild pitch. But Crips fanned Janvrin. With two outs, Hollis singled to left field and Yerkes scored, Paul Shannon believed that had the umpire being paying close enough attention, Yerkes would have been called out at home plate. The game was tied, 2–2.

In the top of the Sox sixth, Hank Perry socked a triple off Crips into deep center field. He scored easily when Engle singled to left and took second base on a passed ball, the second of the game charged to Fred Abbott. Yerkes bunted Engle to third, who then scored on a sacrifice fly lofted by Janvrin. Marty McHale held the Angels at bay in the sixth and the seventh. The Sox almost scored another run in the top of the eighth, but the first out recorded was a runner thrown out at home plate and two quick outs followed. Boston's 4–2 lead held until the bottom of the eighth.

Carrigan put in Gene Dale, who doled out three bases on balls in a row. There was trouble brewing, and Carrigan called in Ray Collins, who had no time to warm up. Third baseman Roy Akin singled to right field and two men scored, the runner on first making it to third base. A sacrifice fly pushed the Angels into a 5–4 lead.

When Carrigan put himself in the game in the eighth, Merton Burke thought he made a difference. Carrigan, he wrote, "jacked up the whole outfield, coached them on to the job, and shut out the Angelesians twice while he coaxed in a run in the ninth and another in the tenth. Carrigan is a heady piece of energy, and the minute he took hold of the boys, a change in their work was noticeable."[21] Burke of the *American* and Shannon of the *Post* were the two among the Boston sportswriters who had stayed behind with the Colts, thinking their readers might be more interested in learning about the prospects than the regular players.

With one out in the top of the ninth, and Elmer "Shorty" Criger (Lou's brother) on the mound, "Babe" Sheehan doubled to left field and Perry singled in pinch-runner "Bullet" Jack Thoney to tie the game. In the top of the 10th, Riggert slashed a "savage liner" to right-center field for a triple and scored on an infield single by Janvrin between first and second. The Sox had a 6–5 lead.

Carrigan had hit in Collins' spot, so he asked Buzick to throw the 10th and saw the bases get loaded when Engle momentarily fumbled one ball, Howard singled, and Buzick walked Akin. There was nobody out. But the Sox escaped unscathed. The *Times* wrote, "Deal lined a scorcher to Yerkes. If it had gone four feet one way or the other, the Angels would have won the game." Phillips grounded out to Yerkes, and Perry caught a fly ball to retire the side, a "remarkable catch" said Shannon, by the center fielder "who always seemed to be in the right place."[22] Riggert had made a nice play earlier, fielding a base hit so rapidly in short left that he was able to throw out the runner coming in to second base on a force play.

Bill Carrigan wasn't being diplomatic when he was quoted in the *Times* saying, "To tell the truth I don't think we really won the game." Umpire Finney may not have been fully awake throughout the entire game. Carrigan was thinking of the fourth inning, when Yerkes scored on the two-out Hollis single, despite having misjudged and thinking the ball was being caught. He trotted around third toward home and, Carrigan said, "the left fielder threw Hollis out at second before Yerkes was within eight feet of the plate ... the 'ump' was watching the second base play and didn't see Yerkes.... I thought we'd lost the game a dozen times but baseball luck was with us from the start. We had the luck, The Angels didn't have any." There were two other moments that *Times* writer Grey Oliver noticed and Finney did not. In the bottom of the seventh, with two out, it was the pitcher, Crips, who was due up. But leadoff man Pete Daley stepped up to the plate. Some of the newspaper men hollered, but to no avail. Daley grounded out; Finney then said he was out for batting out of order. Daley led off the eighth, too, even though he'd — in one sense, though not in actuality — already made the last two outs.

The Red Sox had worn their new road uniforms for the ceremonial first game and the automobile parade from City Hall to the new ballpark. After the game, the uniforms were packed up and shipped back to Boston to await the regular season. That evening, when the team got back to the hotel, they were treated to a water polo game between Redondo and Venice and a speed swimming exhibition by the West Coast champion.

In Oakland, the team had enjoyed a hearty welcome, but the conditions were "real New England weather."[23] The sun came out just long enough that they dressed in their uniforms and took a special car out to the ballpark. But when they saw the grounds, the car simply turned around and came right back to the hotel. The rain and a "fierce wind" made it impossible to work out. Some of the men began to give vent to disgust at the weather. Worse, the word was that it might be wet and rainy for much of the month. Some of the pitchers hadn't really been able to get loose yet, and the same went for the throwing arms of a number of the fielders.

The arrival of the Red Sox in Oakland was heralded in an odd fashion, drumming up interest in a game that couldn't be played: "A town crier, dressed in baseball uniform, mounted on a pony, has been riding the streets all day yelling himself hoarse."[24] Oakland was no small town. In the wake of the 1906 earthquake in San Francisco, both people and businesses moved across the bay to relocate and the city more than doubled in size, from what it had been in 1900, to a population of 150,000 in 1910. The *Boston Herald* ran some photographs of the Red Sox Special during the trip west, including one of the group posed around the engine and one showing Engineer Harvey and Fireman Lackland.

March 3

Both games were rained out, in the north and in the south. Those waiting in Oakland got the word early that the grounds were unplayable. "Since the regular team arrived here there has been nothing but rain and high winds," wrote Nickerson in the *Journal*. Donovan got his charges in uniform nonetheless and got in a workout at Piedmont Rink, then had them jog back to the hotel. A century later, it would be nothing less than startling to come across a major-league ballclub running in full uniform through city streets on its way back to the hotel.

For Hooper and Lewis, the Bay Area was home. Both had played in Oakland for the St. Mary's College ballclub, the Phoenix. John I. Taylor's bride had come from San Francisco and it was clear that Taylor had won much favor with the local luminaries.

But for Nickerson, what the team had done was to travel all the way across the country to work out in such indoor gyms as they could book. They might as well have stayed home. In his talks with native Californians, they all agreed that March was "the bad month." "They were dumped into Redondo Beach at a hotel which had been reopened to receive them. All a part of an advertising scheme. The rooms were cold and damp, the food poor and also cold. Could anything have been less cheerful?" Whatever they'd accomplished in starting training at Redondo Beach was being undone through weather-enforced idleness. "Why a club should pass up a splendid camp at Hot Springs, Ark., to barnstorm and cool its heels about Pacific coast hotel corridors is beyond me." He was not a happy camper.[25]

The Colts suffered so much rain they couldn't even work out so they mostly hung out at the hotel reading and playing cards. Burke said, "It rained harder than the Red Sox boys ever saw it rain before" and that they had to content themselves with getting as much exercise as they could in the hotel. "Some got writer's cramp from addressing picture postal cards. Others have lame right arms from moving silver coins and some gold back and forth on a table." When it let up, several went out for a run in the afternoon and several more took the hot water plunge.

O'Brien had been treated in hospital the day before, having had the forefinger of his pitching hand hit in pregame batting practice. Dale had been one of the most promising prospects before the games began, but he'd disappointed so far, "failed to show anything in the way of control or speed." He was perhaps a little under the weather.

Sheehan, the *American* had reported on March 3, was trying to reduce his weight from 310 to 190 pounds. It's unlikely Burke had been apprised of the typo, but he referred to the catcher's weight again on March 4: "Babe Sheehan, the 210-pound catcher, whom President Taylor captured on a million-acre farm out in Illinois, has wrapped himself up in a roll of cotton flannel, and has taken off twelve pounds. His favorite morning diversion is a ten-mile run, after which he eats three pounds of steak, sixteen hot cakes, three cups of coffee, a dozen oranges and a quart of mush. That stands him in well till noon. Seriously, though, he can play ball." (Burke's March 8 column again cited the figure 310.)

Burke was also amused by one that McHale put over on a waiter: "Have you any cirrhosis of the liver?" "Not unless it's on the bill," replied the young man. Whatever they were being served at the hotel, "each and every one of the squad would give their cherished last year's sweaters for one good New England meal. There is a little revolt on at the hotel regarding food." Some of the players were slipping out to walk down the hill to town and buy their own meals.[26]

March 4

Once more, the "glorious climate" of California failed to materialize and both games were rained out again. "But There Is No Joy In Mudville," read the headline in the March 5 *Boston Post*.

The game in Oakland was called off again due to prolonged cold rain, with no letup in sight and wind strong enough to rattle the window panes. Donovan took up the offer of St. Mary's College and the team worked out there in the cage, with a little baseball and a little basketball. Lewis invited several of the men over to his home in Alameda in the evening. He was a graduate of Alameda High School and a 1908/09 Oakland Oaks alum before being selected by the Red Sox in the September 1909 Rule 5 draft. The hotel was rated highly, "warm rooms and baths and good food, a contrast to the beach."[27] General Charles H. Taylor was in town, visiting his daughter in San Francisco.

Oddly, conditions were ideal at Redondo Beach, but rain and hailstones as big as cherries fell heavily enough in Los Angeles that the Angels telephoned the Red Sox and told them not to come — but didn't place the call until noon, so the morning was wasted. The Colts did get in an afternoon workout for a couple of hours, though their bats had been left in the Washington Park clubhouse so Doc Green had to run out to a sporting goods store to buy a few. The grounds were muddy anyway, so it wasn't much of a workout.

The weather wasn't looking up for March 5, either, but the plan was to squeeze in two games by adding a morning game in Vernon. No one was particularly looking forward to a packed lunch at the park in between games. The food at the hotel wasn't winning much favor at it was. "Cold storage eggs wouldn't be so bad if they were decently cooked, and the fruit served at this place would be rejected by any reputable Boston fruit dealer. The most nourishing thing we are getting is fresh air ... the table the Yannigans are provided would goad the inmates of Warden Bridges' college at Charlestown to mutiny. Ever since the first squad left the fodder has been getting worse, bread and water with oatmeal thrown in may be nourishing food for starving Russians but it is not quite what a ball team in training expects to draw."[28]

"We'll make the Athletics hustle," wrote Patsy Donovan in a statement provided the *Sunday American* which seemed out of synch with any developments. He minimized the effects of the long-distance travel and saw a good year ahead. Speaker went fishing and caught several surf perch and a pompano.

March 5

All the day's games were rained out once more, but readers of the *American* back in Boston were cheered to see Ring Lardner pick the Red Sox to finish in second place, offering a detailed position-by-position discussion of the team's strengths and weaknesses.

All this precipitation was becoming a real problem, with the whole coast under the weather and three more games canceled, the two the Colts had hoped to play and the first game up north that the Regulars were still waiting to play. The Vernon game was called off after a steady overnight downpour lasting until 7:00 A.M. It cleared and the team traveled to Los Angeles for the afternoon game but another shower rained down and forced cancellation. Even despite the weather, several hundred fans had gathered outside the gates clamoring to get in. It was Sunday and the various magnates had all been hoping for good turnouts. Many players went to church in the morning and almost all of them prayed for good weather in the afternoon.

The Red Sox Quartette practiced every day under Bradley's leadership and were getting better and better.

Donovan didn't even bother to send his men to St. Mary's and there wasn't any indoor workout up north. O'Neill began talking with Sacramento about getting the Regulars into a game or two with them.

Donovan wasn't planning to switch both teams *in toto* when they changed positions north and south after another week. Hall was going to remain in the south and link up with the Regulars. Donovan wanted to take Janvrin with him on the southern route, to keep him under his wing and also to prevent him from playing too much were he to travel with the Yannigans team. Conversely, P.J. wanted the more veteran Nebinger to get the extra work so planned to leave him in the Bay Area when the two squads switched positions. Nunamaker would be asked to move to the Regulars.

The March 8 game planned for Whittier was called off by the team there and a game against Vernon inserted in its stead.

March 6

"CARRIGAN'S COLTS WIN AT REDLANDS"—*Boston Post*
at Redlands, CA: Red Sox Colts 7, Redlands 3 (8 innings)

The field at St. Mary's was said to only need a couple of hours of sunshine to drain and be good for play, so the Regulars planned to play the college team on the 6th. But the rains did not abate — one report said it rained three inches on this day alone — and some locals were already declaring it the rainiest month in local history. There was no letup in Sacramento, either. The team worked out indoors at St. Mary's for an hour in the cage, then worked up a bit of a sweat playing some basketball in their baseball uniforms (they dressed in the hotel where there were warm baths). After that, all the players could do was "stare at each other across the lobby of the St. Mark. It is getting on their nerves."[29]

Joe Wood was down with a cold, in any event. Benjamin Franklin Hunt had missed the boat back across the bay from San Francisco, where he'd been visiting a friend with whom he'd been prospecting for gold in Colorado during the winter. But there was no baseball to be played in any event. The *Journal's* Nickerson evidently would have preferred to be in San Francisco. He sniffed, "Stopping at Oakland is a good deal like putting the team up at Revere Beach, for it takes a car ride and a ferry trip to get to Frisco." Oakland resident Tip O'Neill had become conspicuous by his absence. "It has been an awful black eye to the climate of California to have the Red Sox get this steady rain."[30]

In the south, there was a respite. The skies brightened and the Colts got in a game, one arranged under the auspices of the YMCA at Redlands, about 75 miles east from the coast and not far from San Bernardino. The 6:00 A.M. wakeup call wasn't too popular, but it was a nice warm day and the trip passed through orange grove after orange grove. It was said to be the first time some of the players had ever seen oranges on trees, rather than in stores. The Colts played against a team composed of the best college players in the area. The college boys, with some minor-league players mixed in, acquitted themselves well.

The local newspaper anticipated that "the YMCA boys will present a fairly strong team to battle with the Bostonians" though admitting that "practice has been impossible on account of the bad weather and the team will go into the field practically without practice." Nonetheless, several of the team had played ball much of the winter with the Bryn Mawr–Redlands team.[31] The team arrived on the Santa Fe shortly after 11:00 A.M. and was served lunch at the Casa Loma. After lunch, they were taken for a drive around the city visiting Prospect Park and part of Sunset Drive. "Every one of the players was amazed at the beauty of Redlands," reported the *Daily Facts* on the day of their arrival.

The game was played on the "spacious high school playground and Redlands society was out in full force, nearly a hundred autos lining the playing field."[32] Pitching for Redlands was Ed McCreery, just a few days from heading to Victoria, British Columbia, to pitch in the Northwest League in his first season of professional baseball. He threw a complete game, allowing 11 hits and walking three. He struck out six Sox. Three pitchers threw for the Red Sox — Dale, Sawyer, and Buzick — and they collectively allowed 12 hits, seven off Dale and five off Sawyer. Nunamaker and Carrigan each handled some of the catching.

Boston scored first, with two in the first inning and two more in the second. Four hits in a row brought in the first-inning runs, but McCreery then struck out Hollis and Janvrin to get out of the jam. A second-inning walk and hits by Nunamaker and Perry plated the two in the second. Despite all the hits they had, the Redlands crew didn't score until the bottom of the fifth when they already faced a 5–0 deficit. The *Daily Facts* writer suspected that starter Dale wasn't always pitching his hardest, but was allowing the Boston fielders to get a little extra fielding practice since he buckled down the two times he'd allowed the bases to get loaded. He recognized that this was Boston's second team and thus they hadn't put up quite as good a game as the Chicago White Sox had on their visit in March 1910.

The first Redlands run came in on a home run hit off Sawyer by left-fielder Deakins over the head of his Boston counterpart Riggert. A triple, an infield out, and a home run out of the park by the shortstop Broadbent gave Redlands its other two runs in the bottom of the seventh. Sawyer had given up both homers and the triple. Not much more was seen of him in 1911. The game ended after eight innings; the Red Sox scored twice more in the top of the eighth. Doc Green served as the umpire (and was presented a five-dollar gold coin in appreciation). Green offered comments on each of the players, "sturdy, well-built boys" all.[33]

An estimated 1,800 to 2,000 fans turned out to see the game, some peering in from outside the fence. Apparently most of the field of play could be seen from outside, "yet it seems to be a point of honor among Redlanders to come up to the ticket office and give up good coin to see an exhibition that they could follow comfortably from the outside of the fence."[34] After the game's conclusion, the team was given a huge box of oranges to take with them on the drive back to Redondo Beach. The men enjoyed the hospitality so much that some of them talked about missing the last train back so they could spend the night. The pleasure seems to have been sincere, and the griping about having had to wake so early and travel so far long forgotten.

March 7

Harry Hooper was supposed to be presented a sack of gold worth $500—no small sum in 1911—in Sacramento but games both north and south were rained out once more.

"RAINMAKER IS BACK ON JOB," headlined the *Boston Globe*. "WORSE THAN EVER IN SUNSHINE LAND," blared the *Post*. "ONLY 'QUAKE LACKING TO COMPLETE MISERY," said the *Journal*. The setbacks caused by the weather led Tim Murnane to say that the players were now not in any better playing condition than they were when they first arrived, after two weeks in camp. Many of them turned to the bowling alleys and worked hard at trying to build their arm strength. The hot plunge continued to offer another form of physical exercise. "RED SOX ARE NOW GOOD SWIM-MERS," headlined the *Herald*. The rains had been so heavy that even should all rain stop, the grounds in Southern California were too much of a quagmire to permit play for at least a day or so afterward. Players were becoming discouraged. Bill Carrigan said the weather had been almost invariably bad from the beginning, with a snowstorm hitting the train even before it reached Chicago. He counted 11 games canceled to date, with the concomitant loss of all the revenue the gates would have provided. Rather than being in better than usual shape when the regular season began, the enforced idleness might produce the opposite effect.

The *American* recommended an appeal for parlor games, phonographs, checkers, and dominoes and said if they didn't get in some baseball soon, they might consider quitting the American League and enter the ping-pong championships. Hal Janvrin, "when not dancing, has favored the party with violin solos." Nunamaker kept active with the player piano; "everybody has vacated his end of the hotel." The irrepressible Nuf Ced McGreevey set out on a new adventure every day, regardless of the weather, and had already been to Catalina Island and Mount Howe, as well as continuing to work on the manuscript for his intended book, *Twenty Years a Fan and Never Stolen a Ball*, which he offered to sell the *American* for a modest $200,000.[35]

The Red Sox weren't the only team suffering bad weather. The New York Americans had a large snowstorm force cancellation of their work at Hot Springs, Virginia.

Happy Hogan and his Hooligans from Vernon (as the *Times* described them) rearranged their schedule to play a 2:30 P.M. game against the Colts at Washington Park, Los Angeles. But it rained again. Wallace Hogan was the manager of the Vernon Tigers.

In Northern California, the Regulars were at least able to get in a short workout on the St. Mary's playing field before another shower came down. Frank Arellanes, suffering from an abscess said to have come from drinking the sulphur waters in Redondo Beach, had it lanced. He was then given a couple of days off to go visit his family in Santa Cruz, but couldn't get there because of places where the tracks had been washed out. Players weren't surprised that Tip O'Neill hadn't shown his face at the St. Mark for the past three days. The Sox had been unable to play for almost an entire week, missing games scheduled from March 2 through March 7.

March 8

"RED SOX REGULARS LOSE TO COLLEGIANS"—*Boston Herald*
at Oakland, CA: St. Mary's College 1, Boston 0

The Red Sox had planned to travel to Sacramento to play the San Francisco Seals, but got the word that the field there was not in playable condition. They were fortunate to be able to get in a game against the St. Mary's College team, one watched by a crowd pegged at 600 or 1,500 fans, depending on the account. The whole college had a total enrollment of 238 in 1911. From those 238 students emerged nine who beat the Bosox. And nine was all it took. It was a "rather slow, sandy field" on which they played.

There was a little something extra riding on the game besides just the opportunity to get in some work. Mindful as he was that St. Mary's had shut out the White Sox, 6–0, in 1910, Patsy Donovan called the college only at noontime and he wagered one of the brothers at the Catholic school that they couldn't shut out the Red Sox. He promised a new hat if they could. "You're on!" said the manager of the Phoenix, and a game that hadn't even been thought of at 11:00 A.M. was planned with no chance for publicity other than word of mouth.

For seven innings, the boys from St. Mary's battled the Boston Red Sox and neither team scored. Pierce had started for the Red Sox and was deemed a little wild; he didn't walk a single batter but he hit two. Hugh Bedient took over after five innings. Taken together, they only gave up five hits. Williams showed a little versatility and caught most of the game.

It was a cohesive St. Mary's team, virtually the entire team having been intact for three years. They'd also been playing ball all winter, so were in very good form. Pitching a complete game was Hubert Leonard, who limited the Red Sox to an equal number of hits (five) and impressed them greatly. After graduation, he pitched in Denver in 1912 (22–9) and then played six seasons for the Red Sox, winning 90 regular-season games and posting 1–0 records in both the 1915 and 1918 World Series. Leonard struck out six and shut out the Sox, with a double by Speaker the only extra-base hit, putting Donovan on the hook for a hat.

The one extra-base hit Boston pitching permitted made all the difference. In the first inning, Pierce had hit third-baseman Billy Wallace. He later hit Leonard — and Leonard hit him. Bedient had taken over starting in the sixth, but kept the scoreless streak going until, with two outs in the bottom of the eighth, Wallace came up to bat. With two strikes on him, Wallace struck a ball deep down the first-base foul line, and only inches fair. It kept rolling between some vehicles parked along the street but Hooper retrieved it from under an umbrella in the street (!) and fired it in. Wallace ran through his coach's stop sign at third base, Wagner didn't handle the ball as smoothly as he might have, and the St. Mary's batter had himself a home run.

In the top of the ninth, Speaker singled. Lewis reached second base, and Speaker took third on Wallace's throwing error to first. A great play by left-fielder Norman Lynch saved the game, and the shutout, when he leapt four feet to catch Wagner's drive and then threw all the way to nab Speaker at home plate. With Lewis on third, Hugh Bradley struck out. Shutting out a big-league ballclub was not a freak anomaly; as we've seen, St. Mary's had shut out the White Sox in 1910, 6–0.

After the game, Donovan, who had stood watching both teams from the coaching line throughout the game, declared that it was no disgrace to have been beaten by such a strong team as St. Mary's. "That boy Leonard is certainly some pitcher and his backstop, Simpson, is a real star."[36]

The gloomy day at the Hotel Redondo saw some of the players work out tossing the ball around, with half of them not even bothering to get into uniform. Several of the men took a long walk to the surrounding hills and didn't return until late. Thoney, Jerry Sheehan, and Frank Smith returned from a hunting trip on the beach with a live pelican. Aside from the plunge, there was only a motion picture house and the beach bowling alley for entertainment. Fifteen people came to see the movie show, 12 of whom were ballplayers, but the proprietor waited in vain for more and then simply decided to cancel the show. The evening ended with a musical program with Buck O'Brien singing and Hal Janvrin playing violin.

March 9

The day's games were rained out yet again. Some of the more veteran pitchers were even suggesting that Donovan send them back to Hot Springs so they could get their arms in shape.

A drizzling rain in the northland and a downpour and steady daylong rain in the south conspired to prevent either team from getting in a game. Donovan had the Regulars work out for an hour at the college, and let the pitchers begin to mix in some curveballs for the first time of the spring. No one expected the next day to be any better. He was philosophical about the weather: "The Red Sox are hooked into bad weather and we must bear it even if we can't grin."[37] The rain was welcomed, however, by area residents, particularly those in agriculture, since precipitation had been below expected levels and overdue. This was not just a little rain spread over many days; "nearly 25 inches of rain have fallen since the Red Sox reached the coast and the weather sharps say that this is a precipitation greater than California has known in the preceding 23 years."[38]

In the entire 1910 Pacific Coast League schedule, which ran seven months rather than the shorter major-league schedule, only one game had been postponed due to rain for any of the California clubs.[39] Some of the Redondo Beach residents began to talk about "appointing a special day of fasting and prayer to pray for a cessation of the rain."[40]

Without any gymnasium facilities at Redondo Beach, Carrigan's crew were again reduced to what kind of exercise they could get in at the bathing pavilion. Most of them played catch on the roadways; the field was too muddy.

Looking ahead, to the trip east, there were other obstacles which began to loom. With games scheduled at both Yuma and El Paso on the border with Mexico, there was question as to whether those games could be played because of ongoing fighting in the Mexican Revolution, particularly just across the Rio Grande from El Paso in Ciudad Juarez. United States Army troops were being built up along the border, and passenger trains blocked to allow the army priority on the rails. Some of the Red Sox marksmen availed themselves of a shooting gallery at the resort, and joked about how they were getting ready to invade Mexico.

Even though they hadn't had much opportunity to play, and some of the pitchers had yet to throw an inning, Treasurer Hugh McBreen was second to none in terms of sunny optimism: "I honestly believe that our boys should win the pennant. We're going after it with the expectation of winning it, and that's the only way to go after anything."[41]

Joe Wood had talked about how carefully he studied opposing batters throughout the game, mentioning how some of the other pitchers kept written notes on the batters they might face. Ben Hunt discussed the importance of physical conditioning on a daily basis and the importance of mental conditioning and confidence.[42]

March 10

"RED SOX YANNIGANS LOSE IN TENTH INNING" — *Boston Journal*
at Los Angeles, CA: Vernon 4, Red Sox Colts 3 (10 innings)

There was no rain in the north, the sun came out, and it even turned warm, but there was no baseball. The field in San Francisco was a "bog" — unplayable. The tenth game in a row was postponed up north (the one with St. Mary's not being a scheduled game). After the men worked out for an hour at the college, athletic director Brother Joseph presented pennants in the college colors to each of the players and to Patsy Donovan. Catcher Harry Simpson of the St. Mary's team had so impressed Donovan that he'd had a word with him about perhaps playing for the Red Sox in days to come.

There was action in the south, though. A baseball game. Not that many people saw it, however, because the morning newspapers reported that the game was called off and "only a small number of faithfuls had the temerity to investigate the rumor that there would be a game."[43] The weather cleared, though, and they got in a game even though it sprinkled several times during the game. Each side used three pitchers — Boston used Moser, O'Brien, and Buzick — but Vernon's Tigers held the Red Sox to just four hits while Boston allowed eight, though not walking a one.

Boston scored first, for one run in the first inning. Leadoff batter Hank Perry pounded a ball to left field which would have gone out of Chutes Park but hit off the top of the fence just a few inches shy of being a home run. With two outs, Yerkes walked and then stole second base, with Perry scooting in the back door on a perfectly-executed double steal. Three hits in a row off Moser brought in two runs for the Tigers in the bottom of the first, giving the "Villagers" (as the *Los Angeles Herald* called them) a 2–1 lead. The Red Sox evened it up in the third.

It was a well-played game with just one error, but a number of flashy fielding plays, with Janvrin showing some glovework, or non-glovework, as seemed more often the case. He was said to have knocked down three liners with his bare hand. One of them knocked him off his feet, but he threw out the runner at first base while he was down on the ground. The Red Sox didn't collect a safe hit after the third inning when Perry's second double of the game set up a run on back-to-back singles by Engle and Riggert.

Vernon took a 3–2 lead in the fifth. The Sox evened it again in the eighth, on two walks, a sacrifice, and a force out at first base. The game went into extra innings. Buzick was on the hill for the Red Sox. Vernon catcher Brown led off the 10th and reached base safely. The pitcher, Stewart, tried to bunt him over to second, but he was forced out, Stewart being safe on the failed sacrifice. Carlisle struck out for the second out of the inning, but Stewart stole second standing up, not even drawing a throw from Nunamaker. Burrell singled to left-center field and, despite a strong and accurate throw from left fielder Riggert, Stewart scored the winning run.

Word was that Thoney's arm was in such bum shape that he couldn't be considered for a big-league berth. A couple of days later, the March 12 *Times* wrote that he "holds the record for hard luck among the big league stars" due to his frequent injuries.

March 11

"VILLAGE TWIRLERS ALLOW BOSTON ONLY ONE HIT AND WHITEWASH
THEM"—*Los Angeles Herald*
at Los Angeles, CA: Vernon 1, Red Sox Colts 0

"OUTFIELD MUD AND ERRORS HELP SOX"—*San Francisco Examiner*
at San Francisco, CA: Boston 6, San Francisco 4

This was the first day that both teams were able to get in a game, the
first time since the large squad split into two divisions on February 28 that
both were able to play on the same day. The Regulars won; the Yannigans
lost.

A large Saturday crowd on a warm sunny day saw the Colts narrowly
escape being no-hit. Having been held hitless for the final seven innings of
the March 10 game and the first eight innings of this one, there had been 15
frames filled without a hit. A Tigers no-hitter wouldn't have been a singular
accomplishment; Vernon used three pitchers: George Schaefer, Roy Castleton,
and Roy Willett (also two catchers, two shortstops, and two center fielders
were used in the course of the game). They made one error, but the Red Sox
made as many as five, three of them by Yerkes (box scores in the *Globe* and
Journal only show three Red Sox errors, two by Yerkes; the *Los Angeles Herald*
shows five). It was Janvrin's fumbling in the second inning that allowed the
lone run of the game. The *Times* called that an error; the *Globe* did not. No
one really worried much about official scorers in exhibition games.

Patterson had opened Vernon's half of the second with a two-base hit
to the wall in right-center field. McDonnell was up next and dropped a
single into left-center field, what Jay Davidson of the *Los Angeles Herald*
called a "crescent-drop over short." The hasty throw went to third to try
and hold Patterson there but it hit him on the leg and then got away from
Janvrin and rolled to the fence, allowing Patterson to score. Vernon never
scored again. Marty McHale took over in the third and gave up four hits
but no one got past second base. Ray Collins threw the seventh and eighth.

In the meantime, Red Sox batters kept going down despite the lack of
any strikeouts all game long. Schaefer walked two and Willett walked one,
as well as hitting Sheehan with a pitch, but Boston batsman got nary a hit.
Almost the only interruption was when the official scorer, Hamlet Oliver,
turned up late — in the fourth inning — and took his seat in the park.

In the eighth, Willett got a scare when he hit Janvrin and then walked Perry, but he managed to pick them both off. In the ninth, Willett got the first two men and was one batter away from a collaborative no-hitter when Steve Yerkes lined a fastball into right field for a single. Janvrin followed with a hard drive right back to the pitcher, but Willett speared it and the game was over.

Happy Hogan was happy indeed to have taken two in a row from the Red Sox, who hadn't scored in their last 16 innings, and crowed that the Tigers would take two more on the morrow.

In San Francisco, the Seals and the Red Sox squared off at Recreation Park in front of what was said to be a crowd of 40,000 fans. Harry B. Smith, the special correspondent for the *Boston Post* covering the Regulars, spelled it out in his story twice: forty thousand hungry baseball fans. The Seals were skippered by Dan Long, a team that included 12 former or future major-league ballplayers. The Red Sox were without the services of Tris Speaker (out with a cold) and Harry Hooper (collecting a trophy and that purse of gold from friends in Sacramento). Pitcher Chris Mahoney filled in for Spoke in center and infielder Billy Purtell filled in for Harry in right. The field was slick, especially in the outfield, and a little soggy in the infield as well. General Charles H. Taylor was present, seated in a box just behind the Red Sox bench. John I. Taylor never made the trip to the West Coast because of an illness of his wife, Cornelia Van Ness, even though she hailed from San Francisco.

Other than the one game against St. Mary's, this was the first game for the Regulars against another team all season long. They'd played three games against the Yannigans in Redondo Beach and that March 8 game against the college. This was, arguably, their first "real" game of the spring, having lost nine scheduled days due to rain and unplayable conditions.

Boston was first on the scoreboard with one run in the first. The Seals matched that, and then took a lead by adding three runs in the third. Joe Wood had perhaps not fully recovered from his own cold; he threw the first five innings, walked six, and was tagged for all the runs, though they were hardly all earned runs. It's his fault his pitch hit Tennant, but Kleinow and Bradley both committed errors behind him.

In the fifth, Larry Gardner hit a two-run homer over the right-field wall to pull the Red Sox to within a run. The error bug bit the Seals in the sixth when a base on balls, a single by Purtell, and two throwing errors let the Sox score two more runs and take the lead. They added the sixth and final run in the eighth on another walk and a long double by Mahoney.

After Donovan and Carrigan traded telegrams, they decided to leave fewer pitchers with the Colts squad than was originally planned, and so Collins, Hall, Karger, and both Smiths would join the Regulars. This left the Yannigans without an experienced veteran pitcher and diminished their chances for victories going forward.

March 12

"RED SOX REGULARS WIN 2 HEAVY-HITTING GAMES"—*Boston Post*
at Oakland, CA: Boston 7, Oakland 5 (morning game)
at San Francisco, CA: Boston 5, San Francisco 1 (afternoon game)

"TWICE DO THE YANNIGANS GET IT NEAR THE COLLAR"—*Boston Post*
at Vernon, CA: Vernon 5, Red Sox Colts 2
at Los Angeles, CA: Vernon 3, Red Sox Colts 1

Even though the Red Sox had been in Oakland for 10 days, this was — finally — the first game played at Freeman's Park. But it was a banner day — four games all on the same date, making up for a little lost time.

Tim Murnane of the *Globe* had looked over the Oakland ballpark during the days while waiting for the weather to break. He felt it a "third-class affair" while, in contrast, Cal Ewing's Recreation Park was a "fine plant, with the exception of a short outfield."[44] In the same paper, the Boston writer said that pitcher Doc Moskiman had asked the National Commission to reinstate him; he'd been placed on baseball's banned list as a "contract jumper" for failing to acknowledge being reserved by Louisville. He was temporarily reinstated in 1910 and appeared in five games for the Red Sox late in August.[45]

It was Sunday in the Bay Area and the weather was nice. Many of the players went to church in the morning, then left the hotel at 9:00 A.M. for the Oakland park, practiced quickly, and started the morning game at 10:15 A.M. There were 4,500 fans who paid to get in.

The Red Sox must have been primed. They scored five runs in the first inning on a walk to Gardner, a single by Hooper, a two-run triple by Lewis, a single by Wagner (who was thrown out trying to get to second), a single by Nebinger, and two-baggers by Bradley and Mahoney before the first batter made an out. The Oaks were lucky to escape with only five runs against them. Hunt gave up single runs in the third and the fifth innings. Pierce pitched the sixth and the seventh and gave up one run in each inning, and it was 5–3, Red Sox. Boston scored one more in the top of the eighth and Oakland scored one more in the bottom. In the top of the ninth, the Red Sox added a seventh run on Larry Pape's double, two outs, and an error, then held on as Pape pitched the bottom of the inning and closed out the game.

Ten minutes after the game ended, they were on their way to San Francisco, departing at 12:30 P.M. and taking lunch on the ferryboat. By 1:45 P.M. the Red Sox reached the San Francisco park and changed back into their uniforms (the same ones), with play beginning at 2:30 P.M. Umpire George Hildebrand traveled with them and officiated both games. He was a native San Franciscan and became an American League umpire in 1913, serving 22 years in that capacity.

Boston's second game went well, too, with the Seals going down, 5–1, in front of a large crowd variously estimated at 7,500 to 9,000. One has to imagine that Treasurer McBreen learned the true count. Again, one big inning made the difference. Neither team scored their first three times up. Arellanes started the game, pitching the first four and giving up only two hits, and Killilay closed it out. In the top of the fourth, Hooper singled to start it up, two balls in a row were mishandled by the Seals shortstop Weaver, and Arellanes singled and the Red Sox had three runs. In the bottom of the sixth, San Francisco got their one run. Wagner hit one out of the park in the top of the eighth, over the left-field fence and a second run scored when Bradley walked, moved to third on Mahoney's single, and scored on an out. Hooper stole three bases. Play in the field was good, too, with the exception of Larry Gardner, who erred once in each game.

The team was on their way back to Oakland by 6:00 P.M., with two wins under their belts, and tucked into dinner at 7:30 P.M. at the St. Mark.

The two games in Los Angeles were meant to be played at 10:30 A.M. at the Vernon park and at 2:30 P.M. at Washington Park, with the Colts then taking the evening train north. The afternoon game drew 5,000 fans;

the mid-morning game drew 1,000. The size of some of the crowds remained remarkable; exhibition games in Hot Springs in 1910 routinely drew 500 or 600 patrons. When the Sox returned to Hot Springs in 1912, some of the games against major-league opponents like the Phillies drew 700 or 800.

Sportswriter Jay Davidson wasn't impressed by the Red Sox second team: "Those scarlet-hosed highbrows from the intellectual seat of the American government, the Boston Red Sox, are fast earning the title of the Joe Grims of the diamond." He was also irritated that Tim Murnane's column in *The Sporting News* had come down on California as a spring-training site just because they'd happened to stumble into the worst weather in 30 years. Where else, he asked, could a ballclub draw such large, profitable crowds when the weather was right as on a day such as this?[46]

Had Hogan put a bet down on the Tigers taking both games, he would have collected. Charlie Smith started pitching the morning game for the Red Sox. His teammates had collected two hits in the top of the first, but couldn't score. Vernon got one run on one hit in the bottom of the inning. Smith walked the first batter, Yorkshire, England native Walter Carlisle, who'd played in three games for the Red Sox in 1908. Smith had him picked him off first but when he ran to second, Hap Myers' throw went astray and he was safe on second. He took third on an out, and scored easily on a single to left.

Boston evened it up in the fourth on two singles and an out. Dale had pitched scoreless ball in the fourth and the fifth, but struggled. Sawyer had taken over after six. The Tigers scored runs off both of them, twice in the sixth. The Sox crept back within a run in the top of the seventh on a triple by Hollis and a single that brought him in. But the Tigers scored twice more for good measure in the seventh.

The afternoon also saw Boston score first, but the *Times* game account said, "The Squabs were probably trying harder to keep from being beaten than they were to win ... the Squabs bunched enough of their bungles in the fifth round to trim themselves."[47] Two singles and an out, and an unguarded third base bag let the Red Sox score first, in the second inning. That was the only run they scored; they only managed three more hits in the remainder of the game. The fateful fifth saw Buck O'Brien taking over from Moser. Two bad errors by fielders behind him, and back-to-back singles brought two Tigers across home plate. In the eighth inning, Vernon got another run without a hit: an error, and out, and two stolen bases including a double steal pulled in the third run.

The rains had washed out some of the tracks and railroad bridges on the coastal railway. Consequently, the games planned against Ventura and Santa Maria were canceled for the 13th and 14th, so the Colts decided to stay over another night and get in one more game in Los Angeles before heading north. The game in Santa Maria could have been a good one, facing the Portland Beavers where they held their spring training. It was also decided that the Colts would be the ones to play in Hanford and Bakersfield, rather than the Regulars.

March 13

"Carrigan's Colts Slaughter Vernon"—*Boston Post*
at Los Angeles, CA: Red Sox Colts 12, Vernon 3

"Regulars Use The Brush"—*Boston Herald*
at Modesto, CA: Boston 5, Modesto 0

It was finally time for a little payback from the Colts after dropping four in a row to Vernon. They were not only chagrined at their own failure to win, but fired up after learning that the Regulars had won two while they were still smarting from losing the pair they played on the 12th. "The men went into today's battle with blood in their eyes," wrote Shannon. Collins, Buzick, and McHale each pitched three innings, Collins letting the Tigers take a 1–0 lead in the first on a walk, stolen base, an out, another out, and a single. The Colts scored twice in the top of the second on Engle's single, a steal, Yerkes' single, and an error. Vernon added another run in the second to tie it, 2–2, when McDonald singled and Hogan himself tripled down the line in right field. Reflecting the nearly impromptu scheduling, the crowd was very small, about 400 in all. There was also some thought that fans were saving their money to await the forthcoming return to town of the Red Sox Regulars.

In the top of the third, the Colts broke the game open. Hollis, Myers, and Janvrin all singled, and Engle hit the first of two doubles. Before the inning was over, they'd all scored. It was 6–2, Boston. Ratcheting up the score, Carrigan's men added six more runs in the fifth. Riggert tripled and Engle doubled and Priepke, Buzick, and Myers all hit safely; combined with a couple of errors, they'd made it 12–2. Vernon scored once in the bottom of the ninth, but to little avail. There was spectacular fielding by both teams that helped make some of the fans feel they'd gotten value for their money.

The Red Sox players went back to the hotel, cleaned up, and caught a 9:30 P.M. train for Hanford, south of Fresno and about halfway to Oakland. It was a 200-mile trip. The northern unit was originally planned to play in Hanford, but the weather had played such havoc with the schedule that things changed around.

The Regulars made a move about 80 miles to the east, a four-hour journey at the time, to play a game against the Modesto Reds. The city of Modesto was a railway stop on the Central Pacific tracks between Sacramento and distant Los Angeles, populated by about 4,500 people at the time. Some of the area was so flooded from the rains that the water was almost up to the rails. The team arrived in the city at 2:00 P.M. and played an easy enough game for about 550 spectators, "nearly one-half of whom sat in their automobiles on the side lines and displayed very little enthusiasm for the game." The Model T had been introduced in 1908 and with its grain, fruit, and nut trees, Modesto must have been prosperous enough to have so many motor vehicles. As it happened, there was little to get excited about for Modesto fans. One of the reasons the crowd was smaller than it might otherwise have been was that "the customary courtesy of closing the stores during the game when a big league team strikes town, was not extended to the Boston Red Sox."[48] The *Boston Journal* claimed the crowd was only 150 people and wondered why the team had made this lengthy round trip to play in a relatively small town when they could have made much more money with another game in San Francisco.

It was a skin diamond. There was very little hitting, with Bedient (eight innings) and Pierce (pitching the ninth) combining to hold the Reds to just two hits, one in the second and one in the fifth. Boston only collected six. The Reds made four errors. The game account in the *Modesto Morning Herald* was written by the *Boston Journal*'s Herman Nickerson. The Boston and Modesto newspaper box scores both showed two hits for the Reds; the *Los Angeles Times* box score showed three, though the accompanying line score agreed there were only two.

With one out in the top of the second, Nebinger singled. He took off for second base as Bradley struck out, and Palm, the Modesto catcher, threw the ball wildly, so Nebinger scrambled to third base. Mahoney, still hitting as well as anyone for the Red Sox, reached on an infield hit to first base, while Nebinger scored.

Duffy Lewis singled to start the fourth. Wagner hit the ball to the first baseman, who tried to cut down the lead runner but threw the ball into center field. The throw in from center was itself off the mark, and by the time the play was over, Duffy had scored and Heinie was on third. Nebinger hit a grounder to the shortstop, who threw the ball home and got Wagner, hung up between home and third, out at third base. Nebinger moved up to second, then scooted to third on a passed ball. A slow roller by Bradley to third base prompted another throw home, but Nebinger slid in and scored — though the catcher was quick-witted enough to fire the ball to first base and still get Bradley! But it was 3–0 for Boston.

Lewis reached in the sixth on a grounder to third that was too hot to handle, and scored on a hit-and-run play when Wagner doubled to left field. In the ninth, Wagner scored the fifth and final run by singling, stealing second, and scoring on the shortstop's error. Modesto pitcher Mobley had struck out six Sox, however, and, save for the errors and the anemic bats, the Reds played well enough. The *Morning Herald*'s own writer felt the game "was not so one-sided as to be absolutely 'town-lot' ball. The local bunch did not put up their usual game, a fact indicated by the error column. Some of these errors were inexcusable and all were responsible for runs." He felt that they had played good ball for non-professionals, the Reds being an amateur ballclub. His sense was that if they'd played their usual game, the final total might have been 3–0, a closer game but still a shutout. Nonetheless, "we should be proud that we held the great Red Sox down to five runs." As for the Red Sox, he wrote, they were pleased to get in a good game against a team that gave them good practice despite being amateurs. After being in town for four hours and 15 minutes, the Red Sox caught the 6:15 P.M. back to the St. Mark.

The game had indeed been practice for those 11 Red Sox players who took part. But it only lasted 75 minutes. More than three times the amount of time had been spent on the rails getting there and returning to Oakland. The point could well be made that, in terms of preparing for regular-season play, the team would have been better served by staying in Oakland and putting in a full day of workouts. Some of the men saw no action at all. The others who did saw relatively little. And it wasn't as though the team coffers were that enriched by the few hundred paying customers.

Speaker had a little fun on the way back, donning the "train butcher's uniform" and selling oranges, chewing gum, and candy. He claimed he got a 10-cent tip.

March 14

"RED SOX YANNIGANS FIND EASY GOING WITH HANFORD"
—*Boston Journal*
at Hanford, CA: Red Sox Colts 9, Hanford 3

"TRIS SPEAKER IS THE WHOLE SHOW"—*Boston Globe*
at Oakland, CA: Boston 10, San Francisco Seals 4

Hanford was the seat of Kings County, a growing dairy, cattle, and cotton-based community in the south central San Joaquin Valley served by both the Southern Pacific Railroad and the Burlington Northern and Santa Fe Railway at the time. They had their own independent league ballclub for a year and a half, the Hanford Braves of the San Joaquin Valley League. The league had begun in 1910 and disbanded a few months after the Red Sox visit, in mid–July, 1911. This was the first of two stops the Colts made as they headed north.

It was a nice day, with "the prettiest of weather prevailing" and the stores shutting down from 2:00 P.M. to 4:00 P.M. for the game.[49] Some 300 to 400 turned out for the game, but the Hanford home team itself was a little short-handed and needed some extra help. Les Nunamaker handled the catching duties and Jack Thoney played left field. Two Sox pitchers took to the field, Marty McHale played in center for Hanford and Buzick played third base. The help didn't end there.

Hanford started with their man Hawley on the mound and Boston got three runs off him in the first. He'd retired the first two batters, striking out Perry and getting Myers to foul out. Then Riggert reached on an error and Hawley hit Hack Engle in the elbow. Yerkes slammed a double, bringing in both, and then scored himself on the second error of the inning. After scoring once more in the second, the Sox put two more across in the third on an Engle single, another Yerkes double, a wild pitch, and another error. The Red Sox picked up two more runs in the fifth, when Sheehan tripled and Perry singled him in. More than 99 years later, it's a little difficult to piece together how the scoring progressed after that. A box score couldn't handle it, and the surviving game accounts are insufficiently detailed.

What happened is that Hanford looked like they could use a little help in the pitching department, so Moser started pitching for both teams. It wasn't just that he switched sides and took over for Hanford. He did pitch the sixth, and seventh for Hanford, but also pitched the sixth, seventh, and eighth for Boston! And he had himself quite a day at the plate, too — he was 3-for-3 for the Red Sox and 1-for-1 for the Braves.

It appears that Moser was charged with all three runs that Hanford scored; Buck O'Brien took over and pitched the ninth, but he wasn't charged with the run the Red Sox scored in the eighth. By that time, he had given way to Boston's Gene Dale who pitched the last two innings for Hanford. Moser walked two and struck out one, but we don't know for which team. Nor is there a surviving account of whether he may have changed jerseys or caps between innings.

Moser had broken into the big leagues in 1906 and was 0–4 for the Phillies, after finishing his rookie year in minor-league ball with a 24–8 record for the Virginia League's Lynchburg Shoemakers. Back for more minor-league ball, he completed four seasons, with 20 wins in 1909 (again for the Shoemakers) and 31 wins (against 20 losses, with a 1.83 ERA) for the PCL's Oakland Oaks. He made Boston's big-league club in 1911 but only appeared in six games, posting an 0–1 record. Around the beginning of September, the St. Louis Browns purchased his contract from the Red Sox. He started two games for the Browns but was bombed on September 3 and 9 and his major-league days finished with an 0–7 record. He may have never had another day as a hitter as he had in Hanford, aside from batting for both teams, that is: his major-league record was .045 (1-for-22).

"TRIS SPEAKER IS THE WHOLE SHOW," blared the *Boston Globe*'s headline describing the 10–4 triumph of Tris and his teammates over the San Francisco Seals. And so he was, playing "phenomenal all-around ball." Maybe he couldn't wait to get going; it was his first appearance of the spring season and he made up for a little lost time, driving in five runs and scoring three. "ALSO DOES SOME GREAT FIELDING," the subhead added. Batting third, he laid down a bunt and beat it out in his first at-bat. Next time up, the bases were loaded and he tripled to the clubhouse in center field; it would have been a home run but for the ground rules. He singled to left field his third time up, advancing Hooper to third. He went the other way in his fourth at-bat, hitting a low line drive caught on the shoestrings by San Francisco's right fielder. Fifth time up: a two-run home run into the unfinished bleachers in center field. He was spectacular on defense, too, with "three brilliant catches ... corkers"[50]

Speaker had only two full major-league seasons behind him, 1909 (.309) and 1910 (.340), and had only begun to approach the prime years that would leave him with a lifetime .345 average. But it was already clear that he was one of the great fielders of his day and newspapers in California had spread his name far and wide. The *Los Angeles Times*, for one, wrote that as a hitter he stood "shoulder to shoulder with Cobb, Lajoie and [Honus] Wagner."[51]

Nebinger sprained his ankle sliding into third base and had to leave the game. Harry Hooper played third in his stead. Four runs in the third inning gave the Sox a lead built on Speaker's three-bagger that cleared the bases. Speaker scored on Lewis's productive out. The Seals tied it up over their next couple of innings, but then Boston scored one or two unanswered runs in every one of the final four innings. The game drew 2,500.

March 15

"RED SOX MAKE CLEAN SWEEP AGAINST SEALS" — *Boston Journal*
at San Francisco, CA: Boston 2, San Francisco 1

"WENT TO PIECES IN THE FINAL INNING" — *Bakersfield Californian*
at Bakersfield, CA: Red Sox Colts 1, Bakersfield 0

The Regulars had one more game to play in the north, and though it was a low-scoring 2–1 win against the Seals, it was Tris Speaker again who drove the offense in the fourth inning. Hooper was on first and Speaker singled; Harry scored when Lewis sacrificed him home, then Speaker scored when Wagner singled. Eddie Cicotte and Jack Killilay combined on a four-hitter, though four Red Sox errors kept up the hopes of the Seals. Frank Browning pitched for San Francisco and at one point struck out Hooper, Speaker, and Lewis.

The Red Sox had swept all the games they'd played against the Pacific Coast League clubs in Oakland and San Francisco. Ironically or not, the only game they had lost was the 1–0 defeat dealt them by the St. Mary's College students.

After the game, Donovan and 16 of the Sox took the train to Los Angeles, due to arrive at 9:00 A.M. on the 16th. Karger, Collins, and the two Smith pitchers awaited them in L.A, as did Hal Janvrin and Chet Thomas, both of whom had been moved up to the first string. Remaining up north were pitchers Arellanes, Hunt, Pape, and Pierce, and Nebinger. They would now come under Carrigan's control. Doc Green had remained in Southern California, and the Regulars had fended for themselves in the days up north. Now the team trainer would have the first-string group under his care. Nuf Ced McGreevey went to visit friends in Portland, Oregon and then traveled back to Boston.

An astonishing incident came to the manager's attention during the game against the Seals. If he'd been wondering where his backup catcher Chet Thomas was, he found out: he was in a hospital. Thomas had played for Oakland in 1909 and both Sacramento and Oakland in 1910. He had a lot of friends in the area and after the game on the 14th decided to dine with a group of friends in San Francisco and go out on the town. Sometime after midnight, he was admitted to a hospital badly beaten about the head and in serious condition. He was lucid and explained that he's been attacked by a "crowd of thugs" and beaten into insensibility. Doctors expected he might lose the sight of one eye. Fortunately, he recovered well and caught 166 games for Sacramento in 1911, making the Boston Red Sox for the 1912 season and five years after that, part of three World Championship teams for the Red Sox and, later, for the 1920 Cleveland Indians.

The game saw Cicotte (six innings) and Killilay (the final three) limit the Seals to just four hits, all singles, though Red Sox fielders fumbled their way to four errors while the Seals made none. The one run the Seals got came in the bottom of the fifth. Ossie Vitt singled to right field, but was forced at second by Buck Weaver. Weaver, a future major leaguer until he was suspended for his role in the Black Sox scandal, stole second and kept going to third base when Gardner couldn't handle Williams' throw from behind the plate. Walter Schmidt, who himself started a 10-year big-league career in 1916, singled in Weaver.

The Red Sox had scored their two runs in the top of the fourth. Frank Browning, who'd been called up from the Seals and pitched in 11 games for the Detroit Tigers in 1910, threw the first six innings for San Francisco. In the first two innings, he struck out Hooper, Speaker, and Lewis in succession. Larry Gardner walked to lead off the fourth. He was forced at second, so now it was Hooper on first base. Speaker "combed the ball along the third-base line" and reached second base, the throw to third almost, but not quite, getting Hooper. Tim Murnane's account continued:

> Speaker then danced around second and short until he got the pitcher a bit frustrated, and Duffy Lewis poled a sacrifice fly to center, on which Hooper made the plate. An intercepted throw from the outfield found Speaker between third and second, but he kidded the man with the ball until the latter made a poor peg to second, and the speedy Boston center fielder was back at that station.
>
> Then on a short hit to left by Wagner, Speaker lit right out for the plate, surprising the youthful left-fielder to the extent that he juggled the ball and made it easy for the runner.

It was the Speed Boys showing off their stuff— Speaker in particular stretching a single into a double, then running from second to home on a single to the left side. There were only 750 fans. Before the game, the Red Sox had been driven around the Presidio and Golden Gate Park, having lunch at the Cliff House.

Bakersfield was the second stop for the Colts on their way north. Four of the men had gone on ahead to Oakland: Bill Carrigan, McHale, O'Brien, and Moser. With Carrigan now gone, the leader for the day was Arthur Cooper, a trusted team executive in the traveling party. The *American* wondered in advance what the turnout was going to be like. "Bakersfield is one of those small towns on the map where they promise to close up the town and attend the game, and then they don't do it; at least that's the card Modesto handed us and Bakersfield is under suspicion."[52]

The San Joaquin Valley Railroad had come to town as recently as 1898 and Bakersfield was a fast-growing city, with a little over 17,000 people in the metropolitan area at the time of the 1910 Census. The city had a baseball team for just one year, the Bakersfield Drillers in the same San Joaquin Valley League of which Hanford had been a part. The Red Sox played against a cobbled-together team at Recreation Park, one "composed principally of minor leaguers trying out for fast company," a picked team, selected by William "Brick" Devereaux. Unlike Hanford, they had enough players that they weren't forced to borrow any from the Red Sox. Pitchers Griffin and Claflin held the big leaguers to six hits, Claflin playing second base when Griffin was pitching and Griffin playing second when Claflin was. The two combined only walked one batter. It was Sawyer and Dale for the Red Sox, and they gave up eight hits while walking three. Neither team's pitchers allowed a run though the first eight innings.

In the top of the ninth, wrote the *Bakersfield Californian*, the "aggregation went to pieces." Nunamaker reached base on "an inexcusable error by Devereaux," advanced when Perry (who had doubled earlier in the game) hit a long, high fly to right field. Bakersfield's right fielder, Barkdaw, made "a pretty one-handed catch" but was disadvantaged by "having only one hand and being unable to field the ball home."[53] The *Californian* picked up the story of how the run scored: "Here the poor work was done that gave Boston the game. Hap Myers sent an easy one to Hoffman, who had but to tag first base. One of his brother infielders shouted 'first base,' indicating where the play was to be made, and Hoffman becoming confused thought one of the other players intended to cover the bag and he meekly tossed the ball to the first station when there was no one within twenty feet to receive it. It was rotten baseball and tossed the ball away."[54] The home team was unable to score in the bottom of the ninth.

5

The Grand Switch

March 16

"Tigers Go Against Too Much 'Class'" — *Los Angeles Examiner*
at Los Angeles, CA: Boston 3, Vernon 1

"Red Sox Put One Over On Vernon" — *Boston Globe*
at Oakland, CA: Oakland 4, Red Sox Colts 2

The grand switch had now taken place; the Colts were now in northern California, staying at the St. Mark, and the Regulars were playing in southern California, though no longer based in Redondo Beach. Hugh McBreen had traveled from Northern California to Los Angeles, arriving on March 14 to prepare for the return of the Regulars to the south. He switched hotels, and booked the party of 35 (which included the "war correspondents," the sportswriters traveling with the team) into the Westminster Hotel, which was much closer to Washington Park than the 40-mile trolley ride they'd had to take to and from the previous games. It was also free from the cold breezes right off the ocean.

It was, though, in the eyes of Nickerson, a hotel with "far from comfortable quarters." Nickerson was also put out by a rocky ride from San Francisco which had cost a lot of sleep for a lot of the party, and by "much confusion" in checking in. Purtell played third base, but was still suffering a bad arm which Nickerson attributed to the "damp rooms and damp beds" at Redondo Beach.

The morning's *Los Angeles Times* gave John I. Taylor credit for building a strong team: "If there ever was a championship aggregation in the shell, it looks as though Donovan had got the goods.... Going on the theory that championship clubs are made out of youngsters and not veterans, Taylor has proceeded to grab everything he could lay his hands on in the youngster line. In fact, no magnate in the baseball world has spent more money than this same John I. Taylor." The paper predicted it would be Connie Mack's Athletics and the Red Sox who would be duking it out for the pennant. Nickerson was by no means as optimistic: "Unless some brains are given the team as a whole, and unless Patsy Donovan makes a shift at first base I can't see where the team has a chance to butt into the first division." Bradley was still holding down the first-base slot that had been Jake Stahl's. His opinion was no doubt a bit colored by Brad's error and a couple of other "bush league stunts" which showed poor judgment in this day's game. John I. Taylor said, "I am not losing any sleep over the first-base proposition. There is only one first-class first baseman in the league anyway, so we are just as well off as any of the clubs except New York."[1]

The first team the Red Sox took on — just a few hours after they arrived at 10:00 A.M. and dropped their bags in their rooms — was Vernon. They beat the Tigers, 3–1, behind superb five-hit pitching by Joe Wood and Frank Smith. The 2,500 assembled saw almost as many errors as hits, four by Vernon, but the Tigers pitchers held the Sox to six hits. Larry Gardner led off the first inning with a triple to right field. Hooper singled him in, but then dozed for a moment and got himself picked off second base, wasting Speaker's single which followed. Vernon tied it up in the second, starting when Bradley cut in front of Gardner and dropped a high fly ball hit to first base, and then saw the runner advance to second on a sacrifice. A strikeout followed, and then a comedy of errors ensued which ended up with Gardner throwing the ball home and seeing it sail over Bunny Madden's head. There were just two errors, but they were bad ones. Nickerson wrote after the game, "[T]hey played the game as if they possessed heads of mahogany with cement foundations."

Ex-Sox player Walter Carlisle, leadoff batter and center fielder for Vernon, tripled to start the third but the next man up hit one right back to Wood, who threw the ball home to erase the threat. In the fourth inning, Lewis doubled to the center-field fence and Wagner singled him to third. Purtell sacrificed successfully; Duffy scored and Heinie had second base. Hugh Bradley doubled off the fence in left field and it was 3–1 with no scoring for the remainder of the game. Vernon manager Hap Hogan attributed some of the loss to the lack of practice on signals among his team, which had gotten its signs mixed up a few times.

Karger underwent a surgical operation on his ear, which had been bothering him for more than 10 days. He originally thought he'd gotten salt water in it when first arriving at the beach, and he'd consulted a specialist in Los Angeles as early as March 8. What the ailment truly was remained unreported in the press. Burke of the *American* wrote on the 14th: "Purtell's lame arm was secured by sleeping in a damp room and Karger's ear troubles were occasioned by the heated swimming tank. Nearly the whole squad got cold, and nothing but lame arms and sore muscles seems to have resulted from the hot baths which at first it was expected would be a great benefit. Since getting away from the beach the boys have improved in health and condition."[2]

The weather was now — finally — good and warm in both places.

The Colts arrived from Bakersfield, had lunch, took a special car to Freeman's Park, and dropped a well-played game to the Oaks, 4–2. Thoney doubled to the right-field fence in the second and scored, and Perry tripled in the fifth after Pierce had walked, but there were only two other hits for Boston in the game. Moser started the game, pitching against his former teammates (but at least not pitching against his current ones as he had in Hanford). It was only in the fourth that the Oaks scored — twice, off Pierce — and in the seventh off McHale, the first on a double, driven in by a hard hit that Hollis prevented from becoming another double with his quick throw to second, and the second on a home run by Monte Pfyl over the right-field fence. Manager Harry Wolverton was pleased with the result, though he knew the Speed Boys with the real speed were playing down south and that the Red Sox Colts were a little weak with the stick.

March 17

"RED SOX REGULARS MAKE BAD SHOWING"—*Boston Post*
at Los Angeles, CA: Vernon 4, Boston 2

"YERKES AND RIGGERT STAR IN THE YANNIGANS' VICTORY"
—*Boston Journal*
at San Francisco, CA: Red Sox Colts 10, San Francisco 4

Stickwork wasn't in short supply on Friday, as the Red Sox Colts pounded out 13 base hits, scoring 10 runs. Yerkes had a 4-for-5 day, all singles, while Riggert both singled and hit a long home run over the right-field fence. Former White Sox southpaw Harry Suter baffled the Red Sox over much of the first three innings, striking out six batters and allowing just one run in the second thanks to an error by the Seals catcher. San Francisco scored twice in the second off Arellanes, who struggled enough to consider himself fortunate that there were only two runs scored. Riggert's leadoff homer in the fourth tied it, then Boston took the lead in the fifth inning when new pitcher Frank Miller managed to load the bases and then walk Hollis. He did the exact same thing in the sixth — load the bases and walk in a run, this time giving the base on balls to Boston pitcher O'Brien. Hank Perry was up next and he hit a single to center which scored two more. The Red Sox added four more runs before the game was complete. It had been a bit of a sloppy game, though, with three errors for each side.

In Los Angeles, there had been some talk of rescheduling play to the morning because of a boxing match that night at the Vernon Arena for the lightweight title between Ad (Adolph) Wolgast and challenger (and Los Angeles native) George Memsic. The scheduled 20-round fight ended in nine when the referee stopped the battle before Wolgast annihilated Memsic. Red Sox trainer Doc Green was in Wolgast's corner. Karger, Wood, Speaker, and the Piano Mover were all at ringside. Oddly, for an event that had been well-publicized, both boxers and the officials were arrested on charges of participating in a prize fight. A judge later ruled it had been a boxing exhibition and not a prize fight.[3]

The ballgame was held as originally planned in the afternoon, with Vernon coming out on top. There were seven errors in the game, "ragged ball" indeed. A first-inning double by Gardner, a single by Hooper, and a productive out by Lewis gave the first run to the Red Sox. With two outs in the bottom of the fourth, the Tigers tied it on a double off Bedient, a wild pitch, and Bedient blocking a ball hit toward Gardner with both runners safe. In the fifth, the Tigers added two more when, with two outs and runners on second and third, the weaker-hitting Carlisle was intentionally walked in favor of pitching to Burrell, who had already hit well in the clutch in the young spring season. Burrell doubled, clearing the bases, and giving Vernon a 4–1 lead. The Red Sox picked up one more run in the eighth on an error and a Heinie Wagner double. The Tigers outhit the Colts, 10 to 5. Nickerson was still down on the Red Sox Regulars, leading his story: "Slow thinking, poor judgment, and poor baserunning, with the slushiest kind of throwing, all bunched, was enough to hand today's game to Vernon, a team, by the way, which has its eye on the ball and can hit. If any of the 400 or more fans thought they were looking at the 'Speed Boys,' they changes their thinks suddenly and passed out a little josh along that line." It was, he added, "one of the rottenest exhibitions of the trip, fought with about as much class as you would find on some sand lot (apologies to the sand)."

Life at the Westminster was better than at Redondo Beach. It was in the center of the city, which was appreciated, and they were "being petted and pampered with cooking like mother makes at home. All New England cooking has put the boys in the sweetest frame of mind and whetted their appetites."[4] No matter that most of the players were from places outside New England, it was clear that Hotel Redondo cooking was below expectations. A couple of the players were nursing minor injuries. Wagner had a bone bruise on one finger and a "badly injured foot," but not so badly hurt he was going to take himself out of the games. The men were starting to get tanned now that the weather had turned. They just weren't playing good baseball. Paul Shannon seconded Nickerson, though a bit more gently. He did allow as how if they didn't get cracking, "the respect of California fans for the American League clubs may vanish like smoke." Worse, the race for the AL pennant might not find the Red Sox in contention.[5]

March 18

"RED SOX REGULARS BRACE UP"—*Boston Post*
at Los Angeles, CA: Boston 5, Vernon 0

"YANNIGANS BEATEN IN SWATFEST"—*Boston Post*
at San Francisco, CA: San Francisco 14, Red Sox Colts 6

The tables were turned in both of the games of the day. The Seals flipped a 10–4 defeat into a 14–6 pummeling, and Vernon was shut out, 5–0. Charley Hall finally appeared in a game, the one in Los Angeles, despite being 20 pounds overweight, and threw the last three innings of the game Killilay had begun with six blank frames. Donovan and Wagner had worked out the men for two hours in the morning, so thoroughly they didn't have time for lunch at the hotel. Madden caught the whole game, and was thought to be improving every day—after all, the goal of the exhibition season. Boston's fielders were given credit for strong defense behind a shaky Killilay, who walked three and "was in a hole most of the time." Wagner, Janvrin, Hooper, Lewis, Speaker, and even Bradley were all singled out for Murnane's praise.

The two runs in the first were just what it took to win. Hooper singled with one out. The Vernon pitcher tried to pick him off but threw the ball away instead. Lewis singled him in. A walk followed by two errors helped Lewis around the bases and home. Two more runs scored in the second, this time after two outs. Again, it was a Hooper single which started things off. Speaker doubled past Carlisle in center field, and made it all the way around the bases. Carlisle was assigned an error. Lewis pulled off a flashy double play in the first, catching a sinking liner and firing to Bradley at first before the baserunner could safely retreat. Both Janvrin and Hooper made fine plays, too, though Hooper got picked off a base for the second time in three days.

Wagner's single, Janvrin's sacrifice, and a two-base hit by Bradley brought in the fifth run, in the fifth inning. It wasn't a big turnout for a Saturday, some 2,500 people, though the *Boston Herald* said that fans were pleased when John I. Taylor had insisted that regular pricing be maintained (the White Sox had doubled the prices charged on its tours). In any event, many fans preferred to wait and save their money for championship games in the Pacific Coast League season rather than pay to see untested recruits trying out to make teams from back East. The typical recruit wasn't any better than the PCL regulars, if that good.[6]

The Red Sox Colts hit the ball well and often, with 13 safeties to their credit, and got off to a quick 2–0 lead on a walk, an Engle single, and a double off Yerkes' bat. But the bottom of the third saw the Seals score a dispiriting six times with only one or maybe two solid hits. There was a walk, a couple of infield hits, a Texas Leaguer that dropped in, another infield fly that fell right behind second base, and a freak ball that hit the ground and hopped over Priepke's head at second. "High Pockets" Hunt was replaced by Sawyer, whose first pitch in the fourth was banged out of the park by San Francisco pitcher Pat Eastley; it was the first of four more runs rung up in the fourth.

The Seals collected 20 base hits—16 singles, three doubles, and a home run by the pitcher. And just one walk in the entire game. The only two errors in the game were Boston errors. One of the few good things about the game was that Thomas was not only back from the hospital but able to catch the last four innings; it hadn't been a simple beating, he explained—he'd been held up by highwaymen who'd robbed him.

Tim Murnane filed a column which appeared in the next day's *Boston Sunday Globe*, offering reflections on the state of baseball in California with just a little over a week remaining before the trek back east. One quirk he commented upon was the obsession of fans with youth:

> After a man has played six or seven years they call a player a has-been, veteran, old-timer, and other endearing names, forgetting the fact that some of our greatest players have been tied up to the big leagues for 10 or more years and are still the big attractions, such as Mathewson, Young, Lajoie, Davis, Plank, Bender, Leach, Clarke, Donovan, Crawford, Bransfield, and many others I could name.
>
> They are well satisfied with the game put up here by the minors for the reason they have not seen the great players of the big leagues at their best. The California players simply lack age to become better ball players.

The venerable columnist went on to compliment John I. Taylor for finding prospects like Killilay and Nebinger, Nunamaker, Perry, and Riggert. Murnane then took a slightly different tack, saying that the older players on a team like the Red Sox should not count on years in the game exempting them from competition. "The day for the youngster has come and the man trying to get away with a smile and a bluff has lost out. I regret to say that most of the players address their manager as 'Pat.' A little more dignity would look better, and even Pat should insist on a more dignified name for the leader of a big league club."

Burke stuck to his theme of a more contented crew. "A few days ago there were sore in limbs and body and mentally distressed to the point where each and every man was nursing a little private grouch. Presto, a change of food and a warm ray of sunshine and the boys step into line with angelic dispositions and ambitions to become big leaguers. A baseball player, next to an emotional actress, is the most delicate mechanism yet recorded by the Smithsonian Institute. Manager Patsy Donovan and Treasurer Hughie McBreen have to be diplomats, sociologists, psychologists, and mind readers, as well as having reading knowledge of palmistry and phrenology to keep things running smoothly in camp."[7]

Though he'd signed up Williams as a catcher, Donovan was seriously thinking of stationing him at first base. Stahl was gone, of course, but neither Bradley nor anyone else had a lock on the position. The infield was the area of most concern. Engle was being worked some at first. Third base was by no means certain; Purtell was questionable and neither Janvrin nor Yerkes were seasoned enough.

March 19

"ROUGH HOUSE WAKENS UP RED SOX PLAYERS"—*Boston Journal*
at Los Angeles, CA: Boston 6, Vernon 3 (10 innings)

"DOUBLE DRUBBING FOR THE 'MISFITS'"—*Boston Post*
at Oakland, CA: Oakland 4, Red Sox Colts 2 (morning)
at San Francisco, CA: San Francisco 9, Red Sox Colts 1 (afternoon)

A week after their four-games-in-one-day Sunday, the Sox pulled off a trifecta of sorts, losing two of the games while just salvaging the third in extra innings. The Colts dropped a game in Oakland in the morning, then traveled to San Francisco and lost there by a big margin. Engle was out with a bad knee, Riggert had to leave the morning game when he hurt his ankle, and the biggest loss of the day may have been Yerkes, who badly injured his ankle trying to slide into home in the afternoon affair. Thomas moved from catcher to take Riggert's place in left field and Sheehan came in to catch.

George Pierce pitched for Boston in the Oakland game and allowed just one run on three hits in four innings of work. Pierce had played in the minors for four seasons, but later in 1911 ran up a 2–13 record pitching for Providence and Buffalo in the Eastern League. Why the Chicago Cubs took him to the big leagues in 1912 is worth looking into, but beyond our scope here. He was 13–5 in 1913, and lasted six years, winning 36 and losing 27 with a 3.10 earned run average. It was the only run for either side until the seventh. Moser had taken over for the Red Sox, and was glad to see Yerkes single, move to second on a sacrifice, and score easily on Priepke's double down the right-field foul line. Unfortunately, Priepke was caught a full 10 feet off second base by the hidden ball trick. It was, even in 1911, dubbed the "old hidden ball trick." One wonders when it had ever been new. Three Oaks hits, a walk, and a throwing error by Buzick (who was playing third base instead of pitching) resulted in a three-run rally in the bottom of the seventh. Myers singled and Yerkes doubled in the top of the ninth, the score becoming 4–2, but that was as close as the Sox could get. That some 5,000 fans turned out for an exhibition game was a further testimony for the thirst for baseball in the area.

The team packed up and crossed the bay to play the Seals at Recreation Park. This, too, was a low-scoring game until the later innings. The Seals got one run in the bottom of the first, the only run scored off Larry Pape in four innings. Carrigan caught the game for Boston, giving way to Nunamaker near the end. The Sox had tied it up in the top of the fourth when Myers worked a one-out walk. Yerkes singled and Myers went first-to-third. Buzick, playing third base again due to a shortage of healthy players, singled and Myers scored easily, Yerkes doing the first-to-third move. Then Buzick and Yerkes tried for a double steal, but it doubly backfired — Yerkes was not only out at the plate but out with the injury suffered while sliding into the plate. He had to be carried off the field with an ankle already badly swollen. Paul Shannon felt certain he'd be out for the rest of the spring and possibly longer. He didn't get back into another game for a couple of weeks. Yet another pitcher took to the field, Arellanes taking over at third base and Buzick shifting to shortstop. The Seals took a 2–1 lead in the seventh off O'Brien, but the floodgates opened in the eighth when the Colts did almost everything they could do to lose, including a couple of errors and O'Brien walking in one run and then hitting the next batter to force in another. Five runs scored before he recorded the first out. After seven runners crossed the plate, it was 9–1 Seals and not as enjoyable a ride back to the St. Mark.

In the last of eight games between Boston and Vernon, as many as 5,000 fans turned out for the game. Vernon held the series lead, 4–3, heading into this game and it took a hard-fought battle for the Red Sox to even things up at 4–4.

Patsy Donovan was already thinking ahead. There were four games planned against the Los Angeles Angels before the trip back east, and he wanted to trim the two teams down to a combined 30 players, leaving many of the men behind in Sacramento, where the Red Sox apparently had some form of working agreement with the Sacts.

Pat had Eddie Cicotte and Joe Wood pitching for the Red Sox, with

Kleinow and Madden doing the catching. Starting for the Tigers was Al Carson, a right-handed spitballer who'd closed two May 1910 games for the Chicago Cubs but was otherwise a career minor-leaguer. Carson only allowed Boston one hit through the first five innings.

The Tigers put up two runs in the third. Carson himself started the scoring all by himself, with a hard-hit grounder that hugged the first-base line and skittered all the way to, and under, the bleachers seats before Hooper could get there to cut it off. It was the first home run hit in the new ballpark. Vernon scored another run in the third, the only runs that either team scored until the eighth inning. After Carson's homer, Carlisle walked, then went from first to third on Lee Burrell's hit to right field, and came home on a force play at second base. It was 2–0, Tigers, and that held through the first seven. The Sox had meanwhile lost Hooper, who twisted his ankle. Chris Mahoney came in to replace him, and played a key role in the Red Sox scoring the tying run in the eighth. Hal Janvrin had himself a 3-for-4 day, but it was a walk he worked that put him on base in the top of the fifth. Two outs followed, and he moved up each time, then scored on a gift when Carson uncorked a wild pitch.

It was still 2–1 after seven, but then the Red Sox tied it up. Gardner doubled (he had a three-hit day, too, with two singles and the double), and came in on Mahoney's single to left. The score was tied, and maybe it took a little "rough house" to get Boston's blood going. Wood got the first man in the bottom of the eighth, but Brashear singled and was sacrificed to second. Wood offered a wild pitch of his own, as Brashear took third base (or the sacrifice followed Wood's wild pitch, accounts in the *Globe* and *Times* differ). What happened next, the papers pretty much agreed. There was no instant replay to go back and see it again. With two outs and the score tied, with a man on third, Coy hit the ball to Janvrin at third. As Brashear lit out for the plate, Hal went for the prescribed force play and fired the ball to first, but it was a low throw and hit the ground. Bradley stretched but couldn't quite reach it. "It bounced just at the end of his fingers, ran up his arms to his chest and there he grabbed it," wrote the *Times*. "Bradley gathered it in with his arms," said the *Globe*. Umpire Finney first called Coy out, then reversed his ruling and said he was safe, the question revolving around Bradley's control of the ball as the runner reached first. The safe call gave Vernon a 3–2 lead. It was the right call, wrote Shannon.

Bradley and Gardner and team captain Wagner all protested, and Tris Speaker came flying in front center field to join the fray. "Just what business he had there arguing with an umpire when Wagner is supposed to be the official field captain and kicker, will have to be determined in an international guessing context," remarked the *Times*. Having a designated arguer didn't work in this case. Wagner argued strenuously enough, but Speaker was so relentless he got the heave-ho from Finney, tossed from a spring training game. Still, he refused to go, Speaker advancing the novel argument that a player can't be ejected from an exhibition game. There were two umpires working this game; the head ump affirmed the call. Speaker refused to leave and went back to center field, at which point (nearly 15 minutes into the brouhaha) Finney waved to the grandstand and summoned a policeman to come to the field and take Tris off it. Donovan went out to center to talk with Tris and bring him in. Once the policeman had vaulted onto the field itself, it was time to go. Charley Hall took over in center. The Tigers now held a 3–2 lead. Janvrin was given an error on the throw.

The *Times* writer credited Boston for tying up the game once more in the top of the ninth. Losing the game in the eighth was not going to sit well. "This would have been an awful score to telegraph back to the sacred shrine of the magnificent baked bean," he wrote. "A hot wave suddenly swept over Boston." Duffy Lewis led off and smashed a ball hard off the left-field wall, a two-bagger. John Raleigh (who'd been 1–10 with the Cardinals in 1909) then hit Wagner square in the back. Janvrin loaded them up, reaching on a bold and beautiful two-strike bunt to third base. Hugh Bradley was set to be the hero, but he bounced a ball to the second baseman, who fired it home in time to get Lewis at the plate. The catcher, Drummond Brown, fired the ball to first base to get a double play. There were two outs, but Brown had forgotten to guard the plate. He was unaccountably standing six to 10 feet from home after unloading the throw, and didn't notice the alert Wagner round third base and, seeing home plate undefended, streaked for home. The catcher and the baserunner reached the plate about the same time. Brown had the ball on the return throw from first-baseman Patterson, but Wagner slid into the base safely and the game was tied at three apiece. It should be noted that the *Journal* account says the ball was returned to the pitcher and, in effect, Wagner stole home on the pitcher.

In the top of the 10th, the Red Sox unloaded for three runs. Gardner singled to left. Brown pounced on Mahoney's sacrifice bunt but threw wildly to first. Hall (in for Speaker) singled to center. Lewis hit a sacrifice fly to bring in the first run. Wagner hit to right field and Janvrin hit to center, and it was 6–3 for the Red Sox. In the bottom of the 10th, the *Times* man wrote, "Hogan's men were like a lot of cats with their heads in pitchers."

March 20

"CARRIGAN'S COLTS BEAT SANTA CLARA"—*Boston Post*
at San Jose, CA: Red Sox Colts 3, Santa Clara College 2

"REGULARS FIND EASY MARK IN THE POMONAS"—*Boston Journal*
at Claremont, CA: Boston 7, Pomona 0

It was higher education day for both Sox squads. The Colts went to San Jose and took on Santa Clara College at Luna Park. Still understaffed, with Perry and Riggert and others unavailable to play, the Red Sox had Arellanes play third base again and Buzick at short. When Priepke was hit by a pitch in the fifth and had to leave the game, Engle moved from his unaccustomed spot covering left field to take over second-base duties, Nunamaker went out to center field, and Nebinger (back now) moved from center to left, despite being an infielder to begin with. Dale and Sawyer pitched, and the Santa Clara nine out-hit the Red Sox, eight hits to six. The Red Sox were deemed the home team, perhaps because the ballpark was a couple of miles outside the city itself. The *San Jose Evening News* reported 500 fans.

Dale's first-inning error, sandwiched between two singles, helped set up a run for Santa Clara, McDonough's long drive scoring Ybarrando. Engle doubled with two outs, and Nebinger singled. The college team took the lead again in the third. The bases were filled with two singles and a walk. Another single scored provided Santa Clara a 2–1 lead, but Dale struck out the next two batters to retire the side. Dale gave up six hits in his five innings and walked four, but struck out six and initiated two double plays. Sawyer struck out six Santa Clarans, too. Boston scored twice in the bottom of the fifth on a single and two errors, the second of which was Santa Clara spitballing pitcher Barry's wild throw to third base, which let the go-ahead run in — or, as the *Evening News* explained, "presented the Beaneaters with two runs and the bacon." After the game, the Red Sox returned to Oakland.

The Regulars went to college, too. They arrived in Pomona at 10:17 A.M. on the Southern Pacific and were given an automobile tour of the valley, dining at noon at the Pomona Tavern. They paraded in the autos and in uniform down Second Street and then drove to Alumni Field, located about four miles outside of Pomona, in Claremont.[8]

It was an easy 7–0 complete-game win for Hugh Bedient. Donovan was apparently ready to let some of his pitchers begin to air it out, though Bedient seemed to be toying with the collegians, "tossing up the ball and then, with men on bases, striking out the youngsters as he liked." Both teams had eight hits. Bedient struck out 12. The Red Sox played error-free ball, remarkable in that the college grounds presented "a rough, sandy field, with small stones scattered about." The Pomonas were perhaps klutzy to begin with. They committed eight errors.

The setting was a nice one, Murnane glowing about the mountains "capped with snow, while summer weather prevailed in the valley." The college boys came across as a bit insufferable to him, and perhaps it wasn't only Bedient who enjoyed taking them apart. They were "about the windiest lot of kids ever discovered. However, the Red Sox soon took the conceit out of the youths to the displeasure of the girls present."

It would be nice to see a scorecard from the game. It featured Tris Speaker on the cover. There were exactly 760 fans who paid the 50-cent admission price. Sixty percent of the proceeds, in other words $228, went to the Red Sox. They made out well in the citrus department. A two-hour automobile ride through orange groves preceded lunch, and each player was presented a carton of oranges. During the game, oranges were tossed over the wire fence to the players, "Speaker eating several, as well as a bag of peanuts while playing the outfield."

It was, all in all, "the most farcical of games" according to the grumpy Herman Nickerson, who called it another "training trip stunt ... another link in the chain of jokes so far.... We simply went into the backwoods of California to play a game of ball for the express benefit of a few students and the Board of Trade.... As an outing it was all that could be asked for.

Still I thought this coast tour was to condition the men. This part of it certainly did not help. A two-hour workout on the ground of Los Angeles would have been something worth more. Playing games of this character is little short of lunacy."[9]

Some of the men were excused from the trip and toured Catalina Island. There were hints that one or two feigned a charley horse so they'd be left behind from the trip to Claremont. Karger and Madden, Cicotte, Lewis, Hooper, and sportswriter Merton Burke took in the island and saw flying fish, seals, submarine gardens, divers, goldfish, and sea lions. They were so taken with the place that there was even talk of the team playing a game there. Ten years later, Chicago Cubs owner William Wrigley built a ballfield and clubhouse in Avalon and for the next 30 years had the Cubs train on the island.

On March 20, the *Boston Globe* ran a piece showing the batting and fielding averages for all the men on both teams. It also summarized where things stood as the team assessed the players hoping to make the final cut. Almost certainly written by Murnane, the piece read, in part:

> The team has picked up a few newcomers who are bound to remain in the big show. Two of the new men are outfielders and to date have done better work than the two veterans whom they are seeking to replace. These promising players are Riggert and Perry, and there is no doubt of their being retained after the spring trip is over, for they have exceeded the fondest hopes of manager Donovan by their excellent all-round work.
>
> Three others of the newcomers who have shown to advantage and who look good for retention are Yerkes, shortstop, a Carolina League start, Mahoney, formerly of Holy Cross, who has been playing centerfield, and Nebinger, a third baseman, who has caught the eye of coast fans and the baseball writers by his sure, all-round work at the third sack....
>
> Engle looks to be the selection for first base this season. His work on the coast has been satisfactory to manager Donovan, and the young man has put his whole heart in the game, with the result that he is batting better than last season or any other since he was introduced into major league company. He has both Myers and Bradley beaten for the first sack in a walk.
>
> Speaker has been doing his usual superb hitting and he leads the regular members of the team in batting [he was .448 at the time].... Both Wagner and Harry Hooper are going very well, Lewis and Gardner have not so far given very good accounts of themselves, but no doubt will be as effective as ever when the bell rings for the opening game.
>
> Though Janvrin and Priepke have shown up strongly in the field, they have been weak with the stick, and the chances are they will see more of the bench than the field.

The pitchers have been taking things easy, with the exception of the ambitious youngsters. Neither Collins, Hall, Karger, Wood, F. Smith, C. Smith, Arellanes nor Cicotte have over-exerted himself. The baseball men speak very highly of Killilay, Pierce and Pape.

The catchers are acquiring form slowly. Carrigan is not yet hitting in his old form, while Madden is several points shy of his usual work. The latter is catching well, but not meeting the ball with any degree of success.

March 21

"RAIN PREVENTS AN AWFUL SLAUGHTER"—*Boston Post*
at Redlands, CA: Boston 7, Redlands 1 (5 innings)

"HITS BY CARRIGAN AND HUNT WIN OUT"—*Boston Post*
at Sacramento, CA: Red Sox Colts 3, Sacramento 2

Redlands was ready to see "the real bunch," the Regulars, following the March 7 visit of the Red Sox Colts. The home team was largely the same team as before, though they may have looked different since they were all decked out in borrowed University of Redlands uniforms. One or two of the Boston newspapers inaccurately thought them the university team. The game was again played on the high school grounds, lunch was again held at the Casa Loma, and the same drive around the city was laid on.

The people of Redlands had maybe been miffed a little bit back on March 6 when it was the Colts team and not the Regulars who came to their city. Perhaps now that the first-stringers had come and played, their hurt feelings were assuaged. Many fewer fans turned out, though, much less than half the attendance of the first visit. The weather was a little threatening. Between 500 and 800 showed up to watch the game. The Redlands team was augmented by Vernon pitcher Roy Willett. Joe Wood umpired.

Gardner's single, two productive outs, and a wild pitch gave the Red Sox a run in the first. With one on in the second, Janvrin hit a ball that the left fielder misplayed and Hal was able to haul around the bases to score, too. It went to 4–0 in the third on a home run by Mahoney, who tripled in the fifth to help the Sox score three more times. In the bottom of the fifth, the Redlands boys got a run, averting a shutout when Frank Smith (who'd pitched for the White Sox in the 1910 game in Redlands) let up two hits and Wagner's errant throw struck a player in the back rather than getting him out. The Red Sox were adding to their totals in the top of the sixth with another home run, by Bradley, a single by Kleinow, a double by Smith, and a single by Gardner when the skies opened and torrents of rain washed out the game (and all that hitting.) The three additional runs they had scored to that point did not count. The two-mile ride back to the hotel in Redlands was in a heavy downpour. Nickerson was not amused. "To play this wonderful game and collect perhaps $100, the boys were called at 7 A.M. and will not get back to Los Angeles until after 8 o'clock. Quite a stretch for so insignificant an effort. Still it is in keeping with the P. T. Barnum tour of the United States."[10] Cicotte added another sticker to his bags, one for each hotel the team had visited, be it for lunch or otherwise.

The promoters were left slightly in the hole due to the more meager gate receipts. At least the rain had held off long enough to get in a regulation game. Tris Speaker provided the best moment in the game. "He saw a high fly coming toward him. He was eating an orange at the time, turned around completely, in the meantime secreting the orange in his glove. He caught the ball with the upper part of his mitt, calmly surveyed it a moment, then juggled the orange out of the glove and went on eating much to the amusement of the crowd."[11]

Upon leaving Redlands, Red Sox Treasurer McBreen said the team would never again base itself in a coastal resort but would select an inland town instead.

The state capital hosted Carrigan and the Colts for the first of two games in Sacramento. Both were well-played, low-scoring, one-run games. Frank Arellanes started the Tuesday game and pitched the first four innings, allowing a run in the first (on a walk, passed ball, and a sacrifice) and a run in the fourth thanks to a double by "Chicken" Farrell and Lerchen's well-placed single. It was 2–0, Sacts, and the *Sacramento Union* said those two runs looked as big as a mountain."[12]

Ben Hunt threw the final five innings, allowing none. Hunt was the first man up in the sixth. The *Sacramento Bee* described him being "just as long and lanky as ever" and said he "celebrated his advent with a beautiful rap which send the cork over the right-field fence"—in other words, a home run, hit on the first pitch he'd seen from veteran minor-league pitcher Jack Fitzgerald. As he "ambled around the bases grinning broadly," he'd put the Red Sox on the board; the Sox were down 2–1.[13] Both Boston pitchers were former Sacramento pitchers, and both Hank Perry (who played center and had an 0-for-3 game) and Hap Myers (0-for-4 but with 17 putouts at first base and nary an error) were former Sacts, too. Local fans hooted when Boston's starter got tagged. As it happens, Arellanes didn't make the Red Sox in 1911 and was back with the Sacts from 1911 to 1913.

Ferrell, who'd been with the Red Sox earlier in the spring but then turned over to Sacramento, made a spectacular fielding play at one point and had a double to his credit, too. The Sacts managed seven hits to Boston's eight, and might have scored another run or two but for over-aggressive baserunning and good Red Sox fielding which added up to three Sacramento runners being thrown out at home plate. Myers was hurt in the game, and had to come out, Carrigan going to play first base and Nunamaker donning the tools of ignorance. Riggert was back and had a pair of hits, as did Bill Carrigan, the second one a "screaming" two-run double down the left-field line in the top of the seventh which took the Sox from a deficit to a 3–2 lead, the final score. The *Union* readily conceded that the "big league understudies showed up in good form," but that it was a one-run game demonstrated that the dopester who would discount the Sacramento team might have reason to rethink his evaluation.[14]

March 22

"LEWIS SHOWS HOME FOLKS HOW TO HIT 'EM"—*Boston Journal*
at Riverside, CA: Boston 5, Riverside 0

"PERRY'S TIMELY WALLOP YIELDS THE WINNING RUN"—*Boston Journal*
at Sacramento, CA: Red Sox Colts 2, Sacramento 1

The game in Riverside only lasted one hour and 35 minutes but the planning beforehand was impressive. Hoping to serve patrons who wanted to see the game at Evans Field, the Santa Fe Railroad agreed to put on special trains to serve people in outlying communities and to hold the return trains until after the game in order to accommodate travelers. The team representing Riverside "has been picked from all over Southern California and is composed of some exceptionally good players," wrote the *Riverside Enterprise*. Profits from the game were going to the summer camp fund of the YMCA.

The Red Sox party was due to arrive at 10:45 A.M. for the 3:00 P.M. game, but the Red Sox had tried to call off the game due to the threat of rain. Riverside had extensively advertised the game and declined. Slow to get going, the Sox missed the intended train and had to take another which actually arrived at 1:00 P.M. and the group went directly to the Mission Inn for lunch. They were then shown around the city before heading to the high school grounds ("very rough and grassless") where the game was held before 1,500 spectators, the largest crowd to have ever watched a ballgame at Riverside. There was a "brass band made up of Indians" (from the Sherman Institute) to greet them and to enliven things throughout the game. The field was enclosed by a barbed-wire fence, but "there were more spectators on the hills surrounding the field than paid to come inside." Tim Murnane was appreciative of the courtesies shown by the good folks of Riverside who "did everything to make things pleasant for the boys." But he was critical of the field. Some of the players stayed in Los Angeles and worked out there for a couple of hours. Murnane's feeling was that they got more out of the day than did those who traveled the 150 miles roundtrip and got in the limited amount of playing time inherent in a single game. "The practice work is missing," he wrote, "and the Red Sox are much worse off than if they remained in town for practice, as the grounds have simply been sandlots." It was inside baseball they needed to work at, not just pitching and swinging away. However unfinished the field may have been, neither team made an error and the *Journal*'s Nickerson wrote that Riverside's "fielding was far superior to that of any of the semi-professional teams previously encountered."[15]

Ray Collins had been up in the air before the game—literally. While the others were on their quick tour of the city, he and Hooper, Cicotte, and Charles Smith took a ride in a hot air balloon. Collins came back to earth and pitched the first eight innings for the Red Sox and gave up eight hits; Killilay threw the ninth and allowed one. Riverside third baseman Broadbent had a three-hit day. Crandall, who threw for the Riverside team, gave up 12 hits, but for years afterward could point to retiring Tris Speaker all four times he batted. Duffy Lewis, on the other hand, was 4-for-4 with a home run, a double, and two singles. Wagner was 3-for-4, and started two double plays. Mahoney had a double and a triple. Donovan said he was pleased with the day's work. Boston scored twice in the first inning, and once each in the third, fifth, and eighth.

The *Riverside Press* enthused that fans got their money's worth, both in watching the two double plays and just seeing how the big leagues "smote the spheroid." The *Press*, the afternoon paper, headlined its story "CRANDALL HOLDS SOX" (the major leaguers only scored five times). The next morning's *Enterprise* reprised the theme: "LOCAL PLAYERS HOLD RED SOX TEAM DOWN." The Red Sox reached Los Angeles at 8:00 P.M. that evening. Despite their short stay, Paul Shannon wrote that Riverside was "the most charming of all the places visited."[16]

SABR's Andy McCue noted that Riverside's first baseman was named Tortes (Tortez in one or two box scores) and offers a well-educated guess that he might have been related to Riverside native John Tortes Meyers ("Chief Meyers") who played in the major leagues for the Giants and Dodgers from 1909 to 1917.

The game at Buffalo Park, Sacramento, was almost as briskly played, lasting an hour and 20 minutes, and another tight one-run game between the Sox and the Sacts. Again, Sacramento scored in the first inning; this time, that was the only run they got. It was, reported the *Sacramento Bee*, "a snappy game, with no errors and few safe hits."[17]

It was the second errorless game in a row for Sacramento. Riggert made seven (six, per both local papers) putouts on balls hit to him in left field. Marty McHale pitched for the Red Sox and gave up a run to Sacramento in the first inning. Van Buren (the same Deacon Van Buren who had played briefly for the Brooklyn Superbas and the Phillies in 1904) singled, stole second, and then scored on Patsy O'Rourke's double (the same O'Rourke who had appeared in 53 games for the 1908 St. Louis Cardinals). Other than those two hits, there were only two more allowed by McHale in his four innings; Moser only allowed one. The Red Sox only had four hits in all.

Boston scored in the third inning, tying the game. Buzick singled to left field and was sacrificed to second by Sheehan. McHale walked. Perry grounded to shortstop Lerchen, who threw McHale out at second base. A delayed double steal brought Buzick home from third base when the return throw from the second baseman went a little wide. The Sox scored once again in the fifth when McHale walked and Perry tripled to left-center field. That was all the scoring, but the game was resolved.

The *Sacramento Union* wrote, "The game was lost, but defeat came at the hands of a worthy opponent. The Boston Red Sox in their two games in Sacramento have presented the strongest lineup which they have sent onto any western diamond this year. In the games around the bay last week in which Boston came in for defeat after defeat, their infield was in several cases made up of utility and battery men and the jumble was not conducive to good ball playing and team work." Because the Sacts had barely lost back-to-back squeakers, there was "cause for rejoicing even in defeat when the defeat comes at the hands of a team of the Red Sox strength."[18]

The *Los Angeles Times* opined on Donovan's plans for the season to come. He still had 21 pitchers under Red Sox control and it was coming time to make choices. His plan was to get the number down to nine. The *Times* thought the seven sure choices were Hall, Cicotte, Wood, Karger, Collins, Frank Smith, and Charlie Smith. Of the remaining 14, only two could be chosen, likely from among Arellanes, Pape, Killilay, Bedient, Buzick, and Mahoney. Almost every one of the 21 was a quite young player.

March 23

"RED SOX REGULARS WIN A CLOSE GAME"—*Boston Post*
at Los Angeles, CA: Boston 3, Los Angeles 1

"WEIRD PITCHING COSTLY FOR COLTS"—*Boston Globe*
at Oakland, CA: Oakland 10, Red Sox Colts 5

The Los Angeles Angels and the Red Sox began a four-game series. They'd been in the Golden State for a month now, but with the team split into two squads, it was much more difficult to assess the relative contributions of the various ballplayers with an eye to Opening Day of the regular season. This aside, given all the games they'd played to date, the Sox were more in form than Frank "Pop" Dillon's Angels, who were fresh from their own spring preparations, not having played in real games.

It was a bright, sunny, warm day and the Sox had a morning workout on the field, then took on the Angels. There were only 11 hits in the game, six by Boston and five by Los Angeles. Both teams threatened in the first inning, but a double play rescued both pitchers, Ed Karger for the Red Sox and Flame Delhi for the Angels. The latter had mounted the bigger threat, the bases loaded with one out on walks to the first and third batters, with a sacrifice in between and Janvrin's infield error (one of two he made). First-baseman Dillon himself flied to Duffy Lewis and Duffy's throw to the plate caught Roy Akin. Speaker singled and scored on Lewis's double to the left-field fence, and the Red Sox had a 1–0 lead in the fourth.

Bradley singled in the fifth and Karger slammed Delhi's pitch well over the left-field fence; Murnane wrote that the report of the bat hitting the ball sounded like "the yell of a yellow dog"—whatever that means. It was quite a blow, "the ball cleared the top of the fence by a room full of daylight," wrote the *Times*, which went on to say it "knocked a bird's nest from the upper branches of a big tame pine tree and dropped into the Luna Park where the elks gazed at it in wonder." Clearly, this was an impressive home run—though the *Los Angeles Herald* tried to diminish it by calling it a fluke and emphasizing the work of the Angels' Charley Moore, the "newest member of the Angel family." Moore, in addition to two doubles and a single, "was the hero of a pair of as beautiful circus stunts as were ever seen outside a tent."[19]

Karger's home run gave Boston a 3–0 lead, but he may not have collected on a prize he won. A notice painted on the fence said that any player to hit one over it would win a "Joy Ride to the Beach." By this time, the players had seen quite enough of the beach. The home run was unexpected, too. Angels magnate Hen Berry had several times told the Los Angeles papers, "There will be no home runs put over THIS fence." There had been another 15 feet put between the plate and the fence, and another 20 feet of height added over the prior dimensions. "The only way they will ever get a ball over will be to climb the fence and drop it over," said Berry. Karger's drive went "high over the fence, to the left of the scoreboard, it went, dropping out of sight behind the twin pine trees."[20]

The Angels pitcher, Delhi, drove in his team's only run in the bottom of the fifth. Charley Moore, who later enjoyed five games with the Chicago Cubs in 1912, hit a double. Delhi then doubled, too, or so it seemed. "It was a resounding poke that the fence stopped from going into Main street, but in running around the bags Delhi evidently became so elated over his marvelous performance that he forgot to step even near first base. While he was standing on second, tickled to death, rude and unfeeling Duff Lewis threw the ball to the infield and Bradley howled out that he wanted it." So said the *Times*; the *Globe* estimated he missed first base by two yards. The umpire ruled him out, and the inning was over. Akin blundered, blowing another scoring opportunity in the eighth. He singled to right, and took second on a ball that bounced in front of the plate. After Eddie Teck struck out, some of the Red Sox mistakenly thought it was the third out of the inning and began to run in from their positions. Akin walked off second base and Kleinow fired the ball to the bag, getting him out when he saw himself trapped and decided to at least try for third base.

Watching the game from a box were former heavyweight boxing champion James Jeffries and auto racing pioneer Barney Oldfield, who'd set the world record at 70 mph in 1910 but then improved on his own record ranging up to 131 mph. Jeffries had retired undefeated in 1905. He knew Sox pitcher Frank Smith and invited him out to his nearby alfalfa farm after the game. Once upon a time, years earlier, Smith (born in 1879) had considered taking up boxing instead of baseball, but "a jolt on the jaw by Jeffries" convinced him otherwise. Smith was accompanied on the entire spring trip by his wife and son (who the El Paso paper called "Frank Piano Mover Smith, Jr.").

Oaks fans at Freeman's Park were treated to a blowout, as they trounced the "Irregulars" by a 10–5 score. The *Oakland Tribune* headline was blunt: "OAKS MAKE RED SOX LOOK LIKE BUNCH OF BUSHERS." It was Pape and Pierce for the Red Sox and neither of them had anything. Nunamaker and Carrigan were the two catchers and neither of them had much on the ball, either. Oakland runners stole three bases, and Carrigan was charged with a passed ball. The Oaks executed several hit-and-run plays. The Colts had scored first, two runs in the second, on a leadoff walk, a sacrifice, a triple by Nunamaker, and a single by Perry. But thanks to Pape's "weird box work," Oakland scored two times in the second, third, and fourth innings, then added four more in the seventh. Pape had been one of the most effective pitchers for Boston, but was "wild and ineffective." He just didn't have it this day. Pierce, who followed, was just as bad — "wild as a hawk."[21] Maggert's bases-clearing double in the seventh accounted for three of the four Oaks runs which really put the game out of sight. The Oaks hits were not little ones, either, but "good healthy wallops that carried the ball to all corners of the lot, with speed and vengeance."[22] Riggert homered leading off the sixth for another run for the Red Sox, and Myers ran and slid three times to work in one more. He'd walked, stole second, slid again into third base on Buzick's out, then tore for the plate as Carrigan grounded out short to first.

Tip O'Neill was wrestling with the schedule for the northern route back east. The faculty of the University of Nevada at Reno had voted to cancel the game planned there for Monday the 27th as well as the rest of their baseball schedule to punish the team for having played an outsider (a non-student ringer) in one of its recent games. The grounds where the Salt Lake City Skyscrapers played were in poor condition, so the games there on the 28th and 29th were also in doubt. While appealing to the authorities in Reno, O'Neill was trying to book other suitable dates. Three Colorado colleges had written and asked for games: Salida, Canon City, and Trinidad. O'Neill was trying to work it all out.

March 24

"WOOD MAKES COAST FALLS CRY 'ENOUGH'"—*Boston Journal*
at Los Angeles, CA: Boston 11, Los Angeles 4

"SOX PLAY BASEBALL LIKE SAM SOOZAY AND GYPSY ED"—*Oakland Tribune*
at San Francisco, CA: San Francisco 9, Red Sox Colts 3

Grey Oliver of the *Los Angeles Times* started his column with these words: "It would be better for the noble sport of baseball if nothing was said about that struggle yesterday out at Washington Park." He ended by writing, "For the love of Mike, it is to be hoped that there will not be anything like it again today." Paul Shannon was more blunt: "It took but one short inning this afternoon for the Red Sox to settle satisfactorily any idea that the Los Angeles fans may have cherished that the Angels were of anywhere near big league calibre." The inning was the first inning, when Boston put a "5" on the board.

Donovan had the team work out at some length in the morning. In the afternoon game on a very warm day, Smoky Joe Wood struck out nine Angels in six innings and left the game in the hands of Charley Hall, turning over an 11–0 lead. He'd given up four hits. Hall was not as sharp, and was touched for four runs. Murnane wrote that he looked as though he was out of condition. Of course, Wood might have felt he could cruise after his teammates scored five runs in the top of the first. Angels starter Babe Thorsen, preparing for his third season with the team, had a sore arm. Gardner led off with a double to straightaway center, Hooper and Speaker both singled, Hooper back tentatively after a charley horse several days earlier. Lewis sacrificed the two runners ahead, and Wagner tripled to left. Janvrin made the second out, but Bradley signed and Madden doubled. The fielding was apparently execrable, with Los Angeles scribe Jay Davidson writing, "Only four errors were charged against Dillon's tossers in the entire game, but leniency by the official scorer accounts for this, as there must have been at least 18 misplays in the first round."[23] Finally, Wood grounded out to end the inning. The Sox scored four more runs in the third, Wood singling to drive in the last of the four. That was enough for Dillon, who pulled Thorsen from the game but it was a game that was out of hand by then. "So heavy was the Red Sox fusillade that the Angels were compelled to change pitchers in the middle of an inning," marveled Shannon. Gardner had four hits and Bradley had three. Hall had still not gotten himself into condition and was hit hard, including three doubles and a triple, and he walked four.

The references to Sam Soozay and Gypsy Ed ring no bells in the collective memory 100 years later, but the meaning behind the Oakland headline was clear. If it required explication, sportswriter Bert Lowry offered one, referring to the "farcical games" that the "bunch of Green Goods players" known as the Red Sox Colts brought to the Bay Area. He wrote, "If you want to see a comedy — a bunch of bushy bushers — and have a good laugh, grab a San Pablo car and go out to Freeman Park."[24]

The Colts actually out-hit the Seals, 11 hits to nine, but were losers once more, dropping the game by a large margin, 9–3. McBreen arrived back in town to take over the team as it prepared to travel back east, but it was a lackluster performance. A "direct wire" to the *Los Angeles Times* called it a "dull game," posing the idea that "the miscellaneous recruits who make up the second squad of the Boston Red Sox ... took as much interest in the ball game today as they would in a 'drop-the-handkerchief' contest." The Seals mauled Walter Moser with four hits for four runs in the first inning and added two more in the second, and a seventh run in the third (thanks to three Red Sox errors.) Declining quantities of runs per inning, to be sure, but Carrigan had seen enough and brought in O'Brien. He gave up two more runs in the middle three innings. Nebinger had driven in Perry and Hollis for two runs in the third, and Thoney, pinch-hitting for Moser, had driven in one in the top of the fourth. There wasn't any scoring at all after the fifth.

In Reno, it looked like things had been worked out that the ban on the college players had been lifted and game there could be played as the first stop on the route back east. McBreen was trying to arrange an alternate field in Sioux City, Iowa, and that was looking good, too.

As if this transcontinental trip wasn't enough, Taylor and McBreen had already started looking ahead. "RED SOX MAY GO TO ORIENT NEXT YEAR," blared a headline in the *Boston American*. After a month in California, with memories of some of the bad weather having faded, optimism reigned. Donovan declared, "This trip was beneficial. My boys are in better shape than they ever were at the opening of a league season, and most of them are in better baseball form than is usual at mid-season. I'm for California all the time." John I. Taylor, though, had also talked about sending the team around the world for training in 1912. McBreen proclaimed, "Honolulu, Philippines, and Japan for me next year."[25]

March 25

"COLEMAN, FORMER STREET CAR CONDUCTOR, HOLDS SLUGGING RED SOX HELPLESS; GILL LOSES GAME"—*Los Angeles Herald*
at Los Angeles, CA: Boston 4, Los Angeles 3

"RED SOX REGULARS LUCKY TO WIN OUT"—*Boston Post*
at San Francisco, CA: San Francisco 4, Red Sox Colts 3

As the two Sox teams were readying their run east, there was a minor flurry of activity on the telegram wires. McBreen sent Donovan an early message, before the morning workout, asking for assistance in personnel: "The papers are roasting the boys badly and they seem demoralized. Several men too light. Hollis and Priepke no good. Send help, Mahoney and others." Hooper was still not prepared to go full-bore, so Donovan couldn't spare Mahoney. Charley Hall didn't show up so Donovan sent Collins and Karger to McBreen. John I. Taylor had planned to send Mahoney to Sacramento, but Donovan was "sweet" on him and planned to suggest that Perry go to the Sacts and that he keep Mahoney (Mahoney had appeared in two games as a pitcher and one as an outfielder for the 1910 Red Sox; neither Mahoney nor Perry played in the majors in 1911). Pinch Thomas was designated for Sacramento. McBreen also said the uniforms the Colts had were wearing out, so Donovan sent a dozen new ones to him. Whatever interest the Red Sox had had in Doc Moskiman, they had no longer. As for Hall, Donovan had about run out of patience with him, and Murnane wrote, "Hall may be allowed to remain at his home in Ventura until he is ready to show a disposition to play ball."

Two one-run games marked March 25. The Sox just edged the Angels, 4–3, and it was far from easy, even though they were facing a couple of semipro pitchers, Coleman from the Motormen's League and Gill, who was a waiter at a Pasadena hotel and pitched the last three innings.[26] The Red Sox scored one run in the second after an error, a walk to Janvrin, a force out at the plate on a ball hit to third base, and then a single by Kleinow which brought Janvrin home. Frank Smith pitched a complete game for the Red Sox, settling down after surrendering three in the bottom of the second on a couple of walks, two hits, and a ball that went astray when Wagner tried too hard to pull off a double play. Only two Angels got as far as second base, and none any further, for the remainder of the game.

Boston got its second run with two outs in the fourth when Janvrin walked again, then ran to third on Bradley's hit to left field. When Bradley raced for second base, he drew the throw there and Janvrin ran home, Bradley running on to third after the ball was thrown home. Everyone was safe, though Brad hurt his ankle "making the craziest kind of slide" getting into third base and Mahoney pinch-ran for him, with Rip Williams taking over at first base.[27] When Coleman, the street car conductor, left the game after six, the Angels were ahead, 3–2.

Subbing for Bradley may have been the opportunity Williams had been waiting for, to show what he could do where Bradley hadn't been as strong. Gardner led off the eighth, bunting for a hit. Hooper — still lame, but in the game — sacrificed him to second, and Speaker drove in the tying run with a hard-hit ball into center field. Tied entering the ninth, Wagner walked and Janvrin sacrificed to send him to second. Williams singled to left and brought Heinie home.

The Seals won their fourth game in a row from the Red Sox, by the same 4–3 score as the game in L.A., collecting all four of their runs off Arellanes in the second inning on three hits, a base on balls, and Nebinger's costly error that allowed the batter, catcher Walter Schmidt, a complete circuit of the bases after he singled and Arellanes cut off center-fielder Perry's throw toward the plate, hoping to nip the runner at third and fired it so hard to Nebinger that the third baseman couldn't hold it; the ball rolled into left while Schmidt chugged around the bases.

In the fifth inning, the Red Sox scored all of their runs on Riggert's single, the error made at shortstop on Myers' grounder, and Bill Carrigan's three-run homer over the right-field fence. Sawyer walked five but didn't allow a run. Perry was part of the reason the Seals didn't score again. In the seventh inning he caught a ball right up against the fence in center field and in the eighth he threw out a runner at home plate. But they still held the margin of victory after the Red Sox failed to score in the top of the ninth.

Meanwhile, there were warnings that some domestic difficulties might be in the offing. Five days earlier, when the team had passed the day in Pomona, there were those gift boxes of oranges that each had been presented. A story out of Los Angeles, which broke in the May 25 papers, harked back to those boxes of oranges which the Pomona Board of Trade had given to each ballplayer. It seems that "the girls in the packing house" learned who the boxes were intended for "and each fair maiden decided that it was a chance to give the little god of romance an opportunity." They slipped love notes inside, "heart throbs" in the parlance of the day. But the ballplayers took advantage of the well-packed fruit to take the 25 boxes to the express office and generously sent them to wives and girlfriends back home. When word leaked out what had been inserted within, some started rehearsing their explanations and others hoped for something to happen to the express rail car out of Pomona.[28]

As the team prepared for its final day of play in California, Burke predicted that the Red Sox would do better than the fourth or fifth place finish many of the "scientific writers" were predicting. Burke's response:

> They're wrong. They may be very good mathematicians, and no doubt they have used up many perfectly good lead pencils figuring out the probability, but there is one thing you can't figure on paper, and that is the human equation.

The particular human equation in mind concerns the attitude of the Boston players toward each other this year, and toward their team and also the personal ambitions of the men.

For the most part the Boston boys are very young. Last year some of them were not seasoned as much as they should be to play the game to the limit. They are improving with age. Lewis and Hooper are particularly in evidence in this respect. They are playing better ball than they ever did before. Gardner, the young second baseman, is also a comer.[29]

Burke was a year ahead in his thinking. The sabermetricians of the day had it right, but it would be 1912 when the Red Sox would break out and win the World Series, which they did in four of the next seven years, from 1912 to 1918.

March 26

"SPEED BOYS WIN SLOW VICTORY FROM ANGELS"—*Boston Journal*
at Los Angeles, CA: Boston 12, Los Angeles 4

"WHOLE FLOCK OF PITCHERS FAIL TO LAND YANNINGS"—*Boston Journal*
at Oakland, CA: Oakland 6, Red Sox Colts 5 (11 innings) (morning)
at San Francisco, CA: San Francisco 8, Red Sox Colts 0 (afternoon)

"The Sox will never return to Southern California again to train," wrote the *Los Angeles Times*. Patsy Donovan and party were due to leave on the late evening train heading to Yuma, Arizona. There was the distance itself, too far from Boston, not just the dismal weather than ruined the first couple of weeks. For players who had families back east, it could take nearly a week to get home should a child or wife become seriously ill. But the players were now in pretty good condition, with few sore arms or injuries. The *Globe* focused on the very good weather in the most recent 10 days and said the Red Sox "have rounded into midseason form." Tim Murnane said Carrigan's Colts were not in such good shape and he disapproved of splitting the team into two. He also praised the quality of play, the pay, and the appreciation shown baseball in the Pacific Coast League. Vernon's Hogan was "a manager of major league caliber" and the umpiring particularly good, better, he felt, than the National League. Because the climate permitted year-round baseball, he believed California would become more and more productive in turning out quality players. Most of the parks were too small, not large enough for the inside-the-park home run. "The best one can get at the cramped up little box at San Francisco is two bases to right and three bases to the other field." Not even the old South End Grounds in Boston was as small. The PCL season was to begin on March 28. The Red Sox had three more games to play, a final one against the Angels and one each against Oakland and San Francisco.

The Colts had a bad day. The first game was a lengthy one, running to 11 innings, though it still only took two hours to play it. McHale started the game for the Red Sox and pitched the first four, leaving with Boston behind, 2–1. But he's the one who dug the hole for himself by failing to cover first base in the bottom of the third inning on a ball hit between first and second, fielded by Priepke at second whose throw went to the stands and left runners on first and second. Izzy Hoffman's single brought them both in. Oakland got two more off Moser in the fifth. The Red Sox were down, 4–1, but scored four runs of their own in the top of the eighth to take the lead, three of the runs coming on Buzick's bases-loaded triple. Oakland scored once on John Tiedemann's double in the bottom of the ninth and it was 5–5. Buck O'Brien pitched the 10th and also the 11th, until Tiedemann came up again and hit what we now call a walk-off home run.

The Colts couldn't get a run against the Seals, only managing five hits while striking out 10 times. Carrigan used every pitcher he had. Hunt, Pape, and Dale pitched for the Red Sox, Hunt being particularly poor allowing eight hits in four innings while walking three and throwing a wild pitch. The Seals scored two runs in the second, two in the third, and two in the fourth. After Pape took over for Hunt, they scored two runs in the fifth. The *Los Angeles Examiner* story referred to the Boston Tired Boys.

The Regulars won their game, 12–4, the last game they played in the state of California until March 22, 1959. It was, Tim Murnane wrote, "their best game of the season." The headline over H. M. Walker's story in the *San Francisco Examiner* suggested another story: "THREE BUSH BOYS MASSACRED BY RED SOX." He wrote that the three pitchers Pop Dillon asked to pitch, "all of them green enough to put out a prairie fire," were "allowed to trespass upon the territory usually reserved for a pitcher of class. One of these three buds got away without being killed. The other two were mangled beyond recognition."[30]

Boston scored once in the first and once in the fifth. Charlie Smith pitched five (his first outing with the Regulars since coming up from L.A.) and Wood pitched one, and the Red Sox had a 2–0 lead. Williams was playing first base for the injured Bradley. Paul Shannon felt he'd injected "added life and ginger" into the game and that he'd "showed up like a second Jake Stahl."[31]

Killilay pitched a perfect seventh and eighth, while the Red Sox scored four times in the seventh and twice in the eighth. Lewis cleared the bases with a triple. They added another four in the top of the ninth, and it was 12–0 by the time the Angels came to bat in the bottom of the ninth. The 5,000 fans, at least the ones who stuck around to the end, saw a little bit of a comeback by the Angels in the ninth. Hugh Bedient strode to the mound and walked the first two batters on eight pitches. A double drove them both in. A single, another walk ... nine men came to the plate and four scored before he closed out the game. Bradley's injury from the day before was worse than it had been thought, a strained tendon.

The Red Sox Regulars had won 16 games and lost only one. The Colts, on the other hand, didn't show well at all. Baum, writing in the *San Francisco Examiner*, was determined to be kind in what he defined "the most disastrous series ever experienced by a so-called major league aggregation." As they left for Reno, he wondered how many of them would make it, saying it all depended on how charitable John I. Taylor was inclined to be. Some of them would be lucky if he covered their fare home, he said, adding, "We omit further comment for fear of hurting somebody's feelings."[32]

At the close of the Coast trip, the two standouts at the plate were Mahoney (.383) and Riggert (.347). Engle and Wagner were both .338. Lewis was hitting .324 and Gardner was .300. Riggert's 45 total bases were 10 more than the next closest hitter, Duffy Lewis.

"This trip has been an absolute success in every way," crowed Patsy Donovan. "I am delighted with the condition of the Boston players. We are ready to go into the big games at once. Our pitchers are in fine shape, even better than at any time last season." There was one sour note, though, reflected in a headline in the *Journal*: "Pitcher Hall Quits Without Permission." Donovan had intended to send Karger and Hall to join the "northern team" but Hall had absented himself, going to his home in Ventura without leave. Donovan sent Ray Collins with Karger instead. Sheehan was left to join the Vernon ballclub, and Thomas was sent north to Sacramento.

Donovan wrote a column in the March 26 *Boston American* looking at the season ahead, but didn't go out on any limb. He said that nothing but first place would do for his team, but acknowledged that the other seven AL managers felt the same way. He praised a number of the players individually, and stated, "Our outfield is the best in the country, bar none. Tris Speaker likes to have a little fun on the job, but he is a demon when sharp work is needed." As to the pitching staff, he felt that he had a strong and deep staff already in the best of condition, Joe Wood in particular. Even though he named some names, overall he expressed reluctance to get into the whole staff in detail:

> A manager cannot tell what he thinks of each player's work. That would never do. If I were to say that such a player is a star and ought to have been in the big league long ago he causes the financial department a lot of bother. If I say a player is no good and should be replaced, he refuses to work his best for me any longer. When a man doesn't do his best, I stir him up by trying another man in his place occasionally. That usually does the business. Silence is golden on this job.
>
> There are some things, however, that I always feel safe in saying. I never have any fears of giving Wagner a swelled head. I consider him the best shortstop in the world. Wagner would play whether sick or well, and play his hardest under all conditions. I have known him to insist on getting into the game when he ought to have been in bed. He has fighting blood. I place great confidence, too, in Bill Carrigan. He has done wonders managing the colts this season on the coast.[33]

Donovan's choices were reported elsewhere in the paper as Lewis, Speaker, and Hooper in the outfield, Gardner on second and Wagner at short. Purtell at third base, assuming he recovered from his current layoff but with Nebinger to back him up, and Bradley at first base. Should Brad falter, he had Engle and Williams ready. In addition to Engle and Williams and Nebinger, he had utilitymen in Janvrin, Perry, and Riggert. He had four catchers: Carrigan, Kleinow, Madden, and Sheehan. And 11 pitchers in mind: Wood, Hall, Karger, Collins, Hunt, Cicotte, Killilay, the two Smiths, Pierce, and Buzick. Clearly, that would put him over the limit when it came time to trim the rosters, but it was a team about which he felt very good.

The Regulars took the 10:15 P.M. Southern Pacific to Yuma to play the "desert rats." McBreen led the Colts in a 9:00 P.M. departure for Reno, already known as a divorce colony. Despite all the rainouts, revenues weren't bad and Taylor ought to recoup his investment in the lengthy trip if they drew decent crowds as they played their way back east.

6

Heading Back East

March 27

"INDIANS WATCH RED SOX VICTORY"—*Boston Post*
at Yuma, AZ: Boston 17, Yuma 5

"YANNIGANS FIND EASY PREY IN THE RENO COLLEGIANS"—*Boston Journal*
at Reno, NV: Red Sox Colts 14, University of Nevada 4

The Yuma game was what the *Globe*'s Tim Murnane, traveling the southern route, dubbed a "joke game of ball." It was also the first game the Red Sox ever played that took place outside the United States proper. Arizona first became a state, the 48th state, almost a year later, on February 14, 1912. At the time the Red Sox played there, it was officially the Arizona Territory. The territory was originally acquired by the United States in the Mexican-American War of 1848, supplemented on its southern boundary by the Gadsden Purchase of 1849. It was originally called the New Mexico Territory and embraced both of the current states of Arizona and New Mexico. Most of the Anglo immigrants who moved into the area came from the southern states of the United States, and during the Civil War period, Arizonans voted to secede from the Union, becoming a territory of the Confederate States of America. Just 33 days after New Mexico became the 47th state, President William Howard Taft signed the bill making Arizona the 48th state.

Yuma County's population in 1910 was 7,733, but there may not have been that many self-confident baseball players among them. The local boosters group, who had enticed the Red Sox to schedule a game in Yuma, was "unable to get together more than four local players with nerve enough to face the Boston sluggers." There had been a nice welcome, the Red Sox arriving in time for breakfast at the Hotel Gandolfo. There were Indian ponies waiting for the players at the train station, and Tris Speaker and Joe Wood mounted up and led the others on a parade through the town (automobiles were available for those who were skittish or preferred not to travel on horseback). As they made their way through the streets, they saw one hotel that bore a sign reading, "No charge on cloudy days." They were told there had only been three inches of rain in 1910.

It was a hot day, not just a warm day. After breakfast, local business-men took the players for an automobile ride to visit the Yuma irrigation project's plant in the desert which fed water to fields of alfalfa. Before the team started out to the park, the town band played in a circle in front of the hotel while the players showed off some San Francisco dance steps — the turkey trot, the bunny hug, and the grizzly bear.

Some 350 attended the game, 300 of them from Troop A of the United States Cavalry which was encamped on a park in town, prepared to defend the populace against any border crossings by Mexican revolu-tionaries or brigands. Making up the rest of the audience were "Indians right off the reservation, in gaudy garments, heads bound up in bandana kerchiefs; Mexicans, half breeds, dogs, and other living things gathered to watch the free show until you felt like one of the animals in the zoo. The ball park was a joke. No sand lot ever held more sand; the grandstand was a bleacher, with a covering formed by palm leaves."[1] The chief medicine man of the Yuma Indians sat next to trainer Doc Green in the right-field seats. Shannon was bemused by the setting. "Few big league ball players have ever performed amidst stranger surroundings, with full-blooded Indi-ans watching from the bleachers, an army encampment for the left-field boundary, a big horse corral in centre field, and an outfield composed mostly of cactus, sage brush, and glittering sand."[2]

Writers can't be blamed for the headlines placed over their stories by editors back in the newspaper office, but the *Journal's* headline set a new low for anything yet uncovered in researching Boston baseball: "RED SOX ENTERTAIN INDIANS AND GREASERS."

The lack of Yuma ballplayers was a problem which had to be addressed; it was already likely to be a lopsided affair for a major-league ballclub to take on local men, but for one team to only have four players would have been absurd. And they certainly needed a pitcher. The solution was simple enough, and allowed more of the Red Sox to get some game time: the Yuma team added Charley Hall leading off and playing first base, Billy Purtell batting second and playing center field, Duffy Lewis in the cleanup position and playing shortstop, Red Kleinow catching and batting fifth, and Hugh Bedient pitching and batting seventh. Burke wrote, "What possible good it could have done to stop off at Yuma puzzles. It broke the journey to El Paso; that was all, and gave the boys a box score that is a wonder."[3] One of the Yuma players was apparently a newspaperman who'd boasted of being a ballplayer in his past, and who Heinie Wagner had to persuade to suit up.

Pitching for Boston was Eddie Cicotte. He allowed 14 base hits and five runs. Though 10 of the 14 hits were by erstwhile Sox players, each one of the four Yuma men had one hit to his credit. Whether the four hits by the Yuman humans were as a result of Cicotte's generosity is unknown.

Michael T. McGreevey, with mustache and waving cap, poses with Boston Red Sox players in front of a locomotive as the Red Sox Special heads west through Yuma, Arizona (courtesy Boston Public Library, Print Department, McGreevey Collection).

The field was so sandy that outfielders had a hard time running down routine fly balls. And the outfield presented a different sort of hazard — the center-field fence was made of barbed wire and Purtell tore his shirt. Murnane said that only one of the Yuma players, a Mexican, knew the game. Some of the local residents knew Duffy Lewis, though. He'd played in Yuma three years earlier, sometime when he was not otherwise active with the Alameda ballclub in the independent California League.

Why Bedient had such a rough outing is unclear almost 100 years later. He was hammered hard, 31 hits and 17 runs. He had his way with Janvrin (1-for-5) and even held Speaker to a 3-for-6 day, but Rip Williams was 6-for-6 and Cicotte was 5-for-5. Harry Hooper had four hits. Speaker homered and there were six doubles, but the other 24 hits were singles. The only player who stole a base was Cicotte. At 6:00 P.M. the train pulled out for El Paso, scheduled to arrive at noon on the 28th just in time for a ballgame there.

The March 30 *Arizona Sentinel* reported on the game, though there was no acknowledgment that the Yuma team was a little shorthanded (a majority of the players being loaned them by the opposition), and the final score reported downplayed how lopsided the final score was. No boxscore was presented; the paper was perhaps not used to running boxscores, but a boxscore would have revealed both these things. The story read, in full, including the understated run totals:

> A splendid game of the national sport was pulled off in Yuma Monday of this week when the Boston Red Sox of the American League crossed bats with the Yuma boys. It was a very fine exhibition of this popular sport and the Red Sox carried off the honors with a score of 8 to 3.
>
> The Hub boys were given a good time while in Yuma and they expressed themselves at being highly pleased with our city, surrounding country and our hospitable people. If they have their training of the coast another year they expressed themselves as being desirous of playing in Yuma at that time.
>
> Duffy Lewis, a former Yuma ball payer, who is now one of the stars of the Red Sox, played with the local team and his long hit and near home run was one of the features of the game. Danny Maddox's strike at the umpire was another popular feature of the game.
>
> This has been a great advertisement for Yuma, as the team made no other stop in the Territory, which is another proof that Yuma is the best city in Arizona.

There was another lopsided score in Reno, a fast-growing city of 17,000 which had almost doubled in size since 1900. There was enthusiasm preceding the game. The *University of Nevada Sagebrush* anticipated the forthcoming game in its issue of February 27. "The Boston Red Sox is a famous team, and will be in Reno for several days, and the game with them will no doubt be the hardest of the season. The stores in Reno are planning upon a half holiday on the 27th [of March], in order to attend this baseball game." Two weeks beforehand, the paper optimistically declared that "the chances for the 'bean eaters' are terribly slim."[4]

The game was originally to be played on the Mackay Athletic Field at the university, but because of the aforementioned faculty ruling it was scheduled for the state park between a picked team from Reno and the Red Sox. The *Reno Evening Gazette* explained that the game would take place "in the late afternoon in order to allow the students of the university, Reno high school, and the public schools an opportunity of witnessing some real baseball. The star players of the university team, which made such a fine showing against Stanford and California universities in their recent trip, will make up part of the team to go up against the Red Sox."[5] The *Nevada State Journal* said, "Most of the business firms intend to close their stories from 2:30 to 6:00 P.M."[6] Two days later, the venue was moved back to Mackay, and set for 3:00 P.M.

Ed Karger threw a complete game against the college nine of the University of Nevada at Reno, limiting them to six hits while the Colts racked up 16 hits. Riggert was 4-for-5, two of them doubles (one of them banged off the roof of the clubhouse but was a two-base hit by the ground rules). But there was a loss in the game: in the sixth inning, a foul tip ripped Bill Carrigan's thumb open, requiring several stitches. Nunamaker was the only other catcher on the Colts, and would have to handle all the duties from this point on. The Red Sox made four errors, playing in summerlike weather on a very rough and ragged infield in a beautiful setting with snow-covered mountains around. The Nevadans only made two errors, though there were many balls they simply didn't get to — errors of omission as opposed to errors of commission. The *Boston Globe* story said that they "were a few chips shy in knowledge of the fine points of the game," though there were some good players among them. One was the shortstop, brother to Hap Myers. Hap himself got spiked in the game, "and had a mighty bad gash," wrote the *American*.

In Reno, the *Evening Gazette* wrote that despite the fact the game was one-sided it was "interesting and exciting throughout and brought forth considerable cheering from the crowd."[7] The *Nevada State Journal* agreed: "In spite of the disparity in the score, the game was enjoyable and brought out some brilliant plays from the local team. From the standpoint of errors the home team was better, having but two, while the Sox had four."[8]

The *Sagebrush* found a silver lining, too: "The Boston Red Sox team No. 2 came, saw and went away. They did not shut out our boys as they have many teams in California. The score does not tell the story because Knight walked only two men while Karker (sic) walked five." Math may not have been the strongest subject at UNR. The student paper's line score showed Nevada with 16 hits, instead of six. It showed Nevada making 10 errors and the Red Sox making nine. The actual figures were two and four. And Knight walked three, while Karger walked seven.

The train pulled out of Reno at 10:00 P.M., headed for Salt Lake City with an arrival time of 3:30 P.M., possibly too late to play Tuesday's game.

March 28

"Red Sox Loaf, But Easily Win Game"—*Boston Post*
at El Paso, TX: Boston 9, El Paso 1

"Yannigans Hit Out Victory In Clash With Mormons"
—*Boston Journal*
at Salt Lake City, UT: Red Sox Colts 9, Salt Lake City 2

The train from Reno to Salt Lake arrived on time at 3:30 P.M., and the game was played after hustling to the ballpark, but there was time to warm up and maybe the whole team didn't get to the park on time. "Enough players were rushed to the park in a sightseeing automobile to make up a team," the *Globe* reported, "and the game was started shortly after 4 o'clock." Awaiting them at Cummings Field on the University of Utah grounds was a new team in a new league, the Salt Lake City Skyscrapers of the Class D Union Association (the league lasted four years, disbanding in early August 1914); the Skyscrapers finished in second place each of the four years). The team was owned and under the command of 13-year major league veteran Duff "Dick" Cooley, and managed by Cliff Blankenship, who'd played in 95 big-league games during 1905–09. Their season was still a month away and they had only been together a few days when they had to face the Red Sox.

Starter George Hummel ran into difficulty in his two innings of work, and left losing 7–0, despite giving up just four hits. He only walked two, but the problem was in defense. He was "plainly nervous and excited," said the *Salt Lake Tribune*, and made the first error of the game. His teammates made seven more errors in the course of the game; seven different players are represented in the boxscore's error column. Although the grounds were rough, the only two Red Sox errors were both on catcher Les Nunamaker. The Red Sox, the March 29 *Desert News* reported, "worked like a well-made machine and showed plenty of ginger." The Red Sox started Ray Collins and he allowed just three hits, though one was a home run by Conway, the left fielder (Engle homered for Boston). Single runs in the fourth and fifth were charged to Collins. Dale finished up for the Red Sox. The *Salt Lake Tribune* printed photographs of Hap Myers and Larry Pape. Salt Lake was building a new ballpark, where the Union Association games would be played; construction began this very day.

The official population of El Paso in 1910 was 39,279, but the city was swollen by a large number of American and other refugees from Chihuahua who had come to escape the insurrection in Mexico. A lengthy article in the *Boston Globe* said that 98 percent of Chihuahuans favored the Revolution. There was fear in El Paso, just across the Rio Grande from Ciudad Juarez, and none of those interviewed wanted their name to be used. The regime of Porfirio Diaz was in trouble and there were rumors that an attack of the rebels on Juarez was planned for Sunday, April 2, just five days in the future. There were news reports of thousands of non-combatant refugees heading north for the U.S. border. Pancho Villa's invasion of New Mexico didn't happen until March 1916. The Red Sox might nonetheless be glad to get out of town and not find themselves captured by revolutionaries.

Despite the possibility of an impending battle just across the border, there was some sense of calm in El Paso. "Locally there is more excitement today over the visit of the regulars of the Boston Red Sox baseball team than there was over the war, for the visit of a big league team is a rare event here, and everybody who could get away for the afternoon went out to see our boys play ball." It wasn't the first time that major-league baseball had come to El Paso. For each of the three previous seasons, the White Sox had stopped to play a game, and "the valley ranchers have been accustomed to plant their crops by the date set for these annual baseball games and baby naming has been postponed until the arrival of these worthies from the windblown burg on the drainage canal." But there was no White Sox visit on for 1911 and when Boston was scheduled in their stead, "the tentative tears of the troubled populace was assuaged."[9]

The Red Sox arrived about noontime. The game was set for 3:15 P.M. Admission was 50 cents per person. About 1,000 people were able to attend, about half of them soldiers. The game was played on a skin diamond at the fair grounds, built inside a race-track enclosure at George Washington Park. The visit was arranged under the auspices of the Ancient and Arabic Order, Nobles of the Mystic Shrine (the Shriners). The local team was "an amateur, semiprofessional, and professional team from El Paso and its environs."[10] "The day was very warm and the dust very heavy," wrote Murnane.

A few weeks before the game, the *El Paso Herald* noted that the team would be one assembled for the purpose. "Nothing has been done to organize a baseball club for the year and as far as known, none will be made. A team is to be organized to play the Red Sox from Boston on March 28 but this will be only a temporary organization including a number of the professionals who have been spending the winter here. As the Red Sox will be here but one day, the team will be but one day old when it disbands after playing the Bostonians."[11]

"RED SOX LOAF, BUT EASILY WIN GAME" read the *Boston Post* headline. The Sox might easily have doubled their score. Joe Wood pitched the first five innings, and Jack Killilay the last four. The El Paso team got three hits (all off Wood) and just one run, in the fifth. Purtell played second base, so Gardner could take the day off (he'd become ill in Yuma). Purtell committed two errors, unable to throw the ball more than five yards, according to Murnane, "his arm dropping at his side after every weak attempt." Shannon said it would be a long time before Purtell got back in the lineup again, and directly attributed the weakness in his arm to the damp conditions in his room at the Hotel Redondo. One of his errors, a passed ball, and two singles scored El Paso's lone run, though the writers agreed that Madden had blocked the plate and the runner never touched it. The umpire was Red Sox pitcher Frank Smith and the decision was a gift. Later in the day, Smith swallowed his chaw of tobacco, "so the boys feel somewhat repaid."[12] Scoring the run was El Paso center fielder Dunson, who'd apparently just come to town a day or two earlier.

Second-inning singles by Wagner and Janvrin ("Janbran, the little angel face," per the El Paso paper) set up a squeeze that brought in Heinie. The Sox played with "dash and snap," declared the *El Paso Morning Times*. Joe Wood tripled in the first two Red Sox runs, then scored on an out, for a three-run second inning. The Red Sox doubled the score in the sixth on a three-run Harry Hooper homer after Williams had doubled and there was a hit batsman. Janvrin got back his batting eye, 3-for-5 with a double. Hooper had two singles to go with his home run. El Paso didn't have a team in Organized Baseball until 1915. This one was pulled together to provide opposition to the Red Sox. The star of the game was the third baseman, who had two of El Paso's three hits and executed three notable fielding plays: R. E. Beaton of Woburn, Massachusetts, an instructor at the El Paso Military Academy. Beaton had played varsity baseball for Wesleyan, as had pitcher/first baseman Marrinan. A soldier or two helped fill out the El Paso lineup; one of them, Phil Smith, was "considered the best catcher in the army," according to the *Morning Times*.[13] The next day's *El Paso Herald* headlined, "NOT MUCH GAME, BUT PLENTY FUN."

Tris Speaker went 0-for-5 in the game, so any parents who'd held off baby-naming may have by-passed Tristram and settled on Joe, for Joe Wood, or Hal for Janvrin — or maybe gone with the local, R. E. Beaton.

After the game, Kleinow took the train to Pueblo, Colorado, to join the Colts there, since Carrigan's injury prevented him from catching. Williams could catch, as could Bradley, but really it was left to Tommy Madden to do the catching since Williams' best position by far was first base and Bradley was "in bad shape" and limping about, using a cane. Shunning the opportunity to cross the border, the "players refused to take chances by crossing the international bridge into Mexico." After dark, the Boston players took the train to Abilene, Texas.

It wasn't the first time a Boston baseball team had played in El Paso. On February 13, 1894, eight players who comprised the "Bostons" beat El Paso, 15–3, in a game before about "three dozen people, including those who stole in, or overlooked from elevations."[14]

Tim Murnane wrote a summary of the season to date calling the trip to date a success. Datelined El Paso on the 28th, it didn't run in the *Globe* until April 2. Murnane revealed a little more of the poor condition of some of the fields, and maybe a little East Coast chauvinism as well.

From a financial viewpoint the trip of the Boston team to the coast has been fairly successful, considering the fact that the first week of the scheduled games was lost through bad weather.

The failure of the second team, which was in charge of Bill Carrigan, to win when stacked up against the strong teams of the coast at Los Angeles and San Francisco made it a weak drawing card during the last week, but the regulars did a good business.

The fact that the regulars left the coast in perfect condition for their best work was some satisfaction. All the pitchers were in prime shape. This is at least two weeks earlier than ever before, and will mean much to the Boston team in the early stages of the race.

The regulars paid a visit to Modesto, to find a poor ball park, a weak team, and few fans.

Three days in succession we journeyed to Pomona, Redlands, and Riverside located in the orange belt. We were given automobile rides, and shown the interesting breaks in the mountains, the glittering snow fields above the clouds, the valleys filled with golden sunshine, but there we found the poorest kind of ball parks, fenceless and grassless, with small crowds who had little knowledge of the game.

These games were all arranged by eastern people, who are trying to make the colonists realize the beauties of the national game.

At Oakland the weeds were a foot high in the outfield, while at Vernon, a suburb of Los Angeles, there was simple a make-believe ballground, where "Happy" Hogan's clever team plays Sunday mornings, playing the other games on the park at Los Angeles.

In fact, the Vernon and Los Angeles clubs are joint owners of the fine ball park at Los Angeles....

Los Angeles and Frisco seem to be the backbone of the Coast league. By keeping the teams in those cities up in the race, the attendance is good and the clubs are making money.

Cal Ewing at Frisco and Henry Berry at Los Angeles practically control the league. Both are hustlers and very fond of the game. They showed the Boston party every courtesy possible. The press of both cities gave liberal space to the game and the fans seemed fair and good sportsmen.

I found all players in love with the country. They receive liberal salaries for six months' contracts, and few of them go to the big leagues by way of sale.

In this way, the league figures it can build up a strong playing league where the players will become local favorites and good drawing cards....

The team, under Patsy Donovan, left California in the best shape that I have ever seen a team in at this season of the year. The pitchers were curving and, what was better still, the batsmen were forced to face all kinds of pitching.

What looked at one time as if it were going to be a rather gloomy outcome turned out later to be rosy, for no set of players has returned north from a training trip in as good spirits as John I. Taylor's boys.... The journey east will give the boys a chance to take it easy, playing just enough to reach the starting time on edge.

It was the greatest trip ever taken by a baseball club. There were more than 50 in the party, and all were pleased with the results. I can say positively that the club did fully as well in California as was expected. Henry Berry told me that we drew much better in Los Angeles than did the Chicago White Sox last spring. The Boston club, however, failed to pick up the good guarantee in the small towns that Comiskey pulled off.

I am very glad I saw the coast, still I will be more pleased than ever to get to good old Boston with its east winds.

March 29

"Red Sox Show Their Speed To The Texans" — *Boston Journal*
at Abilene, TX: Boston 19, Abilene Redbirds 7

"Salt Lakes Turn Tables On Colts" — *Boston Herald*
at Salt Lake City, UT: Salt Lake City 15, Red Sox Colts 10

Rather than sleep on another overnight train, the Colts actually enjoyed a night in a real hotel and played a 3:00 P.M. game against the Skyscrapers. Only a few hundred fans turned out, which the *Salt Lake Tribune* attributed to the poor playing the day before. The Skyscrapers matched their error total with eight more miscues, but pulled off quite an upset. They had a pitcher from the Washington State League starting for them, Jim Jach, who'd been 15–7 for the Raymond Cougars in 1910. Much was hoped for, but he plainly wasn't prepared to face the Red Sox, even if it was the second team. The Sox got to Jach for one in the first inning and seven in the second thanks to three errors, four hits, and a home run by Engle for a fifth hit. After 2½ innings, Boston had a 9–0 lead and it looked to be a more lopsided game than the first one of the two-game set.

Ben Hunt, known as "Slim," a former Salt Lake City resident, started for the Red Sox and wilted in the third, giving up three runs on a pair of doubles, a single, an error, and a wild pitch. In the fourth inning, Buck O'Brien was landed on hard, tagged for a triple, a walk, back-to-back singles, another triple, a third single, and a wild pitch. Five runs scored and suddenly the Sox held just a one-run lead over Salt Lake. "The bleachers went crazy in their demands for just one more run."[15]

A pitcher that Blankenship had discovered at Fort Casey, David E. Byrd, took over pitching for Salt Lake starting in the fifth and gave up just one run in the rest of the game, in the top of the sixth. That gave Boston a 10–8 edge. The teams had agreed to play just seven innings, so the Red Sox could catch the 7:10 P.M. train to Colorado. Salt Lake struck immediately in the bottom of the sixth — and never had to bat in the bottom of the seventh. The Red Sox did have other pitchers with them, but Boston's business manager Flanagan had seen the early 9–0 lead and sent the others back to the team hotel. With the ineffectual Buck back on the mound, he was hit for a double, saw Nunamaker drop a fly ball in front of the plate, and gave up a double. He got an out on a fly to center field, but then gave up a single, a walk, and a double (the third of the game by Harry Spencer). A grounder gave the Red Sox their second out, but they had already lost the lead. Two more doubles followed, before the bleeding was stanched. It was 15–10, Salt Lake. And Byrd put down the Sox in order in the top of the seventh.

Engle played well and had hit a home run. He was the only one who played well, though, according to Merton Burke. "Perry is getting so fat he hasn't time to chase center field flies. Riggert has forgotten how to catch a ball, and rolling grounders went scampering through his legs without fail. Nebinger could not stop a balloon. Buck O'Brien's arm was sore and they walloped every thing he threw. Nunamaker and Myers distinguished themselves by dropping most everything that came their way." He felt the Colts had expected a pushover and been rudely surprised. He also felt that Carrigan didn't have the full influence over the players that Donovan would have.[16]

The Speed Boys clipped the wings of the Abilene Bluebirds, 19–7, taking the Texans for 21 hits. Truth be told, Red Sox batters collected 26 hits in all, but five of them were hit by Chris Mahoney and Billy Purtell, loaned to Abilene for the game. Both loaned players hit well, Purtell for two singles and a two-run double and Mahoney for a single and a home run that was "the finest of the game going on a line over Speaker's head to the carriage gate for a merry walk-around." Without a doubt, though, Speaker was the batting star of the game, with five hits and nine total bases. Duffy Lewis had two doubles and a single and Hooper had one double and two singles. Even the pitchers hit well. Frank Smith started and hit a single and a triple, and may have grooved a few pitches to Mahoney and Purtell. Charley Hall, who'd been allowed to travel with the Regulars after all, only permitted two hits in the final five innings, and hit two himself, a single and a home run over the right-field fence. A gentleman named Oliver pitched the whole game for the Bluebirds, and it must have been a trying day for him. The "special correspondent" who filed dispatches to the *Herald* wrote, "Mr. Oliver, who is of this town, is a very obliging sort of a ball player, and knowing the Bostons to be in need of a little batting practice served up some good ones."

Abilene's first run was provided by Purtell. When the Sox scored seven times in the third, though, the game was pretty much out of sight. Umpiring the game was the Red Sox trainer, Doc Green. The weather was "extremely warm and there was little shade for the spectators, who crowded on the field a few feet from the foul lines. The ground was sandy and the ball soon became covered with wings." Former major-league pitcher Dave Baldwin recalls using the expression while growing up in Tucson in the 1940s: "We played on hard dirt fields (absolutely no grass) with surfaces like coarse sandpaper that cut the ball's cover. After several hard-hit grounders, the cover would be afflicted with small nicks which looked like little wings sticking out from the ball."[17]

There had been a large crowd — 2,500 — in part because the active United Commercial Travelers fraternal organization had arranged that stores in town shut down for the day. That was about one-sixth of the population.

There was a barn dance in the evening, but a noon arrival, the hot weather, and a full hour of batting practice immediately before the game — mostly working on bunting — had many of the men all done in and they enjoyed sleeping at the Westbrook Hotel.

March 30

"CICOTTE'S KNUCKLE BALL IS ON THE JOB" — *Boston Journal*
at Dallas, TX: Boston 4, Dallas 0

Salida, Colorado, was looking forward to the game with the Red Sox. The March 24 issue of the *Salida Mail* carried a story about the forthcoming visit of the Red Sox against "a local team, which latter team will be strengthened for the occasion." The newspaper added:

> This event is certainly one that will interest every lover of the sport in the city.
>
> The necessary funds have already been raised to have the team stop for the game and arrangements will be made to have all the stores closed the afternoon of the game.
>
> As the baseball season will open within a short time, every man will want to know something of the men who will play in the big league and when the Red Sox come this wish can be gratified. The businessmen are very enthusiastic over the announcement and have expressed a willingness to close their places of business the afternoon of the exhibition contest.

Sadly, the Colts game in Salida didn't happen. The contract for the game had been contingent on the train arriving on time and management canceled the train after the wreck of a freight train in Silt, Colorado held up rail travel in the region. Before the team had left Salt Lake for Silt on the way to Salida, word had been received of the blockage on the tracks. Burke, having chosen to travel with the Colts, was the only reporter on the scene. His account, filed after arrival in Pueblo, was a brief one: "So far as travel goes the Colts allow they have the Regulars beaten to a frazzle. They had a thrilling experience on the way over the great Divide of the Rockies yesterday. The wreck of a silver bullion train tied up traffic in the midst of the mountain gorge and the boys had the time of their lives. A long line of stalled trains poured forth passengers and residents of nearby villages gathered about the scene." He added that some among the travelers became light-headed from the altitude.[18]

They were four hours late by the time they reached Salida. With the cancellation, the Red Sox car continued on through to Pueblo to play on the 31st. Perhaps a few Salida citizens watched wistfully as the train traveled through their town, but there was no ballgame to be had. All these many years later, the townsfolk are still awaiting the return of the Red Sox for a makeup game. The only game played this day was in Dallas.

Dallas was already a large city, over 92,000 people in 1910. Given its famous Fort Worth Stock Yards, the city bordering Dallas was known as Cowtown, Where the West Begins, and the Paris of the Plains with its rowdy "Hell's Half Acre." There were another 73,000-plus situated just next door in Fort Worth. The Sox stayed in a Fort Worth hotel and took the trolley to the 4:00 P.M. game in Dallas. The ballpark, Gaston Park, was the largest in which they had played all year. It was "Tris Speaker Day" in Dallas, and his mother and numerous friends from Hubbard City were on hand. It was a bit of a return for Donovan, too. He had managed the Cardinals when they trained in Dallas in 1903. Dallas was hoping to convince Donovan to let them have Gene Dale back again, even though he was traveling the northern route back; he'd pitched for them and won 10 games near the end of the 1910 season. Dale did indeed pitch for Dallas in 1911 and won an even dozen games. Dallas won the Texas League pennant in 1910, though they fell to fourth in 1911. Speaker had a 2-for-4 day, though nothing like his day in Abilene. He was hit by a pitch and laid down a sacrifice, too.

Eddie Cicotte pitched a complete-game shutout, allowing only two hits, one to Dallas Giants pitcher Jack McAdams (who would get into six games for the 1911 St. Louis Cardinals in his only visit to the majors). McAdams was a real pitcher, not just someone who threw fastballs in the direction of home plate. And Dallas had already played against a few other major-league clubs this spring, beating Detroit 10–0 a few days earlier. It was a scoreless game until the top of the sixth, with only Speaker having reached base through the first five. Then things broke. With one down, Purtell (playing second base for Gardner who was sick, and a little lame to boot) singled and then went from first to third on Hooper's single to right field — really a high fly ball which fell in between two outfielders, either of whom could have caught it. Speaker was up with men on second and third. It was his moment, but perhaps he tried too hard — he popped up. Duffy Lewis lined a single which scored them both. In the ninth inning, Lewis drove in the third Red Sox run (Speaker had singled, a little weakly — again, some thought he was pressing) with a double, then scored the fourth run on Williams' single. Dallas only got two men as far as second base, as Cicotte was dominant, facing only 29 batters and even striking out five men in a row early in the game. With strikeouts, popups, and grounders, Cicotte had a hand in 13 of Dallas's 27 outs.

Among those in the crowd were players from the New York Giants' Yannigans team, which was in town. Then there were the goats. Two goats roamed over the field at one point during the game. They were part of the Dallas team's groundskeeping equipment, a feature rarely seen in 21st century ballclubs.

March 31

"WOOD STRIKES OUT THE TEXANS IN BUNCHES"—*Boston Journal*
at Fort Worth, TX: Boston 4, Fort Worth 2

"RED SOX COLTS JUST BREEZE IN"—*Boston Herald*
at Pueblo, CO: Red Sox Colts 10, Pueblo 4

It was the fourteenth win in a row for the Regulars, playing under a 100-degree sun at Fort Worth in front of about 1,000 fans. Even on this day, catcher Madden wore his rubber shirt under his jersey throughout the long practice beforehand and even during the game itself, and kept it up for the next days, too, shedding several pounds per day. By the time the practice and the game were over, all the players were pretty much done in—except one. For the second day in a row, a Red Sox starting pitcher went nine. Smoky Joe Wood pitched a complete game, striking out 15 Panthers (the *Dallas Morning News* said 16) and walking none. He allowed six hits, three of them by Sam Stovall, brother to big-league right-fielder George Stovall of the Indians. "The attempts of the local sluggers to connect with his jump ball were really pitiable," wrote Paul Shannon, "and there are some pretty fair batsmen on this Fort Worth team."[19] Thirteen of Wood's strikeouts came in the first six innings, before he visibly let up. Shannon said he was still not working at his best.

Boston got a run in the first on Hooper's single, an out, and Lewis's single. They added three more in the third when Gardner (back after a day off) singled, Hooper bunted safely, and Speaker tripled the two in with a long drive into right field. Spoke then scored when Lewis singled to left. Janvrin was having a hard time hitting curveballs, a weakness that didn't augur well for his heading directly to the big leagues.

The Red Sox didn't get a hit after the fifth, and Fort Worth had a chance to tie or win in the bottom of the ninth with runners on first and third, but Smoky Joe sent three straight strikes over the plate and set down the final Panther player. Among those who enjoyed watching the contest was legendary scout Ted Sullivan, ill at a Fort Worth hotel but nonetheless able to make it to the game. The Sox left the hot weather in Fort Worth on the 8:30 P.M. train to Oklahoma City.

There was more drama at the Pueblo game. After a night at the Congress Hotel, the Colts took on a "strong team of independent players" at

Selee Park (named for Boston Beaneaters manager and future Hall of Famer Frank Selee) behind former Western League pitcher Joe Galgano, who held them scoreless through the first three frames. Nebinger got into a game again and set up some scoring in the top of the fourth with a long triple to center field. Engle tripled, too, into left field. Riggert singled, making it 2–0. Priepke reached on an infield hit, and Riggert scored on an infield out. Marty McHale tripled to right-center. Two doubles, two walks, and a single added up to three more runs in the fifth. Pueblo got their first hit of the game, off McHale in the fifth, and put across a couple of runs. They added two more in the seventh, but the Red Sox added single runs in the seventh, eighth, and ninth. With 14 hits and 24 total bases on their side of the ledger, it was a 10–4 victory. McHale pitched a complete game. Nebinger earned headlines in at least one paper, with his double, triple, two stolen bases, and six errorless chances in the field.

The game was almost marred by tragedy when the left-field bleachers suddenly collapsed during the game, bringing about 100 spectators to the ground. Remarkably, no one was hurt. Later in the game, wind blew down a big section of the fence. It was perhaps no exaggeration when the *Globe* account suggested that the park was "badly in need of repairs."

The *Rocky Mountain News* of April 1 had a story headlined "COLLAPSE OF STAND CAUSES NEAR-PANIC AT PUEBLO." The full story read:

> More than 100 men were in imminent danger of serious injury at the Boston Red Sox-Pueblo baseball game this afternoon, when two sections of bleachers gave way under the heavy load they were carrying. The bleacher foundations were weakened several nights ago in the heavy wind that prevailed. Today they were packed to capacity and men and boys were hanging on the posts at the sides. During the excitement of the game a loud crack was heard which was followed by the collapsing of the stand. A dense cloud of dust was sent up and it was several minutes before the fact that no one was injured could be learned. Some persons sitting on the higher parts of the stand were bruised.

After realizing that everyone was not hurt, other than for a few minor bruises, a number of the men re-seated themselves in adjacent seating. About a half an hour later, without any warning — no cracking of wood or anything — this neighboring section of bleachers fell down. Once more, no one was hurt. The *Pueblo Chieftain* noted how remarkable it was that no one was injured given that the bleachers had been packed both times. Further, "small boys had been running under the bleachers all afternoon prior to the accident but fortunately there were none under when the benches gave way."[20] The *Denver Republican* attributed the accident to both the earlier heavy winds and "the excited movements of the fans" which resulted in "more than 100 men thrown in a heap." Paying customers seated in the grandstand were unaffected. Those seated in the bleachers were the "dead heads," people who came "without the formality of purchasing tickets."[21]

The *Globe* suggested as well that the Colts were looking forward to getting to Denver since they would finally begin to play on grass infields. "The Colts have played on some awful fields in the last week, and it is remarkable that none of the players have been injured." Speaking of injuries, Carrigan had the stitches in his thumb removed by Dr. Singer, a Harvard graduate who had built a practice in Pueblo. He was told he could work again in about a week. Kleinow reached the team as planned, preparing to take over some of the backstop duties from Nunamaker. The team slept in Pueblo but the train pulled out at 3:45 A.M. on April 1 for Denver and a 7:30 A.M. arrival. They pulled in 20 minutes behind schedule.

April 1

"RED SOX REGULARS WIN BY 'FREE SILVER' SCORE"—*Boston Post*
at Oklahoma City, OK: Boston 16, Oklahoma City 1

"YANNIGANS UNABLE TO WIN WITH KARGER ON THE SLAB"
—*Boston Journal*
at Denver, CO: Denver 6, Red Sox Colts 3

The Red Sox Regulars arrived in Oklahoma City in time for breakfast and departed just after supper at 7:00 P.M. In between, they had the now-routine automobile tour of the city and a ballgame. It was short-lived joy for the 600 local fans when the Oklahoma City Indians scored a run in the bottom of the second on Downey's "crashing drive to the clubhouse" at Colcord Park, a grounder that sent him to third, and then his steal of home when Killilay wasn't paying him enough heed. He got hit by a pitch his next time up.[22] Shannon credited left-fielder Downey for being "as fast as lightning" but also blamed Killilay: "He has a longer windup than an organ grinder, and this is one of the faults he must eradicate if he hopes to hold men like Cobb and Eddie Collins close to the bag."[23]

Downey's theft tied the game with the Red Sox, who had scored in the top of the first. This occasioned great glee from the local rooters, who "were willing to sing stingingly about the Beaneaters." Razzing the opposition for merely catching up may have seemed a little foolish, but the Red Sox soon disabused them of too much merriment, scoring once in the third, three times in the fourth, three more times in the fifth, six times in the sixth (Wagner's bases-clearing double accounting for half of them), and tacking on two more in the eighth.

There were seven doubles (two by Speaker) and a triple among the 15 hits and not one error, and soon all was quiet. Killilay (seven innings), Bedient, and Cicotte all got in some work. Speaker had a 4-for-5 day. It was quite a ballfield: "Not a blade of grass, not even a stray weed, simply a dirt field, and black dirt at that, in which white uniforms soon became grimy and unsightly with virgin soil, and the major leaguers looked like coal miners after a hard day's work." The park was "a dump of sand, bad to run on, cutting the ball to shreds."[24] The state of Oklahoma had only been admitted to the Union in 1907, but Oklahoma City was a fast-growing, new, and bustling metropolis. As hoped for, the weather was moderate and "delightful." Doc Green umpired the game at first, but when Wagner slid hard into second in the second, he spiked a local player badly in the thigh, so Green took his medical kit to the clubhouse to attend to the man. One of the Oklahoma City players assumed arbiter duties and "gave splendid satisfaction." The *Oklahoman* didn't feel the Red Sox had shown much, other than Tris Speaker (4-for-5), but attributed the lopsided score to the weakness of the Indians' pitching.

Patsy Donovan wrote another column expressly for the *Boston American*, leading off with a sense of unity which perhaps reflected the discord of the year before. "We have a winning combination of players with us this year. There is not a discordant note. We are all for one and one for all." He chose Bradley to play first base: "Of course, we will miss Jake, but we have a young man on the job who, to my mind, is going to open a few people's eyes." And he selected Engle to play third: "The condition of Purtell's arm makes it necessary to make a change at third, and I look to see Clyde Engle fill the bill. He has certainly shown great form this year on the coast." He planned to keep *five* catchers — Madden, Carrigan, Kleinow, Williams, and Nunamaker — recognizing that one or more might need to be loaned out to a minor-league club as the season progressed. Williams, though, was proving to be solid at first base. A couple of days later, Burke wrote, "Williams is a natural-born first baseman."[25] Donovan said he was particularly pleased with Killilay among the new pitchers and was hearing from the other team that Moser was improving all the time. The outfield was, of course, set. As to reserves, "Janvrin will positively be a member of the regular team this year. Another utility infielder I have in mind is Yerkes: he is a first-class man, a hitter, and the best man available for shortstop should Wagner be injured." Perry and Riggert were ahead of Mahoney, but he saw the possibility he might keep Mahoney ahead of one of the others. He closed with his refrain: "We are going after that pennant all right. That's what we are paid for."[26]

The Denver Bears had been looking forward to the visit of the Red Sox, to give them some tough competition. They saw the news, how the Red Sox were mowing down the opposition. The *Rocky Mountain News* advanced the game as early as March 26 saying that President James McGill and manager Jack Hendricks weren't looking for any "love-feast" and that battles royal were expected. Word was that they were hoping the Red Sox would leave Hank Perry behind with him when the Sox continued on; it was said that Sox owner Taylor had promised Denver they could have their pick of the recruits, presumably under some form of working agreement.

On arrival, the team checked into the Metropole Hotel where they spent two nights. A renovated Broadway Park hosted 3,000 fans on a weekday afternoon to see the Bears and the Colts in a 3:00 P.M. game. Both teams battled through six innings, "a snappy, gingery game" against the "cold-blooded Hubsters"[27] with three lone tallies adding up to a 2–1 lead for Denver. The Red Sox scored first on back-to-back triples by Riggert and Nunamaker, though Nunamaker's was helped by a bad bounce of some gravel in the outfield.

The ballpark had a grass infield but it also had a sun that presented difficulties for both teams' outfielders and a footing in the outer garden that was so soft that "it was almost impossible to cover ground on long drives." Kleinow caught, and Nunamaker played first base. Karger pitched the whole game. Nothing stopped Denver from hitting, and they whacked 16 hits in all. The Sox tied it up in the seventh, 2–2, but the Grizzlies came back with a pair, then added two more in the eighth. Nunamaker swung at the first pitch he saw in the top of the ninth and homered to left. Two more Boston men got on base, but the rally fizzled when Thomas grounded back to the pitcher for the final out. "In no department of the game did the Red Sox outshine the locals," wrote the *Denver Post*. This was a strong Denver team; 12 of the 20 players on the roster played in the major leagues at one point or another in their career, including four who played for the Red Sox: Jack Coffey, who joined the Red Sox late in the 1918 season; Casey Hageman, who made the Red Sox later in 1911; Buck O'Brien, who was with the Colts but returned to Denver and went 26–7 before being promoted to the Boston club in 1912; and Hank Olmsted, who'd appeared in three 1905 games for the team when they were called the Boston Americans.

After the game, both teams were the guests of Denver right-fielder Harry Cassidy at the opening of a new movie theater he was launching at Second and Broadway.

April 2

"DUFFY LEWIS' BAT DOES THE BUSINESS"—*Boston Post*
at Wichita, KS: Boston 5, Wichita 4

"YANNIGANS BUNCH HITS IN EIGHTH AND BEAT DENVER"
—*Boston Journal*
at Denver, CO: Red Sox Colts 4, Denver 1

The crowd in Denver doubled in size, and 6,500 fans saw the Colts square it up with the Grizzly Bears in a tightly pitched game on an overcast day, Boston getting only six hits and Denver three. Ray Collins started for the Red Sox, allowing just one hit in the first five innings while striking out eight. Hageman had similarly held the Red Sox to just one hit through five. After six innings, neither team had scored and no baserunner on either side had reached as far as second base. After a single and two advantageous outs, there was a Grizzly on third base in the bottom of the seventh. Coffey hit a routine grounder to Priepke at second base, but Priepke "began to fight with the sphere and the ball, disgusted with his handling, dropped away from him."[28] It was 1–0 Denver after seven full.

Then came the eighth. Hollis walked to start off the inning. Priepke offered amends for the error with a single to right field, Hollis taking third.

Nunamaker's sacrifice fly to right field tied the game. Priepke promptly stole second. Priepke then stole third base, and came in when Arellanes (who'd replaced Collins) singled him in. Hank Perry hit an inside-the-park home run that rolled and rolled and reached the wall in left-center field. All of a sudden, it was 4–1 in favor of the Red Sox.

Another entertaining evening was planned, a nice respite for men now accustomed to hopping on trains within an hour or two after the end of a game. The two teams were provided boxes in the Broadway Theatre for a performance of *The Girl in the Taxi.*

At Association Park, the Wichita game was a tight one, though not a classy one. Frank Isbell owned and managed the Wichita Jobbers (who were consequently sometimes nicknamed the Izzies) in their seventh season in the Western League, in what was intended as the first of two games against the visiting Red Sox. Only seven weeks after this game, on May 22, the Wichita team moved to Pueblo, Colorado, and changed their name to the Indians. The team relocated back to Wichita in 1912.

Hal Janvrin was only batting .184 at the time (Speaker and Mahoney were both hitting over .400), but Tim Murnane of the *Globe* enthused over him at some length: "The boy has the makings of a great ball player. Like all young players he had many faults to be remedied. They are simple ones, however. Trained for sprinting, he wants to get off with the crack of the pistol. Ball players anticipate and beat the sound by carefully noting the position of the man at bat when fielding and the movements of the pitchers when running bases. The great baserunner gets off with a swinging start, for there is no penalty for making a false start as there is in running off the mark." He was 2-for-4 in this game, with a double and a triple. It was a very windy day and Madden apparently had quite a time keeping up with all the breaking balls Piano Mover Smith threw, which often hit the dirt around home plate or went over the batter's head, but he acquitted himself well in that department. Four runners stole second base on him, however. Joe Wood, the Kansan in the group, pitched two perfect innings due to popular demand and struck out three in the process.

The Red Sox perhaps should have scored in the first inning when a ball hit out of the park resulted in two outs. There was already one out when Hooper singled. Speaker then "drove the ball like a shot against the roof of a small house just outside the center fence. It bounded back into the field and Hooper was called out at the plate and Speaker at third." It had hit a tool house, according to the *Wichita Beacon*.

With two out in the third inning, it looked like Gardner had struck out but the umpire called it a walk. Hooper singled, and Speaker was walked intentionally. The bases were loaded for Lewis who drove one to the right-field fence, clearing the bases before he, like Hooper earlier in the game, was out at home plate. The throw to try to get him at third had gone astray but the third baseman chased it down in time to easily get Harry out. Wichita scored once in the bottom of the third and then took a 4–3 lead, to the delight of most of the 1,200 fans on hand, in the fifth. Wichita executed three double plays against the Red Sox "and made them look like a Bloomer Girls team," wrote Nickerson. "The only difference being that Patsy's men didn't wear the yellow wigs."[29] In the Sox sixth, Speaker singled. He was caught off first base, in effect picked off, but made it safely to second despite running out of the basepath. Lewis hit a two-run homer over the left-field fence to give Boston the lead back, 5–4. The "Alameda Kid" had driven in every one of the five Red Sox runs.

April 3

"PERRY'S ERROR IS COSTLY FOR 'YANS'"—*Boston Journal*
at Denver, CO: Denver 3, Red Sox Colts 2

After the obligatory sight-seeing motorcar tour in the morning, the Red Sox suited up for the final game of the set. Denver took the rubber game of the three-game series with a come-from-behind three-run sixth. Taunton's Joe Burns served as umpire. The weather was raw and cold, with snow threatening, and the attendance was off— a "handful of fans" declared the *Denver Times*—and the players only collected 10 hits in all, four by Denver and six by Boston. The Red Sox scored once in the second on a single by Engle, a sacrifice, and a single by Priepke. And they scored once in the fourth; Priepke singled, but despite getting caught off first base he ran to second and was safe when the first baseman's throw to second went astray. He stole third and came home on the third baseman's failure to field Kleinow's grounder. Two Red Sox reached base in the fifth, but both were thrown out on the basepaths. Larry Pape pitched as well as one could hope, permitting just one hit in the first five. There was one amusing moment during the game, when Hap Myers had tucked away the ball hoping to catch Cassidy off base with the hidden ball trick. He saw it wasn't going to work, so he threw the ball back to Pape — but Pape didn't see it coming and Cassidy easily stole second.

Hunt took over starting in the sixth and had some bad luck. He walked Tommy Mee, the first batter, and struck out the second. The center fielder from the first two games, Duke Kenworthy, took over as pitcher but maintained his slot batting second in the order. He singled to left field and it wound up second-and-third as Kenworthy took second on the throw to third. After a strikeout, Perry screwed up and dropped a ball hit to short center. Then Chris Lindsay, the first baseman, dropped in a Texas Leaguer that drove in two and cost the Colts the game. The Grizzlies only had four hits, but won the game, 3–2.

Burke came down on Perry in his game account: "Up to Salt Lake I had Mr. Perry slated for the Regular outfit, but since then he has been very like a bush-leaguer. Personally, I think Mahoney should have the job if it comes to a question between the two, and I think Manager Donovan has leanings that way himself."[30] Apparently, the Red Sox had already tried to buy Kenworthy but failed. He made it to the big leagues and played for the 1912 Washington Senators — but as an outfielder. In 285 major-league games, he never pitched once.

At 10:00 P.M., the sleeping cars left Union Station for Lincoln, Nebraska. Aboard the train, Arellanes blamed the Red Sox dropping two on "the elevation." Correspondent Burke offered material to the *Denver Post*, writing, "The boys have certainly been up in the air in more ways than one. The high life en route, not to mention the trip two miles in the air crossing the great divide, and residence in Denver, which is just a mile high, has probably contributed to their lack of interest."[31]

After the April 2 game at Wichita, lightning danced through the clouds and a downpour ensued, complete with hailstones. The farmers had been praying for rain for weeks, and it rained heavily all night long, "every moment saving fortunes." It drizzled all day, and there was no baseball. The *Wichita Eagle* reported, "Following the storm of Sunday night, Manager Isbell refused to let his players go out for practice work yesterday, and as a result the game with the Boston Red Sox was called off on account of the weather.... Izzy had sworn vengeance on Patsy Donovan and the bunch of beaneaters, and judging from the game Sunday, Isbell's bunch might have 'put one over' on the visiting team if the rain had not soaked the diamond."[32]

It was good to have some rest after an exhausting week playing a game in a different state almost every afternoon, and there was other good news: Bradley had dispensed with his cane, though he wasn't expected to play in a game until the team reached the East Coast. The only real weakness Murnane saw on the Red Sox was that the catchers didn't seem to have much success throwing out baserunners. It was the first day off the Regulars had had since March 9. After playing some billiards and catching up on letters to home, the overnight train to Topeka, Kansas, left at 11 P.M.

April 4

Neither team was able to play, due to rain in Topeka and wet grounds and miserable weather in Lincoln. The Topeka Jayhawks, known locally as the Kaws and presented as such in Topeka box scores, and manager Fred Moore, had already lost a game to the White Sox to rain and hoped to get in at least one of the two games planned against the Red Sox. Some of the ballplayers were happy to get to the National Hotel and have a real bed. The train pulled in during the early morning hours, but was a "deep-sea-going 14-section Pullman, a car that rocked, tossed, and squawked like a pork-packing slaughter house. The men confined to 'uppers' were seasick, and hit their hotel beds with a rush."[33] Speaker had a very bad cold, coughing continuously, one he first caught in California and never quite shaken. It was bad enough to keep him up most of the night for few nights running.

Taking advantage of the time off in the capital of Kansas, the Red Sox made their final plans for opening the season. After the two squads met up in Chicago, and Donovan and Carrigan consulted to rework the composition of each of them, the Regulars would head directly to Washington to open the season there. The two units had not been in touch since they left California, though Donovan read in this day's Topeka papers about the April 2 win in Denver.[34]

The Red Sox number two team would return to Boston and play

against Harvard College at the Huntington Avenue Grounds on April 11. Donovan would travel with the second team while McBreen shepherded the first-string team to D.C. The original thought was to have a grand finale for the tour, with both teams showing up in Boston, but it didn't make much sense to require the Regulars to go there, then to Washington.

Taylor liked the idea of showing off all the new men in Boston, the men that fans had been reading about in the extensive coverage devoted to this prolonged spring training. Immediately after the Harvard game, Donovan himself would take the train to Washington, probably accompanied by Perry, Riggert, and Yerkes.

April 5

"Tris Speaker Ill, On His Way Home"—*Boston Post*
at Topeka, KS: Boston 7, Topeka 0

"Karger's Batting Doesn't Save Yans"—*Boston Journal*
at Lincoln, NE: Lincoln 8, Red Sox Colts 7

After two postponements, the Regulars got out to the Kaw park early to work out. Tris Speaker left for Boston, disappointing Topeka but deciding to take no chances with a cough he'd had which had lingered for two weeks. He just wanted to get to Boston to see a specialist and to recover. Doc Green was out with a cold and a bad back. Joe Wood, the former high school boy from Ness City, had pitched his first professional ballgame in Topeka for the Hutchinson ballclub in 1907, but Topekan fans saw Charlie Smith instead — a very good Charlie Smith.

Conditions were far from ideal. The *Topeka State Journal* wrote, "The field was muddy and the weather chilly. The balls looked like chunks of mud after they struck the ground a few times and had to be replaced." It wasn't just the mud. Paul Shannon wrote in the *Boston Post*, "The Boston players have run up against many a poor park since they left home last February, but the Topeka plant is of the vaudeville variety.... The diamond was six inches deep with mud, the outfield looked like an old deserted pasture, and as for the grandstand, they say that the local management sits up all night praying that the forlorn looking old structure will burn down."[35]

The Sox won their seventeenth game in a row by tackling Topeka, 7–0. Charlie Smith got a boost when the Red Sox scored first, in the first. Gardner walked, then aggressively ran all the way to third base on Hooper's bunt. The ball was thrown wildly there, and he ran around the bases, first base to home plate on a bunt. Smith, wrote *Daily Capital* sportswriter Jay E. House, "was tighter than a purse string" in the six innings he worked, giving up just two hits.

In the fourth inning, Duffy Lewis (who House dubbed the "aurora borealis of last year's American League race") doubled past third base and Wagner doubled into center field, the only two extra-base hits of the game. Williams bunted and the throw went to third, but Wagner was safe. Janvrin squeezed and Wagner scored. Williams scored on a passed ball. A single, sacrifice, and single scored one more in the fifth. Two sacrifice flies brought in two more runs in the eighth. Twice the Kaws got two men on base, in the fifth and in the eighth, but strikeouts ended both innings.

There had been enough big-league teams coming through Wichita that the Red Sox were no novelty. The attendance was reported in the *Topeka Daily Capital* box score as "scattering" but the *Topeka State Journal* optimistically counted 300. The *Post*'s Shannon claimed half that, with many of them being waiters and others from the team hotel. The Topeka paper also allowed that Moore was worried about the slippery ground and consequently the Kaws "made no desperate attempt to show against the Boston team." Topeka made six errors; Boston made one. The paper was impressed both with Janvrin's play and Tim Murnane's "flowing gray locks."

The Red Sox stayed overnight in Topeka and took the 7 A.M. train for the four-hour trip to St. Joseph, Missouri.

The game at Lincoln's Antelope Park was an exciting one. There were some medical comings and goings. Bill Carrigan was back in uniform; though not ready to play, he'd put on some weight in just the time since he'd split his thumb so spent time running around the field. But Arellanes continued to have trouble with abscesses, or boils, this one on his right knee. Perry suffered muscle cramps, a charley horse, and had to leave the game in the seventh. Buzick took his place in center. SABR's Minor League Database lists the team as the Lincoln Railsplitters, but both the *Lincoln Daily Star* and the *Lincoln Evening News* called them the Packers. And, clearly a nickname, the Lopes.

The first run in the game came in the third, when pitcher Ed Karger clouted one over the high fence in center field. A walk, a single, and a double by Hollis drove in two runs in the fourth. Karger hit another homer in the fifth, a line shot over the left-field fence. The fences were deep and it was the first time that any player had homered twice in the same game at Antelope Park. Two singles and a double steal by Myers and Engle made for a seemingly-comfortable 5–0 lead. The Railsplitters got one run in the bottom of the fifth, but with Karger's "terrific speed and jumping benders, he seemed to be almost the acme of invincibility."[36]

Then Walter Moser took over from Karger. Moser was beaten around and let four runs score; first-baseman Jack Thomas was key for Lincoln. Two Lopes singled, then Thomas "proved the trusty willow wielder by slamming the spheroid against the fence for two sacks and a similar number of fares at the plate."[37] Thomas advanced on a muffed infield roller, and stole home on a double steal.

The game was tied. In the bottom of the seventh, Moser let the first two men reach safely and Carrigan called on McHale in relief. Ty Cobb's brother John, right-fielder for the Railsplitters, sacrificed and advanced the two runners. A walk loaded the bases. Bob Unglaub, who'd appeared in 236 games for Boston from 1905 through 1908, was playing second base for Lincoln and both Lincoln newspapers had him as the team's manager at this point in the season. He grounded to Engle, who threw to Priepke to start a double play — but Priepke's throw went wild and both runners scored. Lincoln had taken a 7–5 lead.

With two outs and nobody on in the top of the ninth, Kleinow pinch-hit for Buzick and doubled. Hap Myers singled, but Kleinow had to hold up at third. Myers then stole second, one of three bases he stole in the game including his steal of home in the fifth. Nebinger drove a long double into center field and both runners scored. The game was tied, 7–7.

Thoney had batted for McHale in the top of the ninth; Ray Collins came on in relief but hadn't had much time to warm up. The first batter doubled. Cobb scratched out an infield hit, and Big Bill McCormick singled over third base to score the winning run. Thoney was really only good for pinch-hitting and pinch-running duties, because of his arm. It was clear he couldn't be counted on for the big-league club.

Lincoln was quite a destination for major-league teams this April. The Detroit Tigers had been in town on April 1 and 2, and the Chicago White Sox followed the Red Sox, on April 6 and 7.

Both houses of the Nebraska legislature had passed a bill to legalize Sunday baseball, but the governor unexpectedly vetoed it. He made clear that he wasn't objecting on moral grounds: "It is true that some very powerful reasons have been presented as to why this measure should be vetoed, but I cannot bring myself to the proposition of saying that one man or act of men can dictate a code of morals for any other set of men.... I believe that an executive would be justified in doing this only in a case where the proposed measure is manifestly so vicious as to encourage vice or crime and I cannot bring myself to the conclusion that baseball is productive of either."[38] His problem was with the form of the bill, which left the question unanswered as to what governmental bodies might have authority to make the determination. The Senate overrode the veto, but the House's 56–40 vote to override fell just short of the 60 needed.

Lincoln was the home of three-time Presidential candidate William Jennings Bryan and some of the players "made a pilgrimage" to his home by streetcar. It was noted that some of the streetcars had depressing destinations: Cemetery, Penitentiary, and State Farm. And one of the party, Joe Burns, suffered a lady saying to him, "I don't mind the old men sitting down when ladies stand in the cars, but I hardly expect the young men to." Burns was quick to his feet. He bowed low to all around, and said, "Will the oldest lady standing please take my seat?"[39]

April 6

"KILLILAY EASY FOR ST. JOE NINE" — *Boston Herald*
at St. Joseph, MO: St. Joseph 5, Boston 4

The Colts were unable to play in Sioux City because of a storm that developed on the evening of April 5 and covered the grounds with four inches of wet snow. Though it had melted by 1:30 P.M. in the afternoon, the grounds were too sodden for baseball. McBreen traveling with the northern Number Twos, said all were pleased with the trip. "We had had a great trip. The country was new to many of the party and everyone enjoyed it. Never have I seen good fellowship displayed better than on this occasion. There is no one in the party that is sorry for the trip."[40] The *American* reported that it seemed that most of the players were sorry to see the trip coming to its end.[41]

And in St. Joseph, the winning streak of the Regulars was finally broken. The Red Sox scored once in the second — on two walks, a sacrifice, and Madden's sacrifice fly — and twice in the third. They might have scored another one, but Killilay failed to bunt the ball for a squeeze and Williams was a dead duck at home plate. Killilay had a rough day. He struck out four times in a row without even getting the bat on the ball for a foul — 12 strikes without any bat contact whatsoever. Williams had three singles and two stolen bases. The two runs in the third came when Lewis hit a two-run homer over the fence in center field of Western League Baseball Park (naming rights were not in play).

The St. Joseph Drummers scored one run on three successive singles, even though the catcher Madden caught men trying to steal second and to steal third. The Red Sox got a fourth run in the fourth on a single, a steal, and two sacrifices. The Red Sox held a 4–1 lead after four innings. St. Joe picked up single runs in the fifth and in the sixth. Killilay was still on the mound in the bottom of the ninth. He got the first batter out, but then a single and Barney Reilly's double tied it up, 4–4, and Bob Meinke's clean single up the middle won it for St. Joseph. It was the first loss for the Regulars since March 17. At least they didn't have to spend another night on the rails.

April 7

"Red Sox Regulars Get Their Revenge" — *Boston Post*
at St. Joseph, MO: Boston 13, St. Joseph 0

The Red Sox started Eddie Cicotte and he held St. Joseph to three singles, his second straight shutout, setting him up to perhaps start in Washington on Opening Day. He walked no one and struck out eight. It was such a fine performance that many of the St. Joe fans cheered his work. Scoring six runs in the second inning put the game away early, thanks to three misplays. Mahoney tripled in one run and then scored on another error. Hooper, Mahoney, and Wagner all singled in the eighth, and there were two more errors. The hits kept coming, 16 of them; Hooper had four, while Mahoney, Wagner, and Madden each had three, Mahoney lacking only a home run for the cycle. Burke penned an appreciation: "The more I see of Mahoney the more convinced I am that President Taylor will make a mistake if he releases him. Mahoney is one of the few finds on this trip. He's a star. Perhaps he needs a little coaching and seasoning, but it won't take many games to put him up at the top of the list for headwork, on bases and batting."[42] The Red Sox stole four bases. There were five official St. Joe errors, and the runs piled up until it was 13–0, Red Sox. The team took a 7:00 P.M. train to Kansas City, Missouri, but Cicotte was sent to Washington to be rested and ready for the opening of the regular season.

All the snow in Sioux City had melted before the morning edition of the *Sioux City Journal*, "with the exception of a small strip inside the south fence." The Packers had won the Western League title in 1910 and it could have been good competition, but even after game time was pushed back a bit, cold weather and wet grounds at Mizzou Park again prevented the game. At 7:30 P.M. in the evening, the train set out for Omaha. Just like the folks at Salida, the citizens of Sioux City are still waiting for the Red Sox to play a game in Iowa. They suffered not just one, but two postponements, perhaps doubling their disappointment.

Looking a day ahead, there was a considerable buildup in the Kansas City papers, with banner headlines in the sports sections and even a large photo montage of several of the players in the April 7 *Kansas City Journal*. The White Sox and Cardinals second teams, and the Tigers second team had already played the Blues, with lopsided wins for Chicago (14–0 on April 1) and Detroit (13–3 on April 6); the Blues beat the White Sox, 4–3, on April 2, a loss for Big Ed Walsh. Smoky Joe Wood was a Kansas City native and had pitched for the Blues in 1908. Wood had come to town ahead of the rest of the team. Everyone was hoping he'd be the starting pitcher at Association Park for Saturday's game, reported in some K.C. papers as set for 2:00 P.M. and in others as 3:00 P.M. The Red Sox arrived at Union Station late Friday evening, boarding at the Coates House, and had sufficient time to get it right.

Tris Speaker arrived in Boston around 1 P.M. on Friday and met with John I. Taylor, then went to the Fenway Hospital on Newbury Street and had his tonsils removed. He was in good shape physically and it was hoped that the tonsillectomy would relieve him of the problems he'd been having.

The *Boston Globe* story ended oddly, reading like a piece of propaganda: "Pres Taylor and Speaker had a long and serious talk, in which the player was shown the necessity of the entire team, himself included, playing ball all the time this coming season and sticking strictly to business."

Patsy Donovan was going to suggest to Taylor that the 1911 trip had been too long and that spending night after night on the tracks, in sleeper cars, was just too hard on the players.[43]

April 8

"RED SOX WIN BY MUFFS IN NINTH"—*Boston Post*
at Kansas City, MO: Boston 4, Kansas City Blues 3

"YANNIGAN PITCHER BUMPED BY OMAHA"—*Boston Journal*
at Omaha, NE: Omaha 5, Red Sox Colts 2

"Riot Stops Ball Game" the next day's *Kansas City Post* offered a nice spread on the ballgame, including six photographs. Sportswriter Herb Slater's lead began, "If 'Patsy' Donovan's Boston Red Sox do not win the 1911 American League pennant no one around the circuit will be able to say that they do not possess the 'fighting spirit.' For they certainly do. It's certainly strongly planted in the breast of every member of the team in general and one or two of them in particular. It crops out, too, at the most unexpected moment. And also at the most trivial thing."

It took at least a half-dozen policemen to restore order (the *Post* said it took 19 and a plainclothesman but they may have been engaging in a little hyperbole since they added that it also took the water boy, too). Some of the bugs, as fans of the day were known, came down from their seats and were pressed up against the wire netting that separated off the 25- and 50-cent seats and there was a concern that the more vocal of the fans might spill onto the field.

The whole thing erupted over the Blues re-using some of the "over ripe" baseballs which had already been used in the game against the Tigers two days before. Baseballs of the day were used for as long as they lasted, and sometimes became a little "mushy" if used too long. The Red Sox took exception to what they claimed was umpire McKee giving the worn-out baseballs to the Blues pitchers, and new ones for Boston pitchers to throw to the Kansas City batters. The balls were provided the umpire one at a time by Blues manager Daniel Shay, who was perhaps taking advantage of a rookie umpire, someone umpiring his very first game (the regular league umpire had been "sent away" for some reason). Oddly, the mound was as much as an extraordinary three feet above field level.[44]

Exasperated, the Sox walked off the field in middle of the seventh inning. McKee was a friend of Shay and an inexperienced semipro umpire and some of the fault was laid at his feet for handling matters inadvisably. He borrowed a watch from a friend and ordered them to take the field within five minutes. Unfortunately, he then walked over to the Boston bench to argue with Patsy Donovan. The Red Sox manager was urging his men to take the field; team captain Heinie Wagner was urging them to stay put. Donovan told Billy Purtell to take Wagner's place and lead the men back to play, but Purtell stayed put.

Joe Wood apparently used a word that McKee didn't appreciate, and the umpire swung a right-hand punch at Wood's face. Smoky Joe responded, "hooking and jabbing with both fists" until Blues outfielder Spike Shannon got him in a "hammer lock and a double strangle hold."[45] Shay defused the situation easily enough: he provided a couple of new baseballs to McKee.

The game itself was a corker. Sea Lion Hall pitched the full game for the Red Sox, and coughed up a couple of runs in the bottom of the first. After a walk and a force out at second on a failed sacrifice, Jack Love shot one back in the box that was too hot for Hall to handle and he reached first. Hamilton Hyatt hit one to the scoreboard in right field and Shannon scored easily. Janvrin messed up Red Gardner's grounder (the only error of the game for the Red Sox) and Love scored.

Boston got one back in the top of the second when the Blues shortstop committed the first two of their six errors on Duffy Lewis's ground ball. He made second on one out and took third on a fly ball to center, but then the second baseman mangled a ball off Janvrin's bat and Lewis scored. In the bottom of the second, Kansas City catcher William "Tony" James restored the two-run lead when he "lifted a long cloud-scraper over the right garden wall for a circle of the cushions."[46] It was back to a one-run game soon enough, in the top of the third. Charley Hall ducked from a pitch which hit his bat and popped high up, about 10 feet in front of home plate. James ran out to catch it, but it fell through his hands. Hall had been off and running and was perched on second with nobody out. The third and fourth errors were cashed in when Gardner "clipped a lawn mower single to center."[47] Hall had put on the brakes at third but then raced home when Love kicked the ball around in center. The Blues held the 3–2 lead until the top of the seventh.

Nick Maddox had won 23 games for the Pittsburgh Pirates in 1908 and in four seasons in the big leagues had a 43–20 mark and a 2.29 ERA, all with the Bucs. The right-hander walked Hal Janvrin, who led off the seventh inning. Madden sacrificed himself and bunted Hal to second. Hall hit a baseball that was firm enough to go for a double in right field and score Janvrin. The Red Sox loaded the bases, but couldn't cash in again. Lewis hit the ball back to Maddox to retire the side. Perhaps that was one of the mushy balls. The Sox had tied the score, but perhaps felt they'd been held back from more. At any event, this is when they refused to take the field (Maddox won 22 games for the Blues during the American Association season in 1911 but never returned to the majors).

After order was restored, it took another couple of errors to lose the game. Madden flied to Shannon in deep left field. Shannon let the ball carom off his glove; it hit the fence and dropped to the ground, and Madden made second. Chick Brandom had taken over pitching for the Blues by this time (another former Pirate who was 1–0 in 1908 and 1–0 in 1909). Hall, batting for himself, hit one back to Brandom, who threw to third baseman Jap Barbeau to get Madden, but Barbeau bobbled and dropped the ball. Jap had broken in with Cleveland in 1905, but had also been on the 1909 Pirates with Brandom and Maddox. There were runners on first and third with nobody out. Larry Gardner grounded crisply to Downie at second base, who tagged the oncoming Hall and threw to first base for the second out. The ball to the plate almost resulted in a 4–3–2 triple play, but for Madden's slide into home plate with the run that won the game — after Hall retired the side in the bottom of the ninth. Brandom was 1–14 for the Blues in 1911. With all the action, there had only been seven hits in the whole game, four for the Blues and three for the Red Sox. And once he got past the first two innings, Hall hadn't allowed a run.

There was a game in Omaha, too, one that offered little excitement but pleased the home crowd. Engle and Perry had both been given leave to visit home, and make their own way to Boston. Yerkes' ankle still was subpar, but he played short — with limited range — and managed to hit a double in one of his four at-bats. Ray Collins started for the Red Sox and gave up five runs to the Rourkes, playing at President Bill Rourke's new ballpark, Rourke Park, in front of a couple of hundred fans. The team was also called the Sterlings in the *Omaha Morning World-Herald*, which described the weather as "wretchedly cold" with "real baseball out of the question." Collins' own throwing error in the bottom of the first set up the first Rourkes run. There would have been another run, but Riggert's throw to Nunamaker nabbed the runner at home plate. Nebinger's error in the third set up two more.

The Red Sox had scored first, thanks to a couple of gifts. Thoney led off and reached on the first baseman's error, was moved to second by Myers sacrifice, and scored when the shortstop fumbled Riggert's "easy roller." Hollis tumbled over just when he seemed ready to reach Bill Shipke's long drive in the third. He wasn't charged with an error; Shipke was credited with a triple and two more runs crossed the plate, the two that were on base due to Nebinger. Put three hits together, a sacrifice, and a stolen base and two more runs scored in the fourth. Pape started pitching in the sixth and didn't let up a run, though he did escape a bases-loaded jam in the eighth. The Red Sox scored once more in the top of the ninth when Nebinger doubled and Priepke singled.

McBreen booked the final arrangements. After the last game of the trip in Kansas City on the 9th, the special car carrying the Red Sox would travel overnight to LaSalle Street Station in Chicago and the team would catch an early train Monday morning, getting them back to Boston in time to play Harvard College on Tuesday afternoon at 3:15 P.M. Tickets had gone on sale for the Harvard game.

The Sox squads were coming to the end of "the greatest joy ride in baseball history." It was the longest spring trip ever attempted, and some of the men had crossed the country twice in the process. The team had visited a good percentage of the states in the union, and the Arizona Territory, too.

Were there other adventures in mind? There was even some talk of training in Hawaii. In the days before air travel, that truly would have been something. As late as 1939, Tom Yawkey can be found denying a rumor that the team would be training in the islands in 1940.[48]

April 9

"GARRISON FINISH WINS FOR RED SOX"—*Boston Post*
at Kansas City, MO: Boston 4, Kansas City 3

"YANNIGANS IN GOOD TIE GAME"—*Boston Post*
at Omaha, NE: Red Sox Colts 1, Omaha 1 (tie)

One more game in Missouri and one more game in Nebraska and then it was back home to Boston. Sunday's action saw another 4–3 win for the Red Sox in Kansas City. Neither side won in Omaha.

The Red Sox had a 6:00 P.M. train to Chicago so it was agreed that the game in Omaha would stop at 5:00 P.M. This time about 1,500 people turned out. There wasn't much hitting, and only five walks, but it still took two hours to play. Karger pitched five innings without giving up a hit. In fact, the Karger/Hunt combination had a no-hitter going into the bottom of the eighth.

Rourkes lefty Kid Durbin pitched five innings and only gave up one hit. Two southpaws, 10 half-innings, one hit. And no runs. Durbin's major-league career was mainly as an outfielder (32 games, .275), though he was 0–1 for the 1905 Chicago Cubs. His main claim to fame had been his 32–8 season for the Joplin Miners of the Western League in 1906. Harry Patton came on and pitched the rest of the game for Omaha. He'd thrown four innings for the Cardinals in 1910. It was Steve Yerkes who got that one hit off Durbin. Ben Hunt took over pitching for the Red Sox. After seven innings, it was still 0–0, the tightest game of the spring. In the top of the eighth, Myers doubled to left field. He could have been held to a single but Schoonover in left held onto the ball rather than running it in or throwing it and Myers stretched the wide turn at first into a double. Nebinger flied out. With two outs, Myers stole third base and drew a throw, which Shipke couldn't hold onto. Myers ran home and gave Boston the lead.

In the bottom of the eighth, it was Shipke who got the only hit that Omaha got all day—a Texas Leaguer that fell between shortstop Steve Yerkes and Frank Arellanes, playing center field. Yerkes was still on a tender ankle and Arellanes was a pitcher playing center. It's possible that the Sox could have had a no-hitter if they'd been properly staffed. A sacrifice put Shipke on second. Hunt's wild pitch put Shipke on third. A sacrifice fly to left field by shortstop Kneaves brought Shipke home — though Riggert's throw to the plate had him beat, the ball took a bad bounce and he was safe. Neither side scored in the ninth, though the Sterlings had the bases loaded in the bottom of the ninth with one out. The Red Sox failed to score in the top of the 10th, and recorded one out against Omaha in the bottom of the 10th — but then the game was called due to time, and the score reverted to the 1–1 tie standing after nine. Neither side won but, then again, neither side lost.

The game in Kansas City wasn't resolved until the ninth, a thriller for the 5,000 in the stands. Charlie Smith gave away five or six bases on balls (box score and game account disappeared), but only allowed two hits in five innings. Kansas City scored one in the third, and Boston tied it in the fourth on Wagner's single, two outs, and an error. Killilay took over in the sixth, but a single, a triple, and a single gave the Blues a 3–1 lead. "His huskiness, the umpire" apparently failed to impress Merton Burke with his impartiality. "Victors in spite of his Highness," he wrote, saying that the Red Sox beat K.C. "in spite of the umpire's earnest efforts to win the game for his home town."[49] Joe Wood came in to pitch against the team for which he'd played in 1908. He threw the last three innings and struck out six, not giving the umpire any room to get his goat. Four walks and Lewis's single scored two runs and Boston tied the score. In the top of the ninth, Lewis, Wagner, and Williams combined singles to push the tie-breaking run across. Wood set the Blues down 1–2–3.

Tim Murnane of the *Globe* picked the Philadelphia Athletics to win the pennant in 1911. And they did, by 13½ games over second-place Detroit. No one else was even close. The third-place Indians were 30½ games back. The Red Sox came in fourth, 36½ games out of first place, more or less where they finished the year before.

The *Boston Sunday American* featured bylined stories by Donovan and Taylor, both hoping to boost the interest of fans in The Hub. Donovan noted the youth of the men, "youngsters just winning their spurs." Speaker, Hooper, and Lewis were all three of them just 23. The "old man" on the team was 30-year-old Heinie Wagner. Only a handful of the players were more than 27. Donovan liked that: "A young man full of ambition and energy will work much harder than an old timer. That's why I have so much confidence in the team this year.... This has been a great trip for the team and we are in condition to begin the fight for the pennant at the very start."

Taylor struck a similar theme: "At the beginning of no previous season have I felt more confidence in the Red Sox than now. On the whole it is much stronger than last year's team and will be in the pennant fight from the start till the very end. We are way ahead of last year in the box and behind the bat."[50]

7

Wrapping Up
the Spring Season

April 10

Travel day. It was time-consuming to get all the way back to Boston from Omaha and Kansas City. The two teams met briefly on arrival at the LaSalle Street station in Chicago, the Regulars arriving just minutes before the Colts. There wasn't much time to socialize, less than an hour. "It looked like an old home week festival" for a few minutes, said the *Boston Journal*. "Manager Donovan had not seen some of the boys since those early training days back at Redondo Beach, and he almost had to be introduced to some of them." With a little tongue in cheek, the paper added that Joe Burns, who assumed charge of rounding up the men for the train to Boston, "tried to exclude a couple of the less conspicuous members from the car. He swore that he had never seen them before."[1]

Patsy Donovan left the Regulars and joined the Colts party to bring them to Boston for the game against Harvard, while the Regulars quickly prepared to head out to Washington in order to open the season on April 12. Donovan would join them there in the capital just before the game. Several of the players switched squads at the station. Kleinow, Karger, Collins, and Pape moved from the Colts to join the men heading to Washington, while Bradley, Purtell, Mahoney, Janvrin, and Bedient moved over to join the group going to Boston. To make connections, Donovan had to whisk his charges away. As it happens, the two trains left about the same time, on parallel tracks running neck and neck for many miles — only about 100 feet apart, with players shouting and calling out to each other along the way — before the Colts took the lead just before

Red Sox players at the train station in Chicago. Michael T. McGreevey stands third from right. The player in the light coat fourth from right of McGreevey is Smoky Joe Wood (courtesy Boston Public Library, Print Department, McGreevey Collection).

the tracks parted, and the two trains split off for their respective destinations.

As printed in the *Boston Globe*, the final batting averages for the spring season showed that no given player had appeared in more than the 32 games in which Riggert and Wagner had. Janvrin, Lewis, and Perry had each appeared in 31. The pitchers, of course, appeared in the fewest games — Charlie Smith in only three. Among position players, Pinch Thomas was in just 10 games and Purtell in 11 (despite playing first base, second, third, and center field). Carrigan was in 12, Kleinow was in 13 games, and Sheehan in 14, but everyone else was in 18 or more. Of the 44 men who played for the Sox during spring training 1911, it would be hard to argue that there was one who didn't get a fair shot. Given the large number of games that were played, even if divided into two teams, there were still nine players with more than 100 at-bats and another 10 who had between 60 and 100. It would be a rare exhibition season before or after 1911 which saw 19 players get 60 or more at-bats.

Tris Speaker was the only position player to hit over .400 (he hit .438), though Pape hit .500 (5-for-10) and Hunt hit .400 (4-for-10). Befitting a leadoff hitter with a good (.294) average, Larry Gardner led the team in runs scored with 28. Hooper and Speaker were tied for second place, with 27 apiece. RBIs were not tabulated at the time, not even in individual box scores. Won-loss records weren't maintained for the pitchers, nor were ERAs. There was no tabulation in any of the Boston newspapers adding up strikeouts, bases on balls, or the like. Duffy Lewis led in total bases with 67. Speaker had 61. Riggert had 59 and Wagner had 56. Priepke was the most error-prone, committing 13 errors. Gardner made 11 and so did Buzick. Players with 20 or more chances who were error-free were Sheehan (49 chances), Carrigan (45), Cicotte (23), and Mahoney (20), though of course many of Sheehan's and Carrigan's were accomplished simply by catching a third strike and not dropping it.

Below are the final batting averages of the various position players as reported in the *Boston Journal* in its April 10 edition.

Player	G	AB	R	1B	2B	3B	HR	AVG
Pape, p	7	9	2	5	2	0	0	.556
Cicotte, p	7	15	5	7	0	0	0	.467
Hunt, p	7	9	3	4	1	9	1	.444
Speaker, cf	21	83	25	36	9	3	2	.434
Hooper, rf	25	93	26	38	1	0	1	.409
Mahoney, cf	18	59	15	24	7	3	2	.407
Moser, p	9	10	1	4	0	0	0	.400
Purtell, 3b	8	25	4	9	1	3	0	.360
Wagner, ss	28	106	20	38	9	2	1	.358
Yerkes, ss	16	56	7	20	5	0	0	.357
Lewis, lf	28	109	22	37	12	2	3	.339
Thomas, c	8	15	0	5	0	0	0	.333
McHale, p	9	6	2	2	0	1	0	.333
Williams, c & 1b	18	59	14	17	7	0	0	.305
Engle, 1b & ss	24	96	20	29	3	2	2	.302
Karger, p	5	20	3	6	1	0	3	.300
Perry, cf	28	109	17	32	4	4	1	.294
Hall, p & 1b	8	17	6	5	2	0	1	.294
Riggert, lf	29	113	17	33	4	6	2	.292
Kleinow, c	12	31	1	9	2	1	0	.290
Myers, 1b	25	89	15	25	1	0	0	.281
Gardner, 2b	26	102	24	27	4	1	0	.265
Nunamaker, c	23	57	13	15	0	4	1	.263
Nebinger, 3b	22	85	14	22	6	1	0	.259
Bradley, 1b	16	58	6	15	7	0	0	.258
Thoney, rf	18	41	7	10	2	0	0	.244
Sheehan, c	13	29	2	7	0	1	0	.241
Madden, c	19	67	11	16	4	1	0	.239
Carrigan, c	10	21	2	5	2	0	1	.238

Player	G	AB	R	1B	2B	3B	HR	AVG
F. Smith, p	7	13	1	3	0	1	0	.231
Collins, p	8	14	1	3	1	0	0	.214
Priepke, 2b	24	93	11	19	4	1	0	.204
Buzick, p & ss	17	46	5	9	1	1	0	.196
Janvrin, 3b	28	194	14	19	3	1	0	.183
Arellanes, p	7	13	1	2	0	0	0	.154
Wood, p	7	14	2	2	0	1	0	.143
Sawyer, p	6	7	0	1	0	0	0	.143
Hollis, rf	24	91	7	13	2	1	0	.143
Dale, p	8	8	0	1	0	0	0	.125
Bedient, p	8	12	1	1	0	0	0	.083
Killilay, p	8	12	0	0	0	0	0	.000
Pierce, p	6	3	1	0	0	0	0	.000
O'Brien, p	8	7	0	0	0	0	0	.000
C. Smith, p	3	5	0	0	0	0	0	.000

Team Averages

Batting

REGULARS

	AB	R	BH	TB	AVG	SH	SB
Boston	954	196	294	424	.308	42	44
Opponents	863	61	169	230	.196	14	19

YANNIGANS

	AB	R	BH	TB	AVG	SH	SB
Boston	1049	147	270	379	.256	25	50
Opponents	1028	152	294	385	.286	27	37

Fielding

REGULARS

	PO	A	E	AVG
Boston	740	334	46	.979
Opponents	738	425	81	.935

YANNIGANS

	PO	A	E	AVG
Boston	785	389	61	.951
Opponents	831	425	62	.953

Note: Different newspapers offered different totals, attributable to the number of intrasquad or makeshift games. The figures presented above are from the *Boston Journal*. The *Globe* differed even in the number of games in which players appeared; where the *Journal* showed none with as many as 30 games, the *Globe* had Riggert and Wagner in 32, with Lewis, Perry, and Janvrin all in 31 apiece. The two papers had different averages for different players. The *Globe* had Speaker batting .438 (39 hits in 89 at-bats), while the *Journal* showed him at .434 (36-for-83.) The *Globe* didn't list extra-base totals, but the *Journal* did. Lewis and Karger each had three homers. Speaker, Mahoney, Engle, and Riggert each had two. Riggert had six triples; both Perry and Nunamaker had four. Speaker, Mahoney, and Purtell had three. Leading in doubles was Duffy Lewis with 12; Speaker and Wagner each had nine. The *Journal* offered information regarding sacrifice hits and stolen bases, while the *Globe* did not.

"Coast-To-Coast Trip Was No Bed Of Roses"—*Boston Journal*

Herman Nickerson's summary article on the trip ran in the April 9 edition. It is worth reprinting in its entirety here.

> Few men profit by the experience of others, and the Red Sox have bought their "dope" on California as a training camp, returning just as those who had followed the White Sox predicted they would. The men are bound homeward, tired out with their car riding and playing upon poor ball parks, having covered in this preparatory canter for the race of 1911 more miles than they will be called upon to travel from now until the season closes.
>
> From Feb. 18, when the train pulled out of Boston for New York, until April 11 is a long time to be at work preparing for a season's work. When you figure the distance covered by the men it is remarkable that they are in the shape they are today to battle for a good place in the standing.
>
> Previous to the coast to coast junket the native sons on the team were wont to speak both loud and long of the "glorious climate of California." They were going to show the Easterners something in the way of country, also, and the boom and boost stuff lay heavy on the air. Believe me, these same native sons don't speak of that climate now. If they do they duck, for it is a tender subject with the boys who suffered through the rankest kind of mismanagement.
>
> **How Arrangements Went Awry**
>
> Now, California is a great State and its people the finest ever, only the Red Sox didn't go there in the right manner, nor did they meet the right people. California in March this year was a fright and we struck the frightful places, all picked out by a man who had one whole year in which to arrange the trip. This was the most astonishing part of the whole proceedings.
>
> When we were at Hot Springs, Ark., in the spring of 1910, President John I. Taylor was absent, but he sent word that his team would train on the Pacific coast and that Tip O'Neill had been given the job of preparing for the reception of the squad. That seemed about long enough to notify anyone. Tip O'Neill had time enough to book P. T. Barnum's three-ring circus and menageries for a tour of the world, yet, so far as furnishing comforts for the men is concerned, he might have been the advance man for a "ten, twenty, and thirty troupe."

The only hotel he had booked up to receive the team was at Phoenix, Ari., and that date was canceled.

His big ten strike was in digging up the Redondo Beach Hotel at Redondo Beach, a place gone to seed, but desirous of being renewed in popularity. The hotel was closed up to within a few days of time the boys arrived, after one of the most tedious rides ever planned, in a train crowded with Bush Leaguers bound for the coast.

The hotel was damp, the bedding damp, and the food damnable. The rate was very low, which appealed to "Tip," I suppose. Anyway, it was in direct opposite to the general manner of handling the Boston club as furnished by President Taylor. You couldn't expect much for the rate paid, all of which was part of an advertising scheme whereby the Red Sox advertised Redondo. I rather think they did, but not as expected they would.

During the time the Yannigans were housed at Redondo Beach, playing at Los Angeles, the expense for a car to take the men back and forth was a matter of $25 a day. This spread out with the bill of the hotel would have done a long way toward giving the boys comforts and good food at the hotel in Los Angeles.

First Squad Hurried Away

Manager Donovan and his first squad escaped up the State on March 1, leaving Bill Carrigan with the second squad to suffer alone at that resort. The men didn't get proper food and it began to tell on them. The plainest evidence of this was the improved condition of the boys after a few days spent at the Westminster in Los Angeles.

The Regulars went up to Oakland, which is the Brooklyn of San Francisco, and here they found a good hotel, but it was a poor move from a business standpoint. The location of the team almost hid them from the public eye. Then they turned on the water and the men were forced to work out on the floor of a gymnasium as the guests of St. Mary's College.

This continued for a week or more and was enough to drive the men to drink. Finally the sun shone and games were played, but to light crowds. Floods caused the cancellation of dates and the places picked out for games were in very small settlements against teams that didn't do the Red Sox any good.

In many instances the schedule required the men to arise at 6:30 AM, get a train around 8 o'clock, ride three hours, lunch, play, eat and catch a train, ride three hours and when it was over feel like falling onto a bed exhausted. That may be the way to season ball players, but it strikes me as being about the most foolish thing to do.

Some Better at Los Angeles

When the schedule turned sage and sane and the team found itself at Los Angeles, with a fine ball park to work out on and two pretty fair clubs to play against, then the men began to get some benefit from their efforts. Some, but not much. Perhaps three forenoons were devoted to practice, the rest of the time it was straight baseball.

Now comes the real headwork of the trip. Take a look. Out of Los Angeles, the team played such places as Yuma (not a town, but a disease); El Paso, on a race track; Abilene, a jerk town with no kind of a club, but plenty of sand and hot air. Dallas and Fort Worth were exceptions, but the State of Texas has been worked to death by the major league ball clubs and the fans have no burning desire to see their teams mowed down by the "big stuff." The gate receipts prove this to be true, so if the purpose of this coast to coast tour was to make money, spurred on by the story of what the White Sox collected, it must have been a disappointment.

Old-time ball players will tell you that the present generation of players do not know what a hard training trip really means. These gentlemen say that the managers never paid more than $2 a day at any hotel and that two men slept in one bed, while baths were unknown luxuries. This may be true, and probably is. There are heroes unknown and unsung if this picture is true.

Now, this is the age of great things. Great talk among other things. If you don't believe me, take a trip to California and listen to them tell you how they grow. "Watch us grow!" is the watchword. Being the age of great things, John I. Taylor planned this trip. He didn't take it, so he missed one of the experiences which go to make life varied. He will be able to get tales of the luxuries indulged in by interviewing anyone who made the trip.

P[a]cked into the Pullmans

The team went out on a "Red Sox special," which was described at the time. It returned in two sections, one Southern, the other Northern. The Southern was the regular crowd, and it was packed first into a sixteen-section Pullman, then into a fourteen-section Pullman. There being twenty-seven persons in the party, you can judge how much like those little fishes boiled in oil we felt.

Having a business staff in numbers large enough to handle almost any proposition, the greater part of the time was expended in undoing what had been done and trying to straighten things so the team could proceed. If a trunk was to be sent it required a meeting of the strategy board and when the trunk left a prayer went with it.

Hotels were as glad to see us as they would have been to welcome the smallpox. The bunch would blow into a hotel and it would take the greater part of the day to room the men. The war correspondents were overlooked many times in the shuffle, and, being on the "firing line," by scrapping managed to find quarters suitable for their comfort.

Persons who have never wandered far from their firesides, take it from me, a coast to coast trip with the Red Sox was no bed of roses.

The Final Game of the Long Spring Training Trip

Back in Boston, the Harvard College nine were ready. They'd been working out since February in the Harvard cage and getting in what outdoors work they could as the seasons changed. After the game with the Red Sox, they were going to take a trip south to play a number of games. Harvard had been playing baseball for nearly half a century. Their first recorded season was in 1865, an undefeated 6–0 season. On August 3, 1867, *Harper's Weekly* printed an illustration entitled "BASE BALL MATCH" depicting a Harvard vs. Yale game of 1867.[2] The Crimson were coming off an 8–11 season (with one tie), which had been a disappointment after a strong 13–6 year in 1909. Perhaps the team's greatest year was in 1901, the first year of the Boston Red Sox franchise, when Harvard went 18–2. The 1910 season had been atypical; they'd been 142–68 over the preceding decade (.676). As it happened, the team went 17–6 in 1911.

There had been 11 major leaguers to come out of Harvard already in Organized Baseball's relatively fresh history, among them Walter Clarkson, Eddie Grant, and Ted Lewis. Coach Frank Sexton had just been given a new two-year contract. That would be Dr. Frank Sexton, a graduate of the University of Pennsylvania Medical School, former batterymate of Fred Tenney at Brown University, and a pitcher for half a season with the 1895 Boston Beaneaters (1–5 with a 5.69 ERA, with a .269 batting average). He played parts of four seasons in the New England League and one in the Eastern League. He coached baseball at Brown for a dozen years, and had been hired in the winter of 1910 as Harvard's first professional baseball coach. This was his first season on the job. Team captain was the third baseman, Charlie McLaughlin.

The *Boston Globe* ran a lengthy article on April 10 describing the strengths and weaknesses of the various players on the Crimson. On Palm Sunday, April 9, the area was blanketed with two inches of snow, a rare storm and the first time since 1894 that there had been any significant accumulation as late as that date. The temperature had been in the high 20's.

E. V. B. Parke, writing in the *Boston American*, recalled the previous year's game in which Harvard held down the Red Sox to a 4–1 margin, and hoped for a close game. The *Globe* said it was the best game Harvard played in their poor 1910 season, one of the reasons the college had hired Sexton. "Harvard expects to make a good showing with the Red Sox and if they can't beat the professionals, they at least feel certain of shoving over a couple of tallies."[3] It was a fairly new team; only three of the anticipated first-string players (Robert Potter, R. C. Babson, and Captain McLaughlin) were returning players. They had been working out at the Harvard athletic grounds at Soldiers Field. In fact, they'd worked out more in recent days than had the Red Sox. For a solid week before the April 11 game, they had put in 3½ hours of practice a day. As Nickerson pointed out, a fair criticism of the Red Sox odyssey is that they rarely had time to put in real practice work, and were mostly limited to playing actual games. The games rarely lasted as long as two hours, and were inevitably limited to the men in the lineup and such substitutions as were called for during the games in question. Other than limiting pitchers to a given number of innings in their early outings, it's clear from the box scores and newspaper game accounts that neither Donovan nor Carrigan were using extra players during the course of a typical game just for the sake of giving them all extra work.

April 11

"RED SOX YANNIGANS OUTHIT, BUT BEAT HARVARD 4 TO 2"
— *Boston Post*
at Boston, MA: Red Sox Colts 4, Harvard College 2

The Huntington Avenue Grounds saw the first game in its final year, when the Red Sox hosted the Harvard College crew for a final exhibition game. Back in February, there had been plans for the Red Sox to also play another game on this same day, against the New England League's Lawrence Barristers, but that had fallen by the wayside. Despite the snowfall on the ninth, groundskeeper Jerome Kelley had cleared the snow that day and had the Huntington Avenue Grounds ready to play and in "fine shape."

At 11:45 A.M., the Red Sox second team disembarked from the train at the Huntington Avenue station. Mr. and Mrs. Donovan continued on to South Station for brief welcoming ceremonies, but the ballplayers themselves got off right near the park. One imagines they were a little rail-weary, having traveled for more than 36 hours from Omaha.

It was the very first game of the year for Harvard — they'd only been practicing out of doors for two weeks — but the college team out-hit the Red Sox, seven hits to five. The game attracted some 4,100 fans, on a fairly cold afternoon. About 400 of them were friends of Hal Janvrin's from Boston English High School. The game was interrupted on the occasion of his first at-bat so they could present him with a gold watch. He struck out. The game was played on a soggy field in low temperatures.

Hugh Bedient pitched the first five innings and went in a 1–0 hole in the top of the second when Mahoney dropped McLaughlin's easy fly ball to right, due either to the bright sun, or the soft and spongy field, or both. A sacrifice put the Harvard captain on second. An infield hit put runners on first and third, but the man on first was thrown out trying to steal second. Harvard's first baseman, Hann, doubled over Perry's head in center field and McLaughlin scored. The Red Sox took the lead in the third on a one-out walk to Perry and a balk. Perry took second when Myers' hit back to the pitcher was handled too slowly. He came in on a sacrifice fly by Mahoney. The catcher tried a snap throw to catch Myers off third base and he threw into left field instead. Myers scored. Two runs on no hits.

A walk led to another Red Sox run in the sixth. Riggert was on first, then ran to second on another errant pickoff throw, this time by the new pitcher, Babson, who promptly erred again trying to make a play to third base on the ball Yerkes hit to him. This is when Janvrin blooped in a Texas Leaguer into short left field and drove in what proved to be the winning run. In the bottom of the eighth, Nebinger slapped one so hard to third that McLaughlin couldn't really handle it. Nebinger stole second, and ran to third on yet another botched pickoff by Babson. He scored when the shortstop fumbled a ground ball.

Potter doubled to right field in the top of the ninth. McHale, who had taken over for Bedient, added to the growing list of pickoff miscues by throwing the ball past Yerkes into the outfield. The next ball was hit to Yerkes, who misplayed it and the run scored. The batter, Clifford, who'd reached first safely, managed to get himself picked off, and the last batter struck out. Melville Webb's conclusion in the *Globe* was that if Harvard had not thrown the ball about so much, they might well have won the game. There wasn't a single run the Red Sox scored that hadn't been a direct result of a Harvard error. The Crimson out-erred the Red Sox, six to three.

Over the years, Harvard has played seven games in all against the Red Sox. The first two games were played at the Huntington Avenue Grounds. In 1912, the two teams met in the first baseball game ever played at Fenway Park, 11 days before the first regular-season game. The April 12, 1910, match was billed in the *Harvard Crimson* as somewhat educational:

"Today for the first time in 14 years the University nine will meet a professional nine on the diamond. This is one feature of a general awakening on the part of the athletic authorities, who seem to have come to realize that there is a certain satisfaction in winning, and that it is worth while to give the teams every opportunity for development. The nine will learn much from even one professional game...." The score was Red Sox 4, Harvard College 1. One wonders about the lessons learned in the 21–0 defeat in 1943, however. These are the scores of the seven matchups:

4/12/1910 — Red Sox 4, Harvard College 1
4/11/1911 — Red Sox Colts 4, Harvard College 2
4/9/1912 — Red Sox 2, Harvard 0
4/8/1913 — Red Sox 5, Harvard 0
4/10/1916 — Harvard 1, Red Sox 0
4/16/1943 — Red Sox 21, Harvard 0
4/4/1987 — Red Sox 8, Harvard 0

The 1911 game, thus, gave Harvard the opportunity to wreak revenge on the pros for their 1910 defeat. They would have to wait until 1916, when the college beat the World Champion Red Sox, winners of both the preceding 1915 World Series and the subsequent 1916 World Series.

The 1911 Season

When United States President William Howard Taft threw out the first pitch in the first game ever held at Washington's new Griffith Stadium, the 1911 regular season got underway on April 12.

Had Patsy Donovan declared, "We'll win more than we'll lose," he would have been right, but not by much. The Sox dropped their first two games in Washington, 8–5 (Wood) and 3–2 (Cicotte). The Detroit Tigers got off to a 6–1 start, and even though the Sox at times reached as high as second place, they never spent even one day in first. There was only one day, June 15, when they were as many as six games above .500.

The two longest winning streaks of the season lasted only four games each, until the very end of the season. With six games to go, Boston had a record of 72–75 but they put on a final push and closed the season with six consecutive wins (allowing just nine runs in the six games), leaving them with a 78–75 record.

View of the outfield and the outfield stands at the Huntington Avenue Grounds, 1911. The scoreboard indicates that the Boston Red Sox are playing the Detroit Tigers and losing 3–0. Fans ring the outfield in standing-room-only section. To the upper right the outfield stands of the South End Grounds, where the Boston Braves played, are visible. Note the advertising panel for John I. Taylor's Decatur Motor Trucks (courtesy Boston Public Library, Print Department, McGreevey Collection).

One Last Game for the Colts

Parenthetically, it should be noted that the Red Sox Colts played one more game. They were originally due to have played in Brockton against the New England League team there, the Brockton Shoemakers under manager Stephen Flanagan, who had traveled with the Red Sox on the cross-country trip. The game was not held ("The field itself is a veritable quagmire," wrote the *Brockton Enterprise*), and Brockton played an intrasquad game of its own. On Saturday, April 15, however, the Red Sox Colts played an eight-inning game in Lynn, Massachusetts, at Ocean Park. Known at the Leonardites (after manager Frank Leonard), Lynn beat the Colts, 4–2. The Red Sox scored first, getting both of their runs in the top of the third. It started with Buck O'Brien getting a base on balls. He took second base on a passed ball. Purtell singled to right field, scoring O'Brien, and took second base himself on the throw home to try and catch O'Brien at the plate. Chris Mahoney drove a long double to left field, scoring Purtell.

O'Brien pitched the whole game, but put himself in a deep hole by walking the first two batters in the bottom of the sixth. A single to right field scored Lynn's pitcher, William Harrington, playing in the first season of a 12-year minor league career (he was 21–8 for the Leonardites in 1911). The other baserunner went first to third, then scored on a deep fly ball to right field. The tie score was snapped in the seventh. With a runner on first and two outs, Lynn's catcher partially atoned for his passed ball with a single to center. The baserunner overran the base at second and should have been routinely retired, but Purtell couldn't handle Janvrin's throw from third and he scrabbled back into second safely. After O'Brien walked the pitcher once more, loading the bases, a single scored two runs.

Also playing in the game for the Colts were seasoned travelers Hank Perry, Numamaker, Priepke, and Buzick at first base. Playing right field was Ralph Pond, who's gone down in Red Sox history as one of their true "cup of coffee" players—a grand total of one major-league game in his entire career, filling in for Tris Speaker for the game on June 8, 1910. It was quite a day, June 8. Two other University of Maine ballplayers debuted on the same day, Marty McHale and Hap Myers. The Red Sox committed seven errors that day, one of them being Pond's. It was his one and only big-league chance. He remains unique in Red Sox history as the only member of the team to have fielded at least one ball and recorded a lifetime fielding average of .000. At the plate, he fared better—a single and a stolen base in four at-bats. Pond played for Providence in 1911, his second and last year in the minors.

8

Player Postscripts

Unsurprisingly, **Tris Speaker**'s .334 regular-season batting average led the team. This was a year with *two* .400 hitters — Ty Cobb at .420 and .408 for Joe Jackson. Speaker, who'd been third in 1910 and was third again in 1912, placed ninth in the American League. Among players since 1901, Speaker's career .345 average was one point above Ted Williams' .344, and fourth among all major leaguers, yet he placed first only once, in 1916, when he hit .386 in his first year for the Cleveland Indians. Speaker was in the middle of what is considered to be one of the great outfields of all time. **Duffy Lewis** was in left field and hit .307 with a team-leading 86 RBIs, and **Harry Hooper** was in right, hitting .311 and scoring a team-leading 93 runs. Hooper's .399 on-base percentage was second only to Speaker's .418. The Red Sox hit for a team average of .275 in 1911.

All three men — Speaker, Lewis, and Hooper — are in the Red Sox Hall of Fame. Lewis finished an 11-year major-league career with a .284 average, playing his final three seasons with the Yankees and the Senators. He stuck around Boston for many years, working as traveling secretary for the Boston Braves. Hooper and Speaker are both in the National Baseball Hall of Fame and both have full biographies. Hooper played 17 big-league seasons, with a lifetime .281 mark, and remains the only Red Sox player to have taken part in four World Championships — 1912, 1915, 1916, and 1918.

First baseman **Clyde Engle** appeared in 148 games, more than any other Red Sox player 1911. His .270 batting average was comparable to the .271 which **Jake Stahl** had hit the year before (Stahl came back as player-manager in 1912, hit .301, and led the team to a world championship). Engle drove in 48 runs and had 18 extra-base hits; Stahl had led the league with 10 homers in 1910 and drove in 77. He had 45 extra-base hits. But

Engle's year was a decent one; he played for the Red Sox into 1914. Stahl reverted to his career as a banking executive midway through 1913 when the Sox were playing mediocre ball (39–41) and discord among top executives prompted changes in management and, ultimately, ownership.

Bill Carrigan caught 72 games and Les Nunamaker caught 62. **Jack Kleinow** caught eight games but was released by the Red Sox in early August; he caught on with the Phillies and appeared four more. It was his last year in the big leagues. Madden caught in four games. He was picked up by the Phils, too, at the end of June when the Sox put him on waivers. Carrigan hit .289, second-best of his career (he'd hit .296 in 1909), before breaking his right leg on September 4. His biggest claim to fame was as field manager for the Red Sox. He took the reins for the final games of the 1913 season and then led the team through 1916, winning the World Series both in 1915 and 1916 — his second and third of the three titles the Red Sox won from 1912 to 1916. Carrigan retired after 1916, but was enticed back for three very disappointing seasons in 1927–1929, averaging just shy of 100 losses each year. The two stints demonstrate that a manager is only as good as his players. In his first run, Carrigan's teams won at a .612 percentage but when he came back over a decade later, they were .360. For **Les Nunamaker**, 1911 was his debut year, the first of 12 seasons in the big leagues. He hit .257, played a couple of more years for Boston and then was sold to the Yankees in May 1914. He was part of two world championship teams, the 1912 Red Sox and the 1920 Indians.

Charles F. Wagner was Heinie, not to be confused with Charlie Wagner of a much later era. He had a career for the Red Sox which stretched from the worst season in franchise history (1906) into 1918, when Heinie played three games with the fourth Red Sox world championship team of the decade. He had an "off" year in 1911, and only got into 80 games. There was a lot of movement amongst infielders: Wagner played 40 games at second base and 32 at short. Larry Gardner played 62 at second and 72 at third. Engle played 65 at first base and 51 at third, 13 at second — and even 10 in the outfield. There were eight different players who played first base and seven who played second.

It was **Alva "Rip" Williams** who had second-most of the first-base duty, 57 games, his first year in the majors and the only one with the Red Sox. He hit .239 for Boston, but was sold to the New York Highlanders in February 1912, then packaged in a trade to the Senators that same month.

Larry Gardner hit .285 in the fourth of his 10 seasons with the Red Sox. He was on the 1912, 1915, and 1916 World Series-winning teams, but was traded to the Athletics in January 1918. He played seven more seasons for Philadelphia and Cleveland and finished with a .289 lifetime average.

Steve Yerkes was another player for whom 1911 was his rookie year, though he had appeared in five games back in 1909. He enjoyed a full season in 1911, with 502 at-bats and a .279 average. His two RBIs won Game One of the 1912 World Series and his triple in the third inning drove in the first run and he scored the second run in the 2–1 win over the Giants in Game Five.

Joe Riggert debuted on May 12, 1911, but major-league pitching wasn't easy for him; he got into 50 games and hit at a .212 clip. The next two seasons were spent first in Wilkes-Barre and then in St. Paul, where he played through 1924 save for another three stints in the bigs, for Brooklyn, the Cardinals, and back in Boston in 1919 for the Braves. Hitting .283 that year pulled his major-league average up to .240.

Billy Purtell had been with the Red Sox in 1910, after he and Frank Smith arrived from the White Sox on August 9, in trade for Harry Lord and Amby McConnell, but he'd hit just .208. He appeared in 27 games for the Red Sox in 1911, batting .280 in 82 at-bats. He played full seasons for the International League's Jersey City Skeeters in 1912 and 1913, where his .306 average got him back to the majors with the Tigers. He only hit .171, though. Purtell played in the minor leagues through 1921 and then, after four years away, reprised with a final, full season with the Columbia Comers in 1926.

The "$10,000 beauty," **Jack Thoney**, played in 26 games. He didn't play defense even once, but he had 20 plate appearances (and hit .250). He was used as a pinch-runner on at least four occasions and scored in three of them. The Red Sox sold his contract to Jersey City, where he played through 1912.

Hap Myers was, like Hooper and Lewis, another graduate of St. Mary's College in Oakland. He had spent the spring season with the Red Sox, but he had been drafted by the St. Louis Browns in September 1910, who sold him to the Red Sox on May 11, the same day the Sox sold Frank Smith to Cincinnati. Myers only got into 13 games, but he had 14 hits, batting .368. He didn't play in 1912, worked for the Braves in 1913, then finished his career with two years in the Federal League with the Brooklyn Tip-Tops.

Hugh Bradley hit .317 in limited action (41 at-bats), but he became best known in Red Sox history for one swing of the bat in 1912 — he hit the first home run ever hit at brand-new Fenway Park. Like Myers he ended his career with Federal League play for the Pittsburgh Rebels, the Brooklyn Tip-Tops, and the Newark Peppers, and then seven seasons of minor-league ball.

The youngest player on the spring tour was **Hal Janvrin**. The 18-year-old didn't get a lot of work, debuting on July 9. Nine games, 27 at-bats, a .148 average. While the Red Sox were winning the 1912 pennant and World Series, Childe Harold was playing for the Jersey City Skeeters. He spent five years with the Red Sox and enjoyed two world championships in 1915 and 1916.

Two catchers saw very little work: **Red Kleinow** (eight games) and **Bunny Madden** (four games). Kleinow's first six seasons were with New York, who sold him to the Red Sox in May 1910. He was released on August 5, 1911, signed with the Phillies, and was released by them just days later. Madden was one of those rare Red Sox who were actually born in Boston (there have only been 16 of them). Over three seasons, he appeared in 28 games for the Red Sox, was put on waivers and claimed by the Phillies on June 24, and played in 28 games for them, his last in the majors. He played for 10 more years in the minors, mostly for Montreal. He returned to the Boston area and worked for the New England Telephone Company.

Smoky Joe Wood won 23 games in 1911, 23–17 with a 2.02 earned run average. He was only foreshadowing his stupendous 34–5 (1.91) season in 1912 (3–1 in the World Series), but it was unfortunately a career prematurely ended by injury. He nevertheless won the ERA title in 1915 (1.49) before reinventing himself as a batter with the Indians beginning in 1917; he hit .297 in 470 games over six years.

The Red Sox had a team ERA well under 3.00 at 2.74. There were two 11-game winners (**Eddie Cicotte** and Ray Collins) and one 10-game winner (Larry Pape.) Cicotte, sadly, lost 15 games. He was 1–3 with the Red Sox in 1912, but sold to the White Sox in July so did not experience the joy of Boston's World Series win. Cicotte would have his chances, though, savoring a championship with the 1917 White Sox — and sullying one in 1919, when he and others on the "Black Sox" threw games to Cincinnati. **Larry Pape** was 1–1 in 1912, his last games in major-league ball. His contract was sold to the Buffalo Bisons, but when they in turn tried to send him to a lower level, he quit and went into industry. He gave it one more shot after sitting out a year and played very briefly with Portland in 1914. **Ray Collins** never played for another team than the Red Sox (1909–1915), not even in the minor leagues. The left-hander put up an 84–62 record, anchored by a 2.51 career ERA. A 20-game winner in 1914, he faded in effectiveness in 1915, was relegated to bullpen duty, and chose to retire and begin farming in Vermont.

Ed Karger was 5–8 with Boston in 1911, with a 3.37 ERA. Though only 28, it was his last year in the majors, where he'd put up a 48–67 record over six seasons. He pitched for the St. Paul Saints during the 1912–1915 period, in one game for Houston in 1917 (giving up two walks and a hit in zero innings pitched), and then two final seasons in Aberdeen in 1920 and 1921.

Charley Hall pitched for the Sox through 1913, his best year being his 15–8 (3.02) season in 1912 which helped get Boston into the World Series. The "Sea Lion" (he had a deep, loud voice) pitched 10 and two-thirds innings in Series relief. He kept pitching through 1925, winning 285 games in the minors on top of his 54–47 major-league record. Hall and Frank Arellanes were the two Latinos on the 1911 Red Sox.

Frank Arellanes was the first Latin player for Boston. Of Puebla, Mexico, ancestry, his family had nonetheless been in the country longer than most of the other players on the team. Debuting with the Sox in 1908, he became, in effect, the replacement for Cy Young in 1909, and his 16 wins led the team. He'd only been 4–7 in 1910, however, before being sent to Sacramento. He didn't even make the team in 1911, though he revived to win 22 games for Sacramento in 1912, the third of four seasons with the Sacts. His final years in organized ball were with Vernon in 1916 and 1917.

Jack Killilay put in five seasons of minor-league ball before joining the 1911 Red Sox and he put in five seasons after departing the Red Sox. His one year in the majors was the 4–2 season in 1911 (61 innings, with a 3.54 earned run average) for the Red Sox from his May 13 debut to his last game on September 22. At the plate, he was 1-for-24, but it was a double. He won 145 games in the minors.

The Brockton boy, **Buck O'Brien**, seemed to have some really good games and some really bad games in 1911 spring training. He'd been a 20-game winner with Hartford in 1910, and then was 26–7 with Denver in

1911, joining the Sox in time for a September 9 debut. It was a stunning first month — he was 5–1 with an ERA of 0.36 (only two earned runs in 47 and two-thirds innings). And he had a terrific 1912, too — 20–13, 2.58. In the World Series, however, he was a disappointing 0–2, 5.00, though he was badly served by the way he was used. Between the Red Sox and then the White Sox, he was 2–11 in 1913 before heading back to the minors.

Another 20-game winner in 1912 was **Hugh Bedient** (20–9), but you might not have predicted that given the 8–11 season he had with the Providence Grays in 1911. His big-league debut came on April 26, 1912. Bedient also appeared in four of the games of that year's World Series, and was the winner of Game Five, beating Christy Mathewson, 2–1. He started the deciding Game Eight and held the Giants to just one run over the first seven innings, though it was Smoky Joe Wood who won the game in the 10th. Bedient won 15 games in 1913, and eight in 1914, then jumped from the Red Sox to play for Buffalo in the Federal League in 1915. He pitched in the minors through 1925, a 20-game winner for Toledo in 1921.

Walter Moser had been 0–4 with the Phillies in 1906. He'd built up an enviable minor-league career with 24, 14, 19, and 20 wins, and then a 31–20 season in 1910 with the Oakland Oaks. His return to the big leagues still never produced a win. In 1911 he was 0–1 for Boston in six appearances (three starts), and was sold to the St. Louis Browns on September 1. For the Browns, he was 0–2. After a 12–15 season with Atlantic City in 1913, he left baseball for what must have seemed greener pastures.

Valuable as a member of the Red Sox Quartette, **Marty McHale**, the "Irish Thrush," had been 11–11 with the Brockton Shoemakers in 1910, signed after pitching three consecutive no-hitters for the University of Maine. With Boston in 1911, he started one game and appeared in three others, giving up 10 earned runs in nine and one-third innings. The Sox traded him to Jersey City as one of six players from the 1911 team, all swapped for catcher Hick Cady. Hal Janvrin, Walter Lonergan, Hap Myers, Billy Purtell, and Jack Thoney joined McHale in that trade. The New York Highlanders bought his contract from Jersey City and over three seasons with New York he was 11–27 (3.28). A brief reappearance with the Red Sox in 1916 lasted all of six innings (0–1 in two games). He was sold to Cleveland in May, and was 0–0. He went on to become an investment broker.

And last, and least, two pitchers who appeared in one game apiece,

Charlie Smith and **Frank Smith**. Charlie pitched two and one-third innings and Frank pitched two, not even a half a game between them. Charlie's ERA was 15.43 and Frank's was 9.00. They were both 31 years old. Charlie was sold to Newark in early May and purchased by the Chicago Cubs in August. He pitched through 1914 for the Cubs (a 19–19 record), then had a final 17–8 season with the San Francisco Seals in 1915. Frank Smith was put on waivers at more or less the same time as the unrelated Charlie, claimed by the Browns, but sold to the Reds, who bought out the Browns' waiver claim. He won 10 games for Cincinnati, losing 14, and pitched a few more years winding up his career in the Federal League, before he returned to Pittsburgh and the moving business.

He already had five minor-league seasons on his resume, but **Hank Perry** spent 1911 with the Providence Grays putting up a .343 average. His only time in the big leagues came in 1912, 40 plate appearances for the Detroit Tigers. He never struck out, but he only hit .167 and also never drove in a run. His last year in the minors was 1913, spent with Jersey City and Buffalo.

Chris Mahoney had been in three games with the 1910 Red Sox, two as a pitcher and one as an outfielder. He was 0–1 on the mound, and 1-for-7 at the plate, a single, but showed considerable promise, particularly on the 1911 spring training trip. He played the next three years in the minors, mostly for the Portland Beavers, and had middling success (5–5 on the mound and .262 at the bat) but not enough to continue a career in baseball.

Richard Nebinger is a bit of a mystery man. He played in a total of 38 games for Akron and Fairmont in 1907 and 1908, never hitting higher than .194. He showed some promise in the springtime with the Red Sox, but his 1911 season was spent entirely in the minors (100 games between Sacramento, Oakland, and Chattanooga, wherein he lifted his lifetime batting average to .205). Perhaps worried at seeing it drop back, he left baseball. Whether he was related to the Richard Nebinger who hit .201 in 1958, also playing for three teams in his only minor-league year, we just do not know.

John Buzick played in Lynn, Massachusetts, in 1910 and 1911 but he didn't play all that much. In 1910 he hit .238 and in 1911 he hit .272. What he did after the 32 games in 1911 remains unknown.

Hollis is one of the biggest mysteries of all. Our Hollis was both a pitcher and a right-fielder with the springtime Red Sox. One of the newspapers called him George Hollis, but the only Hollis who seems likely in SABR's Minor League Database is Bradley Hollis. There is not a thing by way of biographical information known about him — not even the year of his birth, or whether he was right-handed or left-handed. Bradley played for the Centralia Pets and hit an even .250 in an even 200 at-bats. He had five homers, but made 24 errors as a shortstop (.901). That may be the reason it was his only season. There had been a George Hollis, a pitcher, but his last year was 1908. There was a C. W. "Babe" Hollis, another shortstop with Calgary in 1913.

In Sawyer's case, we know his name was **Willard Henry Sawyer** and we know he was born September 5, 1888, and was a pitcher from Maine, who played on Hebron Academy's baseball and basketball teams, serving as captain of the 1908 team. Hebron does not show him completing his studies, and he doesn't appear to have ever played minor-league ball, much less in the majors. There's no Sawyer who's even close. He married Avis L. Rand on March 26, 1912, and the couple had three children. He ran a general store in Wilton that had previously been run by his father Willard E. Sawyer. W.H. died in 1967.

Benjamin Franklin "High Pockets" Hunt had a name. And a great nickname, too. He grew up on a farm in Oklahoma and never played baseball until three years before his Red Sox debut in August 1910. He'd reportedly been a drifter, passing through Hutchinson, Kansas, when he joined the team there and won nine games in a month, heading on to Boston immediately afterward. The Sox placed him with Sacramento in 1911, and in June the Sacramento newspaper reported that he was dying of pneumonia with only a slight chance of recovery. Dick Thompson enlisted numerous SABR researchers to try and track down Hunt's details, and the search was a fascinating one (see Hunt's biography on SABR's BioProject site). He survived that scare but, still fairly young, died of alcoholism and tuberculosis in 1927 in Greybull, Wyoming, where he'd run a pool hall.

Information regarding **George Pierce** appears in the game account of the March 19 games.

Jerry Sheehan was left behind in California, and saw duty with three teams in 1911. He hit .256 in the PCL for the Vernon Tigers and San Francisco Seals, the best average of his six seasons of minor-league ball, and

.238 with the Providence Grays. He'd begun with Sioux City in 1907 and wound up his career with the Streator (Illinois) Boosters in the Three-I League.

Chet Thomas was sent to Sacramento where he played for his third season with the team. "Pinch" Thomas made the Red Sox in 1912 and was a small part of that world championship team, and an active part of the 1915 and 1916 World Series winners, too. He was traded to the Athletics after the 1917 season, then sold by them to the Indians where he added a fourth World Series title to his resume. His last year in the majors was 1921.

Gene Dale, that most promising of prospects before the spring season, did make his major-league pitching debut in September, but it was for the Cardinals. He was 0–2 in 1911 and 0–5 for St. Louis in 1913, with some back and forth in the minors, with Dallas in 1911 and then Montreal the next three years. In 1915, he was purchased from the Royals by the Reds and won 18 games for Cincinnati (18–17), finishing his major-league career with a 3–4 season in 1916.

Herman Priepke presented the saddest story. Just a month after the season began, he died in Utica at 11:00 P.M. on May 11 of pneumonia, following a severe cold he had contracted in Oakland. A native of Germany, he'd come to the United States when he was about one year old and settled in LaPorte, Illinois, with his parents. The Red Sox had placed him with the Utica ballclub, and when his health seriously declined, he took to bed, planning to go back to Boston for treatment. He'd already sent his trunk ahead when he developed pneumonia and died at age 31. His wife was with him at the time.[1]

Managers and Ownership

Manager **Patsy Donovan** was born in County Cork, Ireland, way back in 1865. The Donovan family emigrated to America and settled in Lawrence, Massachusetts. Donovan's 1911 season was his last in baseball. He'd debuted as a left-hand hitting outfielder in 1890 and played 17 seasons in the big leagues, mostly with the Pirates and the Cardinals, leaving with a .301 lifetime average. His only postseason experience was in his first year, when he batted .471 for the Brooklyn Bridegrooms in that year's "World

Series" which ended in a tie (of all things) against the American Association's Louisville Colonels. Each team won three games, and they tied. (From 1884 to 1890, the champions of the National League and American Association — the two recognized major leagues — met for a postseason series that was a forerunner of the modern-day World Series, which began in 1903. The 1890 Bridegrooms–Colonels match-up was the last between the leagues, as the Association would fold following the 1891 season.) Donovan was a player/manager for eight years, then managed Brooklyn in 1908 after ending his career as a player. In 1910, he led the Red Sox to a fourth-place finish, down from third place the year before. When Jake Stahl returned to the Sox in 1912, Donovan was discharged and given a role as a Red Sox scout. He managed in the minors for 13 years, and also coached secondary schools in the New England area (one of his student ballplayers was Phillips Andover alumnus George Herbert Walker Bush) and then went on to scout for many years for the New York Yankees. The Donovans married in Lawrence, Massachusetts, on November 23, 1910, and had traveled to Europe on their honeymoon. Mrs. Donovan accompanied the Red Sox party as it crisscrossed the country. They had their first child, a boy, at the end of August 1911.

Attendance at home games suffered badly in 1911. The Red Sox had been second in all of baseball in 1910, riding high with 584,619, not far behind the Philadelphia Athletics', who at 588,905 had led the league. In 1911, Boston fell to fifth place among the 16 clubs, to 503,961, a sharp decline at a time when many other clubs were showing gains over the year before. Fortunately, the interest engendered by the new Fenway Park in 1912 and a first-place finish boosted attendance to 597,096.

John I. Taylor's postscript began while the season was still in progress. American League President Ban Johnson wanted to see Taylor replaced. Under pressure from Johnson, Taylor began negotiations with prospective purchaser James McAleer sometime in August or perhaps earlier (a *New York Times* report dated September 13 said that negotiations had fallen apart "some weeks ago" because McAleer wanted to own all the stock, while Taylor wanted to hold onto some of the stock). Two days later, Taylor announced that McAleer and Robert McRoy, secretary of the American League, had purchased a 50 percent stake in the club. McAleer was a former player and, at the time, manager of the Washington Senators.

Ban Johnson was present at the announcement, and there was little doubt that he had orchestrated the sale.

Even with three games remaining on the schedule, incoming Red Sox president James McAleer announced that he was determined to entice Jake Stahl back to manage the team. He told the *Washington Post*, "I will offer Stahl inducements that I do not think he can afford to overlook. He is still a young man, with a long baseball life before him, and I believe that he will return to the game."[2]

On November 10, 1911, a little over nine months since the Red Sox had passed through Chicago and failed to entice **Jake Stahl** to rejoin the Sox and take the trip to Redondo Beach, Stahl was brought back on board, named as manager for 1912. It was McAleer who made the offer, not Taylor. Stahl said, "I'll be mighty glad to get back into the game again, and especially to be back in Boston. The surroundings will be congenial with McAleer and Robert McRoy at the head of the club."[3] Would it be too much to read between the lines that Stahl had been less than enthusiastic about playing for Donovan and Taylor? The new ownership had sweetened the pot by reportedly granting Stahl a small stake in the ballclub itself to secure his commitment as player/manager for 1912.

Not much more than a month after the 1911 season got under way, Taylor already had grandiose plans for spring training in 1912. He had worked out a plan with the Cincinnati Reds by May. Taylor would "secure a suitable tract of ground within hailing distance of a good-sized city in the South — preferably in Georgia. On this land, the Boston and Cincinnati Clubs will lay out two diamonds near each other so that each club may have its own grounds for practice. A large bungalow will be erected alongside the ball parks by each club in which the players, manager, and training attendants will live during the training season. The clubs will have their own cooks, waiters, and other help ... the right kind of food to eat and plenty of it, which is something they seldom get in a hotel. In the second place, they will be away from the 'attractions' of a city where they are often led into temptations that undo their training work on the ball field.... The bungalows will be equipped with hot and cold shower baths and certain mild forms of amusement will be provided for the players." Of course, they would be under the watchful eye of their manager at all times.[4]

The land located turned out to be in Texas, not Georgia, as the *Sporting Life* edition of September 9 reported, "The Boston Club has closed a deal to do its 1912 spring training at Toga, Texas, 50 miles North of Fort Worth." The very same issue reported on page 5 (the Toga story was on page 11) that the report the Sox had signed a deal to train in Texas was untrue; Taylor was looking at the spot recommended by scout Ted Sullivan. In November 1911, the Red Sox announced they would again be training in Hot Springs, Arkansas, in 1912.

Stahl led the Red Sox to the pennant and a world championship in 1912, but by mid–1913 was feuding with McAleer. On July 14, 1913, McAleer fired Stahl, replacing him as manager with Bill Carrigan.

On November 30, 1913, New Yorker Joseph Lannin bought the 50 percent of Red Sox shares owned by McAleer, McRoy, and Jake Stahl. General Charles H. Taylor and his son John retained ownership of their half. The sale was, no surprise, more or less dictated by AL architect Ban Johnson, angry that McAleer had dismissed Jake Stahl as manager in mid-season. Canadian-born, Lannin had been a bellhop in a Boston hotel, rose in the ranks, and eventually came to own three New York hotels. Lannin became president of the Red Sox. An indication of Johnson's involvement was how McAleer learned of the sale. Joe Cashman told Peter Golenbock that McAleer received a telegram reading, "You have just sold the Red Sox to Joseph Lannin. Ban Johnson."[5]

On September 11, 1919, on a New York witness stand, Ban Johnson testified that he had advanced the money which Robert McRoy put into helping purchase the Red Sox in 1911.

Appendix A

Spring Training
Schedule and Results

February 25	Redondo Beach, CA: Regulars 7, Yannigans 3 (5 innings)
February 26	Redondo Beach, CA: Regulars 3, Yannigans 2
February 28	Redondo Beach, CA: Yannigans 5, Regulars 1 (7 innings)
March 2	Los Angeles, CA: Boston 6, Los Angeles 5 (10 innings)
March 6	Redlands, CA: Red Sox Colts 7, Redlands 3
March 8	Oakland, CA: St. Mary's College 1, Boston 0
March 10	Los Angeles, CA: Vernon 4, Red Sox Colts 3 (10 innings)
March 11	Los Angeles, CA: Vernon 1, Red Sox Colts 0
	San Francisco, CA: Boston 6, San Francisco 4
March 12	Oakland, CA: Boston 7, Oakland 5 (morning game)
	San Francisco, CA: Boston 5, San Francisco 1 (afternoon game)
	Vernon, CA: Vernon 5, Red Sox Colts 2
	Los Angeles, CA: Vernon 3, Red Sox Colts 1
March 13	Los Angeles, CA: Red Sox Colts 12, Vernon 3
	Modesto, CA: Boston 5, Modesto 0
March 14	Hanford, CA: Red Sox Colts 9, Hanford 3
	Oakland, CA: Boston 10, San Francisco Seals 4
March 15	Bakersfield, CA: Red Sox Colts 1, Bakersfield 0
	San Francisco, CA: Boston 2, San Francisco 1
March 16	Los Angeles, CA: Boston 3, Vernon 1
	Oakland, CA: Oakland 4, Red Sox Colts 2

The Colts were now in Northern California, and the Regulars in Southern California.

March 17	Los Angeles, CA: Vernon 4, Boston 2
	San Francisco, CA: Red Sox Colts 10, San Francisco 4
March 18	Los Angeles, CA: Boston 5, Vernon 0
	San Francisco, CA: San Francisco 14, Red Sox Colts 6
March 19	Oakland, CA: Oakland 4, Red Sox Colts 2 (morning)

(March 19 cont.)	San Francisco, CA: San Francisco 9, Red Sox Colts 1 (afternoon)
	Los Angeles, CA: Boston 6, Vernon 3 (10 innings)
March 20	San Jose, CA: Red Sox Colts 3, Santa Clara College 2
	Claremont, CA: Boston 7, Pomona College 0
March 21	Redlands, CA: Boston 7, Redlands 1 (5 innings)
	Sacramento, CA: Red Sox Colts 3, Sacramento 2
March 22	Riverside, CA: Boston 5, Riverside 0
	Sacramento, CA: Red Sox Colts 2, Sacramento 1
March 23	Los Angeles, CA: Boston 3, Los Angeles 1
	Oakland, CA: Oakland 10, Red Sox Colts 5
March 24	Los Angeles, CA: Boston 11, Los Angeles 4
	San Francisco, CA: San Francisco 9, Red Sox Colts 3
March 25	Los Angeles, CA: Boston 4, Los Angeles 3
	San Francisco, CA: San Francisco 4, Red Sox Colts 3
March 26	Oakland, CA: Oakland 6, Red Sox Colts 5 (11 innings) (morning)
	San Francisco, CA: San Francisco 8, Red Sox Colts 0 (afternoon)
	Los Angeles, CA: Boston 12, Los Angeles 4
March 27	Yuma, AZ: Boston 17, Yuma 5
	Reno, NV: Red Sox Colts 14, University of Nevada 4
March 28	El Paso, TX: Boston 9, El Paso 1
	Salt Lake City, UT: Red Sox Colts 9, Salt Lake City 2
March 29	Abilene, TX: Boston 19, Abilene 7
	Salt Lake City, UT: Salt Lake City 15, Red Sox Colts 10
March 30	Dallas, TX: Boston 4, Dallas 0
March 31	Fort Worth, TX: Boston 4, Fort Worth 2
	Pueblo, CO: Red Sox Colts 10, Pueblo 4
April 1	Oklahoma City, OK: Boston 16, Oklahoma City 1
	Denver, CO: Denver 6, Red Sox Colts 3
April 2	Wichita, KS: Boston 5, Wichita 4
	Denver, CO: Red Sox Colts 4, Denver 1
April 3	Denver, CO: Denver 3, Red Sox Colts 2
April 5	Topeka, KS: Boston 7, Topeka 0
	Lincoln, NE: Lincoln 8, Red Sox Colts 7
April 6	St. Joseph, MO: St. Joseph 5, Boston 4
April 7	St. Joseph, MO: Boston 13, St. Joseph 0
April 8	Kansas City, MO: Boston 4, Kansas City 3
	Omaha, NE: Omaha 5, Red Sox Colts 2
April 9	Kansas City, MO: Boston 4, Kansas City 3
	Omaha, NE: Red Sox Colts 1, Omaha 1 (tie)
April 11	Boston, MA: Red Sox Colts 4, Harvard College 2

Not counting the three intrasquad games in Redondo Beach, the Red Sox won 41 games, lost 21, and had the tie game in Omaha. The Regulars put up a record of 27–3, losing only to St. Mary's College, the first game against Vernon, and the April 6 game in St. Joseph, Missouri. The Colts were 14–18–1 in their games.

Appendix B

Train Schedule for the Red Sox Excursion

Boston to Los Angeles

February 18 Depart Boston at 1:00 P.M. from South Station on the New York, New Haven, and Hartford Railroad. Arrive New York City at 6:00 P.M.

February 19 Depart New York at 7:50 A.M. on the Baltimore & Ohio Railroad from the depot at West 23rd Street.

February 20 Arrive Chicago at 9:45 A.M.

February 20 Depart Chicago at 9:15 P.M. on the Chicago, Rock Island, and Pacific Railroad via special train.

February 23 Arrive Los Angeles at 2:45 P.M. via Southern Pacific Railway.

[Travel within California was not included in the February 13 announcement detailing the trans-national arrangements.]

Returning Northern Route

March 26 Depart San Francisco at 9:00 P.M. via Southern Pacific Railway.

March 27 Arrive Reno, Nevada, at 9:55 A.M. Depart Reno at 9:50 P.M. via Southern Pacific Railway.

March 28 Arrive Ogden, Utah, at 12:10 P.M. Depart Ogden at 6:00 P.M. via Denver and Rio Grande Western Railway, arriving in Salt Lake City at 7:00 P.M.

March 29 Depart Salt Lake City at 7:10 P.M. via Denver and Rio Grande Western Railway for Grand Junction, Colorado.

March 30 Arrive at Grand Junction, Colorado, at 5:50 A.M. Depart at 7:40 P.M. via Denver and Rio Grande Western Railway.

March 31 Arrive Pueblo, Colorado, at 8:50 A.M. Depart at 7:25 P.M. via Denver and Rio Grande Western Railway, arriving in Denver, Colorado, at 11:30 P.M.

April 3	Depart Denver at 9:00 P.M. via Chicago, Burlington, & Quincy Railroad.
April 4	Arrive Lincoln, Nebraska, at 1:35 P.M.
April 5	Depart Lincoln at 9:45 P.M. via Chicago, Burlington, & Quincy Railroad. Arrive Omaha, Nebraska, at 11:25 P.M.
April 6	Depart Omaha at 7:45 A.M. via Chicago and North Western Railway.
April 6	Arrive Sioux City, Iowa, at 11:00 A.M.
April 7	Depart Sioux City at 7:20 P.M. via Chicago and North Western Railway. Arrive in Omaha at 11:20 P.M.
April 9	Depart Omaha at 6:00 P.M. via Chicago, Milwaukee and St. Paul Railroad.
April 10	Arrive Chicago at 8:00 A.M. Depart Chicago at 8:25 A.M. via Lake Shore and Michigan Southern Railway.
April 11	Arrive Boston at 10:40 A.M.

[OR Depart Chicago on April 10 at 9:05 A.M. via Michigan Central Railroad. Arrive Boston on April 11 at 11:50 A.M.]

Returning Southern Route

March 26	Depart Los Angeles at 10:15 P.M. via Southern Pacific Railway.
March 27	Arrive Yuma, Arizona, at 8:15 A.M. Depart Yuma at 10:10 P.M. via Southern Pacific Railway.
March 29	Arrive Tucson, Arizona, at 6:50 A.M. Depart Tucson at 1:10 A.M. via Southern Pacific Railway. Arrive El Paso, Texas, at 11:20 A.M.
March 30	Depart El Paso at 5:25 P.M. via Tucson and Southwestern Railroad.
March 31	Arrive Tucumcari, New Mexico, at 4:00 A.M. Depart Tucumcari at 7:40 A.M. via Tucson and Southwestern Railroad.
April 1	Arrive in Oklahoma City at 12:15 A.M. via Chicago, Rock Island, and Pacific Railroad (there was apparently a transfer at some point, perhaps at Tucumcari, despite the departure railroad indicated above.)
April 1	Depart Oklahoma City at 6:55 P.M. via Chicago, Rock Island, and Pacific Railroad. Arrive El Reno, Oklahoma, at 8:00 P.M.
April 2	Depart El Reno at 4:05 A.M. via Chicago, Rock Island, and Pacific Railroad. Arrive Wichita, Kansas, at 9:40 A.M.
April 3	Depart Wichita at 10:25 P.M. via Chicago, Rock Island, and Pacific Railroad.
April 4	Arrive Topeka, Kansas, at 4:20 A.M.
April 6	Depart Topeka at 7:55 A.M. via Chicago, Rock Island, and Pacific Railroad. Arrive St. Joseph, Missouri, at 11:35 A.M.
April 7	Depart St. Joseph at 6:45 P.M. via Chicago, Burlington, &

Quincy Railroad. Arrive Kansas City at 8:40 P.M.

April 9   Depart Kansas City at 6:30 P.M. via Chicago, Rock Island, and
               Pacific Railroad.

April 10   Arrive Englewood, Illinois at 8:05 A.M. Arrive Chicago at 8:20
               A.M. Depart Chicago, at 8:25 A.M. via Lake Shore and
               Michigan Southern Railway.

April 11   Arrive Boston at 10:40 A.M.

[OR Depart Chicago on April 10 at 9:05 A.M. via Michigan Central Railroad.
Arrive Boston on April 11 at 11:50 A.M.]

Source: Itinerary printed in the *Boston Journal*, February 14, 1911. Changes were
anticipated, and occurred, as the trip proceeded.

Chapter Notes

Introduction

1. Bill Nowlin, "Ted Williams and Opening Days," *Diehard*, May 2010.
2. E-mail correspondence, March 24, 2010.
3. *Boston Post*, March 28, 1911.

Chapter 1

1. *Sporting Life*, February 19, April 9, May 7, and September 17, 1910.
2. *Washington Post*, November 4, 1910.
3. *Boston American*, March 5, 1911.
4. Details regarding the history of Redondo Beach primarily come from *Redondo Beach*, an Arcadia book authored by the Historical Commission of Redondo Beach. The book features close to 200 photographs almost exclusively depicting the period from 1900 to 1920.
5. The family genealogy can be found in *The Huntington Family in America*, published in Hartford in 1915 by the Huntington Family Association.

Chapter 2

1. *Boston Journal* and *Boston Post*, January 4, 1911.
2. See the forthcoming Society for American Baseball book on the 1912 Boston Red Sox season, edited by Bill Nowlin.
3. Mention of the discord between Taylor and Lord appears in Hugh Fuller-

ton's February 19 column in the *Boston American*.
4. *Sporting Life*, December 31, 1910.
5. *Boston Post*, January 10, 1911.
6. *Boston Journal*, January 13, 1911.
7. *Sporting Life*, May 7, 1910.
8. *Boston Post*, January 14, 1911.
9. *Boston American*, January 30, 1911.
10. *Boston American*, February 19, 1911.
11. *Boston Post*, February 2, 1911.
12. *Boston Post*, February 10, 1911.
13. *Boston American*, February 28, 1911.
14. *Los Angeles Times*, February 14, 1911.
15. *Boston Journal*, January 13 and February 4, 1911.

Chapter 3

1. A photograph ran in the February 19, 1911, edition of the *Boston American*.
2. *Boston Journal*, February 19, 1911.
3. *Boston American*, February 18, 1911.
4. *Boston American*, February 18, 1911.
5. *Boston American*, February 19, 1911.
6. *Boston American*, February 18, 1911.
7. *Boston Post*, February 18, 1911.
8. *Boston Journal*, February 21, 1911.
9. *Boston Journal*, February 21, 1911.
10. *Boston Post*, March 21, 1911.
11. *Boston American*, February 20, 1911.
12. *Boston American*, February 19, 1911.
In the very same issue of the *American*, John I. Taylor referred to those very same White Sox visits to California, saying that Comiskey "has always had a successful trip."

13. *Boston Journal*, February 22, 1911.
14. *Boston Post*, February 22, 1911.
15. *Boston American*, February 21, 1911.
16. *Boston American*, February 25, 1911.
17. *Boston Herald*, February 23, 1911.
18. *Boston Post*, February 23, 1911.
19. *Boston Journal*, February 23, 1911.
20. *Boston American*, February 24, 1911.
21. For more on Leroy, see the section on him in *Red Sox Threads*. The quotation from the *Boston Post* was in the February 24, 1911, newspaper.
22. *Boston American*, February 25, 1911.
23. *Los Angeles Times*, February 21, 1911.
24. *Boston Journal*, February 24, 1911.
25. *Los Angeles Times*, February 26, 1911.
26. *Boston Globe*, February 25, 1911.
27. *Los Angeles Times*, February 25, 1911.
28. *Boston Post*, February 25, 1911.

Chapter 4

1. *Boston Herald*, February 26, 1911.
2. *Boston American*, February 19, 1911.
3. *Los Angeles Times*, February 26, 1911.
4. *Los Angeles Examiner*, March 2, 1911.
5. *Los Angeles Times*, February 26, 1911.
6. *Boston Post*, February 27, 1911.
7. *Boston Post*, February 27, 1911.
8. *Los Angeles Times*, February 27, 1911.
9. See *Red Sox Threads* for the story of the fight for Sunday ball in Boston.
10. *Boston Journal*, February 28, 1911.
11. *Boston American*, February 27, 1911.
12. *Boston Post*, February 28, 1911.
13. *Boston American*, March 1, 1911.
14. *Boston Globe*, March 1, 1911.
15. *Boston Journal*, March 1, 1911.
16. *Boston Post*, March 2, 1911.
17. *Oakland Tribune*, March 2, 1911.
18. *Los Angeles Examiner*, March 3, 1911.
19. *Los Angeles Examiner*, March 3, 1911.
20. *Los Angeles Herald*, March 3, 1911.

21. *Boston American*, March 3, 1911.
22. *Boston Post*, March 3, 1911.
23. *Boston Journal*, March 3, 1911.
24. *Boston Journal*, March 3, 1911.
25. *Boston Journal*, March 4, 1911.
26. *Boston American*, March 4 and 5, 1911.
27. *Boston Journal*, March 5, 1911.
28. *Boston Post*, March 5, 1911.
29. *Boston Journal*, March 7, 1911.
30. *Boston Journal*, March 7, 1911.
31. *Redlands Daily Facts*, March 4, 1911.
32. *Boston Herald*, May 7, 1911.
33. *Boston American*, March 7, 1911.
34. *Boston Post*, March 7, 1911.
35. *Boston American*, March 8 and 9, 1911.
36. *Oakland Tribune*, March 9, 1911.
37. *Boston Journal*, March 10, 1911.
38. *Boston Post*, March 10, 1911.
39. *Boston Globe*, March 12, 1911.
40. *Boston Journal*, March 10, 1911.
41. *Boston American*, March 10, 1911.
42. *Boston American*, March 9 and 11, 1911.
43. *Los Angeles Herald*, March 11, 1911.
44. *Boston Globe*, March 12, 1911.
45. See also *Boston Journal*, February 7, 1911.
46. *Los Angeles Herald*, March 13, 1911.
47. *Los Angeles Times*, March 13, 1911.
48. *Modesto Morning Herald*, March 14, 1911.
49. *Hanford Journal*, March 14, 1911.
50. *Boston Journal*, March 15, 1911.
51. *Los Angeles Times*, March 15, 1911.
52. *Boston American*, March 15, 1911.
53. The description of the catch comes from the *Bakersfield Californian*, but description of Barkdaw's disability comes from the *Boston Globe*.
54. *Bakersfield Californian*, March 16, 1911.

Chapter 5

1. *Sporting Life*, March 25, 1911.
2. *Boston American*, March 14, 1911.
3. *New York Times*, March 18, 1911, and *Los Angeles Times*, May 8, 1911.

4. *Boston American*, March 17, 1911.
5. *Boston Post*, March 18, 1911.
6. *Boston Herald*, March 19, 1911.
7. *Boston American*, March 18, 1911.
8. *Pomona Progress*, March 20, 1911.
9. *Boston Journal*, March 21, 1911.
10. *Boston Journal*, March 22, 1911.
11. *Redlands Daily Facts*, March 22, 1911.
12. *Sacramento Union*, March 22, 1911.
13. *Sacramento Bee*, March 22, 1911.
14. *Sacramento Union*, March 22, 1911.
15. *Boston Journal*, March 23, 1911.
16. *Boston Post*, March 23, 1911.
17. *Sacramento Bee*, March 22, 1911.
18. *Sacramento Union*, March 23, 1911.
19. *Los Angeles Examiner*, March 24, 1911.
20. *Los Angeles Examiner*, March 24, 1911.
21. *Boston Herald*, March 24, 1911.
22. *Oakland Tribune*, March 24, 1911.
23. *Los Angeles Herald*, March 25, 1911.
24. *Oakland Tribune*, March 25, 1911.
25. *Boston American*, March 24, 1911.
26. *Boston Journal*, March 26, 1911.
27. *Boston Journal*, March 26, 1911.
28. *Boston Globe*, May 25, 1911. Perhaps not all the players shipped the fruit home. Merton Burke said it cost so much that few invested.
29. *Boston American*, March 25, 1911.
30. *San Francisco Examiner*, March 27, 1911.
31. *Boston Post*, March 27, 1911.
32. *San Francisco Examiner*, March 27, 1911.
33. *Boston American*, March 26, 1911.

Chapter 6

1. *Boston Journal*, March 28, 1911.
2. *Boston Post*, March 28, 1911.
3. *Boston American*, March 28, 1911.
4. *University of Nevada Sagebrush*, March 13, 1911.
5. *Reno Evening Gazette*, March 23, 1911.
6. *Nevada State Journal*, March 27, 1911.
7. *Reno Evening Gazette*, March 28, 1911.
8. *Nevada State Journal*, March 28, 1911.
9. *El Paso Herald*, March 28, 1911.
10. *El Paso Herald*, March 27, 1911. The March 29 edition termed it an "impromptu team."
11. *El Paso Herald*, March 10, 1911.
12. *Boston Journal*, March 29, 1911.
13. *El Paso Morning Times*, March 27, 1911.
14. *El Paso Daily Herald*, February 14, 1894.
15. *Salt Lake Tribune*, March 30, 1911.
16. *Boston American*, March 30, 1911.
17. E-mail from Dave Baldwin, March 9, 2010.
18. *Boston American*, March 31, 1911.
19. *Boston Post*, April 1, 1911.
20. *Pueblo Chieftain*, April 2, 1911.
21. *Boston Herald*, April 1, 1911.
22. *The Oklahoman*, April 1, 1911.
23. *Boston Post*, April 2, 1911.
24. *Boston Journal*, April 2, 1911.
25. *Boston American*, April 5, 1911.
26. *Boston American*, April 2, 1911.
27. *Rocky Mountain News*, April 2, 1911.
28. *Rocky Mountain News*, April 3, 1911.
29. *Boston Journal*, April 3, 1911.
30. *Boston American*, April 4, 1911. Two days later, Burke wrote that Perry had "a little grouch he has been nursing against a certain newspaperman, name unmentioned, who doesn't approve of his recent performances."
31. *Denver Post*, April 4, 1911.
32. *Wichita Eagle*, April 4, 1911.
33. *Boston Journal*, April 5, 1911.
34. *Boston American*, April 5, 1911.
35. *Boston Post*, April 6, 1911.
36. *Lincoln Evening News*, April 6, 1911.
37. *Lincoln Daily Star*, April 6, 1911.
38. *Lincoln Evening News*, April 1, 1911.
39. *Boston American*, April 6, 1911.
40. *Boston Journal*, April 7, 1911.
41. *Boston American*, April 6, 1911.
42. *Boston American*, April 8, 1911.

43. *Kansas City Journal*, April 8, 1911.
44. *Boston Post*, April 9, 1911.
45. *Kansas City Star*, April 9, 1911.
46. *Kansas City Post*, April 9, 1911.
47. *Kansas City Star*, April 9, 1911.
48. *Washington Post*, August 6, 1939.
49. *Boston American*, April 10, 1911.
50. *Boston American*, April 9, 1911.

Chapter 7

1. *Boston Journal*, April 11, 1911.
2. *Boston Journal* figures, April 10, 1911.

3. *Harper's Weekly*, vol. 11, August 3, 1867, p. 488.
4. *Boston American*, April 10, 1911.

Chapter 8

1. *Sporting Life*, May 20, 1911, and *Boston Globe*, May 12, 1911.
2. *Washington Post*, October 6, 1911.
3. *Boston Globe*, November 11, 1911.
4. *Sporting Life*, May 27, 1911.
5. *Day by Day with the Boston Red Sox*, entry for November 30.

Bibliography

Newspapers and Weekly Publications

Abilene Daily Reporter
Arizona Sentinel
Bakersfield Californian
Boston American
Boston Globe
Boston Herald
Boston Journal
Boston Post
Brockton Enterprise
Chicago Tribune
Christian Science Monitor
Dallas Morning News
Denver Post
Denver Republican
Denver Times
El Paso Herald
El Paso Morning Times
Hanford Journal
Harper's Weekly
Hartford Courant
Harvard Crimson
Kansas City Journal
Kansas City Post
Kansas City Star
Lincoln Daily Star
Lincoln Evening News
Los Angeles Examiner
Los Angeles Herald
Los Angeles Times
Modesto Morning Herald
Nevada State Journal
New York Times
Oakland Tribune
The Oklahoman
Omaha Morning World-Herald
Pomona Progress
Pueblo Chieftain
Redlands Daily Facts
Reno Evening Gazette
Riverside Enterprise
Riverside Press
Rocky Mountain News
Sacramento Bee
Sacramento Union
Salida Mail
Salt Lake Desert News
Salt Lake Telegram
Salt Lake Tribune
San Francisco Examiner
San Jose Evening News
Sioux City Journal
Sporting Life
The Sporting News
Topeka Daily Capital
Topeka State Journal
University of Nevada Sagebrush
Washington Post
Wichita Beacon
Wichita Eagle

Books

Historical Commission of Redondo Beach. *Redondo Beach*. Charleston, SC: Arcadia, 2006.
Hubbard, Donald. *The Red Sox Before the Babe*. Jefferson, NC: McFarland, 2009.
Huntington Family Association. *The Huntington Family in America*. N.p., 1915.
Nowlin, Bill. *Day by Day with the Boston Red Sox*. Burlington, MA: Rounder, 2006.

_____. *Red Sox Threads: Odds and Ends from Red Sox History.* Burlington, MA: Rounder, 2008.

Stout, Glenn, and Richard A. Johnson. *Red Sox Century.* Boston: Houghton Mifflin, 2000.

Index